D0554305

OMNIVM LVX CIVIVM

BOSTON
PUBLIC
LIBRARY

ACTS OF FAITH

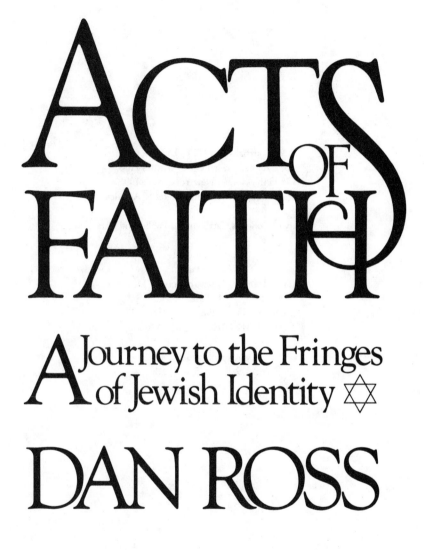

ACTS OF FAITH

A Journey to the Fringes of Jewish Identity ✡

DAN ROSS

ST. MARTIN'S PRESS
NEW YORK

Copyright © 1982 by Dan Ross
For information, write: St. Martin's Press,
175 Fifth Avenue, New York, N.Y. 10010
Manufactured in the United States of America

Library of Congress Cataloging in Publication Data

Ross, Dan, 1951–
Acts of faith.
1. Jews—Identity. 2. Jewish sects. 3. Marranos.
I. Title.
DS143.R58   296.8'3   81-18375
ISBN 0-312-00400-1   AACR2

Design by Manuela Paul
10 9 8 7 6 5 4 3 2 1
First Edition

This book is dedicated
to the memory of my grandfather
Jacob Ross (1892-1975)

Table of Contents

FOREWORD

What is the common factor among the ten Jewish, half-Jewish, and pseudo-Jewish communities described by Dan Ross in his "journey to the fringes of Jewish identity"? The answer, I think, lies in the persistence of the historical memory that in the past they were Jewish, and in the persistence of the conviction that, therefore, they differ to this day from their neighbors. This memory and conviction persisted whether, as in the cases of the "Jewish Indians" of Mexico and the Bene Israel of Bombay, the group in question was caught by centripetal forces which pulled them toward the Jewish people, or, as in the cases of the Chuetas of Majorca and the Dönmeh of Turkey, they were tossed by centrifugal forces away and out from the Jewish core of which they once were a part.

In the case of the former two communities, the desire to become Jews, full Jews, is the crucial issue and testimony to the hold which the Jewish past can exercise even after the passing of centuries. In the case of the latter two, the psychological problem is more difficult. Since these communities have been removed, or have removed themselves, from Judaism and become true Christians and Moslems, why did they preserve the memory of their Jewish origin which, even after many generations, remained sufficient to keep them apart? Why was the last, irrevocable step—simply not telling their children about their Jewish origin and thereby totally submerging into the religious culture of the environment—never taken?

In my recent book, *The Jewish Mind*, I discussed, among other things, the marginality typical of so many Jews living in the assimilationist environment of the modern Western world. Dan Ross's study of communities on the fringes of Jewishness supplies the communal analogue to these individuals, with their problems magnified and generalized. Here we see entire communities occupying marginal positions between Jewishness, on the one hand, and another religious culture—Christianity, Islam, Hinduism, Confucianism—on the other. In some cases, as in those of the Chinese Jews and the Portuguese "not-so-secret Jews" (as Ross calls them), the community tried to synthesize the forces that pulled them in opposite directions. Such attempts, like that of squaring a circle, met with indifferent success; the resulting formation looked similar to, but was never quite identical with, either a square or a circle. A case in point is that of the Chinese Jews, who moved in the direction of Chinese culture. By the middle of the nineteenth century, the identity of the few remaining Jews became almost totally submerged in Confucianism, with only a vague memory of their former Jewishness remaining.

Something similar happened to the Jews of Portugal and Majorca. After their forced conversion to Christianity, their Jewish identity and consciousness were gradually obliterated—to be replaced by the mere memory of a remote Jewish ancestry, coupled in Majorca with a Christian religious fervor.

In Mashhad, Iran, the development was centripetal. Within one generation of being cut off from Judaism by forced conversion to Islam, the *jadid al-Islam*, or "new Moslems," established a secret Hebrew school and fought their way back to Judaism, despite all the dangers involved. A parallel process took place among the Falashas of Ethiopia. They had observed a quasi-biblical religion until they were discovered in the nineteenth century by European Jews, who showed them the way to the Jewish mainstream. The other two varieties of proto-biblical Judaism, those of the Samaritans and the Karaites, are now moving in the same direction: being swallowed up in Israel by the Jewish majority religion.

Dan Ross presents dramatic pictures of each of these ten communities on the fringes of Judaism. He titles his book *Acts of Faith*, not merely as an allusion to the autos-da-fé in which ended many a Marrano Jewish life, but because the very survival of these groups on the Jewish peripheries was an eloquent manifestation of the power of faith—not only in God but in the Jewish people. The approach utilized by Ross is a happy combination of historical research and field study. The result is a series of fascinating portraits presenting both past trials and tribulations and present-day problems and vicissitudes. His book is a significant contribution to our knowledge and understanding of the ten most important communities on the fringes of Jewish identity.

RAPHAEL PATAI

CHAPTER ONE

Mexico's "Jewish Indians": *Neither Indians nor Jewish?*

Past editions of *Mexico on $5 and $10 a Day* steered tourists to a tribe of "Jewish Indians" in a village named Venta Prieta, fifty-five miles before Mexico City on the main highway from Texas. The guidebook had little to say about Venta Prieta other than that one hundred or so Jews lived in it, most of them "unmistakably Indian in appearance."[1] It suggested pausing there to break up the drive from Mexico City, perhaps just long enough to visit their red-brick *templo.*

"We had a lot of visitors because of that book," one Venta Prietan recently recalled. "I think they expected us to be wearing feathers or something."

Among those drawn to Venta Prieta by that guidebook was the present writer, while on vacation in spring 1975. To a young man out for adventure in Mexico, the idea of Jewish Indians seemed incomparably exotic. And what better time to visit than Passover, a traditional season of hospitality, when Jewish travelers all over the world are welcomed into strangers' homes? So, Venta Prieta went on the itinerary for Passover's second night, after a first night spent in Mexico City. Any illusions of sharing Passover with "Jewish Indians," however, were soon shattered.

The village is easily reached from Mexico City via nearby Pachuca, the state capital of Hidalgo. But in Pachuca's tourist information office, a white-haired gentleman with light skin and European features began the process of disillusionment. "Why do all you *norteamericanos* come looking for Jewish Indians?" he scolded. "There is no such thing. Yes, there are Jews in Venta Prieta, but they are no more Indian than I am. We are all Mexicans."

The rebuke had been unexpected. If Venta Prieta's Jews were not Indians, what were they?

The answer came momentarily, after the bus pulled into the dusty village two miles south of Pachuca. Venta Prieta looked like an ordinary Mexican village—cinder-block houses, adobe walls, some

1

trees setting it off from the vast plains around it. The synagogue was easily found at the corner of two unpaved streets. Passers-by pointed it out nonchalantly, as though it were not unusual to find a synagogue in a Mexican village. Built of red brick, it also sported a stone facade, stained-glass windows along one side, and a small garden full of trees and shrubs, all of which was surrounded by a chest-high fence. Colorful children's drawings for Passover were taped on the windows of a smaller building next door. Hebrew letters were crudely scrawled on the drawings, as in all Jewish schoolrooms at holiday times.

Before long there was also a gaggle of children at the gate, staring wide-eyed at their unexpected visitor. They looked no different from other Mexican children. Except for the six-pointed Star-of-David necklaces some wore, they could have belonged to any of the legions of children that pursue a tourist wherever he wanders in Mexico. Well-fed and well-dressed (by rural Mexican standards), there seemed nothing out of the ordinary about them, except that they were Jews.

They were not Indians. The gentleman in Pachuca had been correct. Racially, they were "mestizos" (mixed): members of what is sometimes called the "Mexican" race. They displayed a wide range of racial features; at one extreme they could have stepped out of an Aztec mural by Diego Rivera or José Orozco. But in Mexico, copper skin or Aztec features are not enough to classify you as an Indian, unless you live in an Indian culture. Most Mexicans display some Indian features, but are not considered Indian any more than black Americans are considered African. They are simply Mexicans. But the process of disillusionment was not complete.

An older boy of high-school age agreed to lead a short tour of the synagogue. In the entranceway he paused to touch a mezuzah on the doorpost and briefly brush his fingers against his lips, in the traditional Jewish manner. He reached into an open box in the anteroom and took out two familiar-looking skullcaps, putting one on and handing the second to his guest. The interior was plain and undecorated, but clearly a synagogue. An electric menorah and an oil Eternal Lamp shone in the front. A Holy Ark was adorned with the Ten Commandments. To the rear was a small gallery with an organ. Next door, the second building turned out to be a community center for meetings and festivities. A seder, the festive meal of the first two nights of Passover, had been held there for the entire congregation the night before.

Would a second seder be held there that night, which a visitor might attend?

"Oh, no," the boy replied. "On the second night the seders are in our homes. I'm sorry, but they are private. What a shame you couldn't have come last night."

The tour soon ended, but not—even yet—the disillusionment. Back in Mexico City, further doubts were cast on these "Jewish Indians." Not only are they not Indians, but it turned out that most Jews in Mexico City do not consider them Jewish.

Why not? Because, say the Jews of Mexico City, they never converted to Judaism. To be a Jew it is not enough to practice the Jewish religion. A Jew must be descended from Jews (specifically a Jewish mother) or have formally converted. Although the Venta Prietans claim to be descended from Jews, Mexico City's Jews don't believe them.

To an American who rarely sets foot inside a synagogue—but whose credentials as a Jew have never been challenged—this seemed a strange line of reasoning. Is being a Jew no more than an accident of birth? How can the formal act of converting to Judaism be more important than daily and weekly acts of devotion? Why does an American tourist who never prays belong to the same people as a Mexico City businessman who never eats gefilte fish, but not with a Venta Prietan who reads the Torah each week? If God and gefilte fish are both irrelevant, what can it mean to be a Jew?

Venta Prieta turned out to be just the first of many communities which triggered such questions. That visit touched off the curiosity about unusual Jewish communities which, eventually, produced this book. It was not simply fascination with the bizarre or exotic. Jews who are quaint or live far away are no longer that intriguing. Jews live in all corners of the earth, after all, and they are no more or less exotic than the people they live among.

Rather, this book became a journey to the fringes of Jewish identity: to Jews who do not fit the usual definitions, to Jews whose credentials have been challenged, to Jews who raise questions about what it means to be a Jew—an attempt to comprehend the Jewish people by defining its outer limits. This journey took place in libraries as well as in Israel and Portugal, culminating in spring 1980 with a return trip to Mexico, to attend—after five years' delay—a Passover seder in Venta Prieta.

·   ·   ·   ·

"A Jew must first of all be human," argues an Orthodox rabbi in Robert Silverberg's science-fiction tale, "Dybbuk on Mazel Tov IV."

"Show me that in the Torah," retorts his more freethinking opponent.[2]

The argument was over a question not likely to be faced outside the fictional world: can a six-legged, green-furred creature be a Jew? But while the question is fictional, it is drawn from real life. No one really knows what a Jew is. Despite the generalizations of borscht-belt comedians, not all Jews are raised on a diet of chicken soup and a mother's love. Nor can all Jews trace their pedigrees to the "world of our fathers." All Jews do not have big noses or curly hair. Nor do they all believe in Judaism. There is no single race, culture, or even religion shared by Jews: no kernel of "Jewishness" all Jews can point to and say, "*That* is what makes me a Jew."

What, then, is a Jew?

That, thunders a chorus from the past, is a good question. The traditional definition is that a Jew is the offspring of a Jewish mother (or a convert to Judaism). But this, as others have pointed out, is about as helpful as defining a sheep as the offspring of a ram and a ewe.[3] It says nothing about the *content* of Jewishness. How do we distinguish a Jew from a non-Jew if not by the language he speaks, the shape of his nose, or the God to whom he prays?

The French writer Albert Memmi recalled, in *The Liberation of a Jew*, how he and other young leftists tried to deny they were Jewish, using a "peeling-off tactic comparable to eating an artichoke. We started out with Stalin's definition of a nation: then we considered each trait mentioned in this definition. We asked ourselves: Do the Jews have a common language? Obviously not. Do they share a common territory? Not that either. Do they even have a religion? No! No! Most Jews can't even remember the names of the important prophets! The only problem was that when the peeling was done, the Jew, unlike the artichoke, always found itself intact."[4]

Being Jewish means different things to different people. To Reform Jews, it may be purely a matter of religion (though the religion they practice scarcely resembles that of most other religious Jews). To Yiddishists, it may mean speaking "Jewish." To Woody Allen, it may mean being neurotic. In the Soviet Union Jews are a nationality, like Ukrainians or Lithuanians except that they have no homeland. In Israel they are also thought of as a nationality, but *with* a homeland. Historian Salo W. Baron cited the hypothetical case of identical triplets born in Odessa early this century and still alive today. One stayed in Russia and is a Jew by nationality, another moved to New York and is a Jew by religion, and the third lives in Tel Aviv and is simply an Israeli, to whom being Jewish is otherwise irrelevant. Yet all three are still brothers, bearing essentially the same identity: Jews.[5]

The story is not entirely speculative. Another distinguished Jewish scholar, Gershom Scholem (of whom more will be said in Chapter V), has told about his own three brothers from an assimilated family in pre-World War I Germany. The oldest sought his identity in right-wing German nationalism, the second in assimilation, the third in international communism, and he, the youngest, in Zionism—the only one to think of himself as a Jew. Even after the Holocaust, the oldest (then living in Australia) rejected the idea that he was Jewish. "What?" he asked. "Hitler is going to tell me what I am?"[6]

Others like him were less fortunate. Under Nazi law, a German (or anyone else) needed only a single Jewish grandparent to be Jewish enough for the Holocaust. In the Vilna ghetto Yiddish scholar Zelig Kalmanovitch reflected in his diary in 1943: "A year ago some circles of the intelligentsia in the ghetto sought an answer to the question: what is a Jew? Or, who is a Jew? . . . The majority of these people had never given much thought to this question. Being Jewish was a matter of feeling, some with more, some with less, and some with none at all. . . . Now these various people were driven and locked up in less than four ells of the ghetto. People of different language, different cultures, different interests and beliefs, of different, often contradictory, hopes and aspirations—all had been drawn together as one, under one rubric: Jews. Confined as a punishment: that is, for having committed a crime, and the crime consisted in being a Jew. A great many actually did not know what to say about the crime. They didn't even understand what it meant to be a Jew. Truth to tell, practically nothing came from all this thinking and reflection. It was impossible to find a clear or definite answer to the question: 'Who is a Jew nowadays?'"[7]

As it happened, the Nazis were less casual than Vilna's Jews in defining Jewish identity. They went to great lengths to determine who was eligible for the Final Solution. Ambiguous cases were studied intensively. Kalmanovitch himself, before the Nazis killed him, helped save thousands of lives through his study of the question (see Chapter VII).

The Holocaust was only one chapter (though by far the most gruesome) in the historical saga of Jewish identity. Jews have long been aware they are unique, a people which does not fit ordinary definitions: to some "chosen" but to others simply different. When Jews, known then as Hebrews or Israelites, first appeared in the ancient Near East, they seemed no different from the peoples around them. Like those others, they had their own religion. They freely intermarried with their neighbors. Foreigners became Jewish simply by living among Jews, choosing to live as they did. That included worshipping the Jewish God, just as being a Canaanite meant worshipping Canaanite gods, or being an Egyptian Egyptian gods.

But there was a difference between Judaism and those other religions: monotheism. The idea of one God, by its very nature, has the potential to be not ethnic but universal. Eventually, one would not need to be born a Jew or live in the land of Israel to worship the God of the Jews. Because of this, being a Jew would become a completely different thing from being a Canaanite or an Egyptian.

As long as "Jews" were "the people in the kingdom of Judah," there was no need for them to develop these new forms of identity. It was with the Babylonian exile that this need arrived. For the first time in recorded history, a captive people clung to its national religion in a foreign land, surrounded by other gods. By redefining what it meant to be a people, by tying their identity to a God instead of a place, Jews remained distinct even in exile. The idea of monotheism freed the Jewish people from the limitations of race or territory, transforming it into a community of faith.

As it turned out, the sojourn in Babylonia was just a warm-up for a much longer exile: the dispersion of the last two thousand years. But the new conception of Jewishness formed in Babylonia prepared

Jews for this Diaspora. During Greek and Roman times, these ideas were refined into a body of religious law explaining who and what a Jew is. Recorded in the Talmud and other rabbinical writings, these laws have molded the sensibilities of Orthodox Jews ever since—which is to say virtually all Jews until the last few centuries.

The world of the religious Jew was a world divided into "us" and "them": the Jews and the gentiles. The Jews were a sacred people, bound together not by blood or territory but by a covenant with God. This covenant implied both privileges and obligations. Only Jews were eligible for the Kingdom of God (the best a gentile could hope for was to escape the fires of Hell), but to get there they had to obey all 613 commandments. The covenant was symbolized by circumcision, the ultimate demarcation of Jewishness.

By extension, the covenant was not only with God but between the Jews themselves. Only through the righteousness of the entire community would the Messiah appear and Israel be redeemed. This covenant united Jews more effectively than any ties of race, culture, or geography could have—because it survived the loss of all those other factors. Even such an uncommitted Jew as Benedict (Baruch) Spinoza, the philosopher who anticipated today's "marginal" Jews by refusing to become a Christian after Amsterdam's Jews excommunicated him in the seventeenth century, wrote: "Such great importance do I attach to the sign of the covenant [i.e., circumcision], that I am persuaded that it is sufficient by itself to maintain the separate existence of the nation forever."[8]

Although gentiles were excluded from the Kingdom of God, this was not meant to be discriminatory. Anyone willing to obey Jewish law was encouraged to become a Jew. After a formal procedure including circumcision and baptism, a convert was considered newly reborn as a descendant of Abraham, Isaac, and Jacob. This legal fiction was so complete that he was considered to have no blood relatives. Theoretically he could legally have committed incest with his "former" relatives, if the rabbis had not added a separate law banning it.

Once admitted, membership in the Jewish people was inalienable and hereditary, passed down through the mother. Why the mother and not the father? No one really knows. Some historians explain it as the only way of being positive who the parents are, since you can't be as sure of a child's father as his mother. Others suggest that it was because of rape by soldiers in wartime. This is all speculation. Nowhere in the Bible does it say that a Jew must have a Jewish mother. This custom apparently began after the Bible was already completed. The Talmud casuistically derives it from a biblical passage (Deut. 7:1-4) which, in truth, says no such thing.[9]

Jewish identity used to imply much more than it does today. The Jewish community was autonomous, and all Jews were subject to its laws. This was true of Diaspora life in all times and places until recently: Europe and Asia, Moslem countries and Christian, cities and villages, ancient times and medieval. It does not, by itself, mean that Jews led an inferior or degraded existence. The very ideas of equality and fraternity were inconceivable to the pre-modern mind, for whom each person and community had its rightful place in the order of things. Jews were simply one more "estate" in the medieval community, as were nobles and serfs. They were worse off than some but far better off than others.

It is difficult to comprehend how suddenly and radically all this changed. When Moses Mendelssohn began his literary career in the mid-1700s, the Berlin intelligentsia was set agog by this "young Hebrew who wrote in German."[10] Such a phenomenon had been unheard of. Mendelssohn's heirs in the Jewish Enlightenment plunged headlong into the Age of Reason, tearing down the barriers of language, clothing, manners, and education that had marked off Jews from non-Jews for thousands of years. Suddenly, the Jewish masses were exposed to the intellectual ferment of eighteenth-century Europe.

Simultaneously came the collapse of the feudal system. Feudalism was replaced by the modern secular state: nations of individuals, not corporate "estates." It became impossible for Jews alone to remain a body apart. Civic equality was awarded to Jews—in some cases forced on them—in country after country as Europe restructured itself along national lines. European Jewish emancipation began in France shortly after the Revolution, in 1790–91, and was consummated (on paper, if not in reality) by the Treaty of Versailles after World War I.

Those twin forces, enlightenment and emancipation, spawned the lingering crisis in Jewish identity. Long ago freed from the limitations of race, culture, and country, the Jewish people was now freed from religion, too. Yet—unlike Albert Memmi's artichoke—it remained intact. The covenant between man and man outlived the covenant between men and God.

It did not survive without trauma. Many Jews, without religion, could find no reason to remain Jewish. Mendelssohn's followers and even his children began converting to Christianity, not out of any religious conviction but to overcome social disabilities. It happened so quickly that while Mendelssohn himself was a devout Jew, his grandson Felix, the composer, was raised as a Christian almost from birth. In the course of the nineteenth century more than two hundred thousand Jews, including such notables as Karl Marx, Benjamin Disraeli, and Heinrich Heine, were baptized.[11]

Those Jews who did *not* wish to convert faced a different, unprecedented problem: how to accept emancipation graciously and still remain Jewish. Their dilemma is not easily understood by most Americans, for whom being both Jewish and American is perfectly natural in a multi-ethnic society. But Europe lacked America's melting-pot ethic. In fact, it was in the process of redefining itself along national lines. For Jews to survive in this uncharted world, they had to come up with new forms of identity. The search took different turns in different places.

In France, Napoleon convened a Sanhedrin of Jewish notables (named after the governing body of ancient Palestine) to define their status. At his request it declared that Jews were required to consider their land of birth or adoption their homeland, and to love and defend their fellow countrymen as though they were fellow Jews. The Sanhedrin refused only one of Napoleon's requests: that it endorse intermarriage.

In Germany and America, the ideology of Reform became popular. In the eyes of nineteenth-century Reformers, no barriers separated Jewish Germans from other Germans, or Jewish Americans from other Americans, except their faith.

In Eastern Europe, Jewish nationalism took root. There, Jews were said to be a nationality, entitled to minority rights in whichever country they lived. The ultimate expression of Jewish nationalism was Zionism, which embodied the aspirations of religious and secular Jews alike for a homeland to act out their religious or national identity.

The truth was that no one really knew what a Jew was anymore. As in the Babylonian exile twenty-five hundred years before, Jews survived by redefining the meaning of a people. But in the modern era, each Jew became free to choose his own definition, even if it existed in his own mind alone. The miracle is that Jewish identity survived at all—as though a sudden wind had blown down its foundations yet the bulk of the structure remained standing, somehow suspended in mid-air.

The Jewish people now defines itself *as* itself. Definitions vary, changing shape in different times and places, but Jews continue to exist according to all of them—as though the definition were secondary to the fact. Being Jewish is no more, really, than a shared state of mind. Call it a mutual illusion, if you wish, but it is an illusion which has created its own reality.

This, unfortunately, leaves another question unanswered. Who belongs to this shared state of mind, this mutual illusion?

Until the last two hundred years or so, Jewish identity was rarely in doubt. Everything about Jews was different from their neighbors: clothing, hair, language, religion, education, occupations, laws, music, habits, folklore, the entire way of looking at the world. Today, none of these things may differ. But Jews still exist. The question is, who are they?

For the Orthodox, this is no more in doubt than it ever was. A Jew is the offspring of a Jewish mother or a convert to Judaism.

But for the larger mass of Jews to whom traditional law is no longer the writ of God, it is less certain. Is anyone who *feels* Jewish, who shares the illusion, a Jew? Or has the traditional definition of a Jew retained more validity than other traditional customs, such as separating milk from meat or putting on *tefillin* (phylacteries) every morning, which many good Jews no longer practice?

In Israel these questions are not academic. Jewish identity is an integral part of the Israeli landscape, expressing itself in all spheres of life: citizenship, education, army service, immigration privileges, identity cards, and marriage and divorce. Israel's sense of national identity is as a Jewish state. But without a consensus on who or what a Jew is, the young nation has been embroiled in controversy since its earliest days.

One of Israel's basic laws is its Law of Return, passed in 1950, which acknowledged an unrestricted right to Israeli citizenship for all Jews. (Non-Jews may also become citizens after a period of naturalization.) The Law of Return did not spell out who qualified as a Jew. At first it was interpreted loosely for the benefit of Holocaust victims, many of whom were not Jewish by any but Nazi standards, but had no place else to go. Similarly, when many Jews and "semi-Jews" were expelled from Poland in the 1950s along with their often non-Jewish spouses, all were admitted under the Law of Return. These immigrants posed a problem for clerks in registration offices. For security reasons Israeli identity cards require entries for both religion and nationality. Local clerks in each municipality had to decide how to fill them in. Not until 1958 did Interior Minister Israel Bar-Yehuda attempt a semblance of consistency by sending a directive to the clerks: anyone who claimed to be a Jew should be registered as one.

His directive sparked Israel's first crisis over "Who is a Jew?" An Orthodox political party threatened to quit the coalition government unless the directive was rescinded. Left-wing parties threatened to quit if Orthodox standards were imposed. The cabinet could find no acceptable compromise, so the religious party resigned. Elections were called for the following year.

Before the election, Prime Minister David Ben-Gurion solicited advice from "sages of Israel" all over the world. He sent a letter to rabbis, Jewish scholars, judges, and writers of various ideological persuasions. Is it possible to be a Jew by nationality but not religion, he asked them. Are two-thousand-year-old Talmudic directives too archaic to guide a modern nation? Have the institutions of separatism, so useful in the Diaspora, outlived their purpose in a Jewish state?

The answer of the sages was a resounding no.[12] Nearly all said it would be improper—or at least premature—to stray from the traditional definition of a Jew. As it turned out Ben-Gurion had already reached the same conclusion, but for more prosaic reasons. The results of the 1959 election again made it necessary to include the religious party in his coalition. Their price for participation was a new directive. Clerks were instructed to register as Jewish only "a person born of a Jewish mother who does not belong to another religion, or one who was converted in accordance with religious law."[13] This definition was repeatedly challenged in the courts. The two most famous cases were brought by a Carmelite monk known as Brother Daniel and a navy officer named Benjamin Shalit.

Brother Daniel had been born in Poland as a Jew named Oswald Rufeisen. As a youth he had been an ardent Zionist and an anti-Nazi hero, smuggling arms into the Mir ghetto and rescuing about one-hundred-fifty Jews from its "liquidation." He was later hidden by nuns in a convent, where he converted to Catholicism and decided to become a monk. He joined the Carmelite order with the specific aim of being sent to their monastery on Mount Carmel, a wish that was granted in 1958. When Brother Daniel arrived in Israel he applied for citizenship under the Law of Return. He claimed he was still a Zionist and still a Jew. He pointed out that, according to Jewish religious law, an apostate from Judaism remains a Jew. His case went all the way to Israel's Supreme Court, which decided against him in 1962.

The court ruled that Jewish religious law is not the law of Israel. To be a Jew under the Law of Return, it said, an immigrant must pass a "common-sense" test. He must be a Jew "as we the Jews understand it."[14] Since the average Jew would not consider a Catholic monk Jewish, Brother Daniel did not qualify. He accepted defeat graciously, and became an Israeli citizen through naturalization.

Benjamin Shalit was more successful. An atheist whose wife was not Jewish, Shalit tried to register his children as Jews by nationality with no religion. Again the case went to the Supreme Court, which decided in his favor on a technicality. By a five-to-four margin, it ruled in 1970 that local clerks had no right to record anything but what they were told by citizens.

Again, the religious party threatened to quit the government. This time Prime Minister Golda Meir agreed to amend the Law of Return, giving the Interior Ministry's directive (that is, the Orthodox definition) the force of law. The amended Law of Return also provided full citizenship rights for the spouses, children, and grandchildren of Jews, even though they may not be Jewish (by this definition) themselves.

"Who is a Jew?" remains a political hot potato in Israel, sparking controversies from the sublime to the ridiculous. Religious politicians periodically try to re-amend the law, this time to mandate that only Orthodox conversions be recognized; as of this writing they have not succeeded. In 1978, Prime Minister Menachem Begin's fragile coalition government nearly collapsed because an American-born basketball star's conversion to Judaism was not strictly Orthodox. The coach of a rival team called it to the attention of an ultra-Orthodox political party, which threatened to quit the government if he continued to play basketball without a proper conversion.[15]

Today, Jews all over the world look to Israel for spiritual guidance. The "average Jew" accepts Israel's leadership in deciding who a Jew is. To be a Jew "as we the Jews understand it" now means being accepted as a Jew in Israel. This book is about marginal Jewish communities, not individuals, but the same criteria apply. It is in Israel where their identity faces the acid test.

There are many ways of being Jewish, and many ways of perceiving Jewishness. Each community in this book differs from the mainstream in some fundamental way. They challenge conventional views of Jewish identity, and contradict stereotypes held by gentile and Jew alike. Some cannot be considered Jewish by any reasonable definition. Many have had their credentials challenged, in Israel or elsewhere. Few are clear-cut cases. But all have something to say about not only *who*, but *what*, a Jew is.

.   .   .   .

The village of Venta Prieta first came to the attention of Mexican Jews in the 1930s, when Mexico City newspapers reported a clash there between *israelitas* and *católicos*. The Catholic villagers of Venta Prieta, whose total population was then no more than a few hundred, wanted to use government funds to build a church. Its Jews preferred a public school, which would be of use to the entire village. The controversy turned violent before Mexico's president ruled in favor of a school, and backed up his decision with soldiers. The school, since expanded, still serves both Catholics and Jews, who have gotten along smoothly ever since.

Jewish leaders in Mexico City went to investigate. They discovered a community of whose existence they had never dreamed: a few dozen villagers who gathered each week in a one-room adobe synagogue to worship God with a mixture of Jewish, Protestant, and Catholic prayers and hymns. They knew no Hebrew, and had not been circumcised. Unlike Mexico City's Jews, they were indigenous Mexicans—mestizos. They did not differ from the other residents of Venta Prieta in any way but religion. Some were related to Catholic villagers. Their leader was a Mexico City lawyer named Baltasar Laureano Ramirez, who had formerly lived in Pachuca and still returned to Venta Prieta to preach to his flock.

Mexican Jews and tourists began visiting Venta Prieta. They also visited a second congregation in a poor neighborhood of Mexico City, founded more recently by Laureano Ramirez. Some came to ogle these exotic semi-Jews, others to instruct them in the rudiments of Judaism. Volunteer teachers taught them Hebrew prayers, Jewish customs, and even a few Russian-Jewish songs which they interspersed with their Spanish hymns. Venta Prieta's synagogue was decorated with six-pointed stars, Hebrew inscriptions, maps of Palestine, and drawings based on biblical themes. Most visitors were impressed by the depth of their faith, despite their ignorance of Judaism.

The first of many magazine articles about them appeared in October 1939. It was a lavish six-page spread in Mexico's equivalent of *Life* magazine, *Hoy* (Today). It was entitled *"Indios Israelitas"* and subtitled, *"Los Judíos Mexicanos de Venta Prieta, Hgo."* It reported, for the first time in print, the explanation of their origin which would become so controversial, earning them the hostility they might not have aroused through their religion alone.

The article reported that Venta Prieta's Jews were descended from Spanish Marranos (secret Jews) who had dispersed throughout colonial New Spain, intermarrying with Indian women, like the other conquistadors. Their descendants preserved Jewish customs in secret for hundreds of years, until freedom of religion had been declared in Mexico. These descendants lived all over Mexico, the article continued, but before the Mexican Revolution (1911) they had not been in contact with each other. They were only tracked down through the efforts of Laureano Ramirez, who was described as "the son of Mexican-Jewish parents."[16] He had traveled the length and breadth of Mexico after the fighting ended, and founded a national Jewish organization with chapters in Venta Prieta, Mexico City, and elsewhere. The particular families living in Venta Prieta, it added, had come there in the nineteenth century from the state of Michoacán, where they had been persecuted for being Jewish: the leader of the community had been thrown into boiling water.

The notion that Venta Prieta's Jews were descended from Marranos only added to their exotic charm. It seemed plausible enough at the time, in light of the recent discovery and "renaissance" of Marranos in Portugal (see Chapter II). The following year, the first English-language article on these "Jewish Indians" told a similar tale to American readers.[17] It was repeated again in 1944, in a pamphlet published by an organization called the American Friends of the Mexican Indian Jews, founded by an Arkansas rabbi. The "Friends" placed several more articles in the American press, and collected enough money for a shipment of books to Mexico before disbanding.

This explanation was not challenged in print until anthropologist Raphael Patai published his study of Venta Prieta in 1950. Two years earlier, he had spent three months in the village. By that time the "Jewish Indians" in both Mexico City and Venta Prieta were regular stops on the Jewish tourist circuit. But the two congregations were no longer on speaking terms with each other. A personal feud had erupted between the Venta Prietans and their former leader, Laureano Ramirez. To this day neither side will discuss the dispute.

Patai's writings are the most extensive source of information on Venta Prieta and its Jews. At that time the village had no electricity, no indoor plumbing, and no paved roads other than the Mexico City–Pachuca highway on its edge. The villagers, Catholic and Jew alike, mostly dry-farmed the few acres allotted them in land reform. They practiced carpentry, baked, distilled *pulque* from the sap of the maguey plant, and raised cows, goats, chickens, and other animals. A few commuted to jobs in Pachuca.

Patai counted fifty practicing Jews out of Venta Prieta's 471 residents. They included some of the most respected villagers, including the local magistrate. The president of the congregation, Simon Tellez, was the wealthiest man in Venta Prieta. Nearly everyone was related by either blood or marriage. Only one family, in fact, actually claimed descent from Marranos. The others stated frankly that they had joined from outside, by either marrying into that family or adopting its religion.

Like earlier visitors, Patai could find nothing but religion to distinguish Venta Prieta's Jews from its Catholics. All showed the same range of Indian and European features, all spoke Spanish with the same drawling Mexican accent, and all showed the same casual attitude toward religion—whichever one they happened to practice. What marked off Jew from non-Jew was that the Jews gathered each Friday night, Saturday morning, and Jewish holiday in the adobe synagogue adjoining the Tellez cowshed. The synagogue was furnished with a Holy Ark, a table covered by a white cloth, and four rows of benches. Their prayers were mostly in Spanish, with a few sentences in halting Hebrew. They sang a few tunes learned from Mexico City's Jews, along with some Christian hymns. Men left on their sombreros during services; women covered their heads with scarves or veils. Men and women sat together, and music was provided by a foot-pedal organ. Outside the synagogue, the anthropologist could find no expression of their being Jewish.

Patai was particularly struck by several customs he had never seen in other synagogues. They knelt during important prayers, and the girls cupped their hands in front of them. Whenever anyone left the synagogue he would back out the door, facing the Holy Ark. Patai was also struck by their lack of interest in the new state of Israel, even though his visit took place during its War of Independence and he had told them he came from Jerusalem.

As an anthropologist, Patai was more interested in the community's present than its past. When he asked about their origin, it was not to find out where they came from but where they *believed* they came from—to uncover "the myth which gave content and color to their lives," as he later put it.[18] But the deeper he delved, the more curious he became. He began by interviewing the matriarch of the Tellez clan, Trinidad Jiron de Tellez. She repeated the story she had already told several journalists: that her grandfather in Michoacán had been sewn into a bull's skin and thrown into boiling water for being a Jew. But Patai also looked up the old woman's only surviving sister, who told a different version. This sister, a Catholic, said that their grandfather, like her, had been a good Catholic. He had once been tied up in a bull's skin as a punishment, but not for being a Jew, and he was never thrown into boiling water, either.

Unable to verify either version, Patai looked into an alternative explanation. He had been told in Mexico City that Venta Prieta's Jews had only recently switched to Judaism from the Protestant *Iglesia de Dios.* That church is the Mexican branch of the American-based Church of God, a fundamentalist sect which abstains from pork, observes the Sabbath on Saturday, and claims to be the spiritual heir of ancient Israel. The Church of God, active in Mexico since the nineteenth century, had met with particular success in the Pachuca area. Some of its members, considering themselves "circumcised in the heart" (as opposed to the body), called themselves *israelitas,* a word otherwise used in Mexico as a polite synonym for *judíos* (Jews). Although Patai was unable to get either the *Iglesia de*

Dios or Venta Prieta's Jews to admit they had ever been associated with each other, he found what he calls "irrefutable documentary proof" that Laureano Ramirez had been a leader of the *Iglesia de Dios* before he began calling himself a Jew.[19] Church materials indicate he was affiliated with it until the 1930s: the period during which he lived in Pachuca, began preaching to the Venta Prieta congregation, and supposedly traveled all over Mexico, tracking down descendants of Marranos. In fact, a photograph in the 1939 issue of *Hoy* showed him preaching in Venta Prieta's synagogue above a tablecloth clearly embroidered with the words, *"Iglesia de Dios."* By the end of his visit, Patai was convinced that Venta Prieta's Jews were recent converts from Protestantism.

But at the same time that he was exposing their past, Patai became more and more convinced of their sincerity in the present. "The more I probed the more evidence I found of their deep sentimental attachment to Judaism," he wrote.[20] He found them "fervent, eager, and enthusiastic Jews," even though they differed from their neighbors in only "some very vague and indefinite notions about religion."[21] He later observed: "In their relaxed, typically Mexican way, they took it for granted that they were Jews, although they knew practically nothing of Jewish religion or history."[22]

In the same year that Patai published his conclusions, the *Enciclopedia Judaica Castellana* was published in Mexico City and corroborated him. It stated authoritatively: "There is in Mexico a group of proselytes who are called 'Indian Jews' abroad. The members of this group are no more Indian than the rest of the population of Mexican cities. . . . The majority of this Jewish group comes from the Protestant sect, *Iglesia de Dios.* . . . Because of disputes and for other reasons, some affiliates of this sect decided to consider themselves Jews and have lived as such for some two decades."[23]

These conclusions governed relations between Venta Prieta and Mexico City for the next two decades. Jewish organizations shied away from assisting the villagers. But a few Jewish individuals—impressed by the Venta Prietans' sincerity—instructed them in Hebrew and traditional Judaism. Likewise, Mexican rabbis officially refused to circumcise village children—although individual *mohels* (circumcisers) sometimes agreed. Some of Venta Prieta's Jews attended services in Mexico City. A few formed friendships with Jews in both Mexico City and Pachuca.

The community passed a milestone in 1963, when its first

youth went to Israel. A visiting Israeli doctor convinced the parents of thirteen-year-old Isaac Perez to let him take the boy home with him. Isaac studied in an Israeli agricultural school, served as an army paratrooper, and married an Israeli girl. He came home for two years to teach Hebrew to his family and friends before returning permanently to Israel as a teacher in that agricultural school. Others have since followed him to Israel, though only a few have remained there.

Venta Prieta continued to receive a steady stream of journalists and tourists. Magazine articles also continued to appear: some sensational, some condescending, some gullible, some skeptical. The community began to distrust its visitors. They said that while acting friendly in Venta Prieta, many went home to malign or make fun of them in print. The distrust even extended to Patai when he returned for a second visit in 1964. The villagers refused to welcome him until he proved he was not responsible for any of the offending articles.

After proving his innocence, Patai was astonished at the changes which had taken place in his sixteen years' absence. Electricity, running water, and underground sewers had all come to Venta Prieta. Regular bus service was turning it into a suburb of Pachuca. The old adobe synagogue had been replaced by a modern brick-and-stone structure. More significantly, a new generation of Jews had come of age. The new president, Ruben Olvera Tellez, had been only nine years old during Patai's first visit. But he and his contemporaries had changed the orientation of the community. Rather than insisting on their Jewish descent, they were simply trying to live as Jews.

Though still far from Orthodox, Venta Prieta's Judaism had grown much closer to the mainstream. In many ways it resembled the Conservative movement. Men and women sat on separate sides of the synagogue, as do Conservative Jews. The organ was no longer used (only Reform temples allow organ music). The old artwork had been replaced by a menorah and an Eternal Lamp. Men took off their sombreros and put on Jewish skullcaps; women wore the same lace doily-like head coverings as Jewish women in Mexico City. They used a standard Spanish-Hebrew prayer book, though the service was still mostly in Spanish. Patai also noticed some informal ways they had come to resemble the mainstream. Several villagers worried aloud about intermarriages. A new suspicion toward proselytes existed. And the community's Zionist fervor—completely absent sixteen years before—especially struck Patai. Two maps of Israel were hanging in the synagogue, and several young Jews expressed a desire to join their *compadre* who had already gone there.

This time, however, they were reluctant to talk about their past. "We aren't so much interested in how we *became* Jewish," one young woman told Patai, "but want primarily to live a fully Jewish life."[24] The anthropologist sensed an underlying embarrassment about their earlier claim. When he suggested that conversion would be a logical next step, they were no longer indignant. "At that moment," Patai observed, "it seemed evident that these young people knew that the story of their Jewish ancestry was nothing but a pious fairy tale."[25]

The following year, Venta Prieta received its first friendly overture from official Judaism, albeit an American, not a Mexican, organization. Fifteen teenagers from a Reform youth group visited the village in the summer of 1965. Calling themselves the "Mexico Mitzvah Corps," they spent a month building the community center next to the synagogue and fixing up the courtyard as a garden. Dubious at first, the Venta Prietans warmed to their hard-working guests. The project turned into a month-long *fiesta* as American teenagers befriended their Mexican counterparts and their multilingual rabbi gave Hebrew lessons to adult Venta Prietans. Ever since, the one-room community center—*"el club,"* as they call it—has been the focus of all Jewish activity in the village: meetings, classes, songs, plays, and Passover seders.

The Mitzvah Corps was widely publicized, from Mexico City to New York. But front-page coverage in Mexico City led to a re-airing of the old controversy. This time it was vented more publicly and heatedly than ever before. The skeptics had a zealous new spokesman: a Miami lawyer named Seymour B. Liebman who had embarked on a second career as historian of Latin American Jewry. Liebman made it a personal crusade to debunk the myth of "Jewish Indians." He had spent several years tracking down every legend, story, and rumor connected with them. Just three days after Venta Prieta's community center was inaugurated, his rebuttal appeared in the English-language *Mexico City News*. "The small group in Venta Prieta is neither Jewish nor Indian," Liebman told the newspaper. "If the well-meaning young Americans . . . wanted to do something on behalf of Judaism, the opportunities abound in the United States rather than among people not recognized as Jews in Mexico."[26]

Liebman published the details of his research two years later. It was a lawyer's brief against their descent from Marranos: based on similar facts and coming to similar conclusions as Patai, but without the anthropologist's open sympathy for his subject. He quoted earlier writers out of context to make them appear more hostile than they really were. He also reprinted the old picture of Laureano Ramirez from *Hoy*, darkening the words *"Iglesia de Dios"* to make them stand out. He asserted: "Regardless of all the articles sentimentalizing and accepting the Judaism of the 'Mestizo Jews,' there is but one valid criterion—Jewish law."[27]

Liebman's polemic did not materially affect Venta Prieta's Jews. In fact, for unrelated reasons, the last dozen years have seen their first acceptance by official Mexican Jewry. A new Conservative rabbi arrived in Mexico City in 1968 and became their unofficial "spiritual adviser": Rabbi Samuel Lerer, who leads an English-speaking congregation in a wealthy neighborhood of the capital. Rabbi Lerer performs marriage ceremonies for couples and gives Bar Mitzvah lessons to boys from the village.

"When I first came to Mexico," he recently recalled, "I went to Venta Prieta and asked how I could help. They told me, 'Everyone promises, but no one does anything.' I said, 'Try me,' so they asked me to marry a young couple whose wedding was only two months off. I took up people from my congregation with me and gave them a real Jewish wedding. Everyone was crying: their people, my people, even me. You can't imagine what it meant to them to be married by a rabbi."

Rabbi Lerer now insists that couples formally convert to Judaism before he marries them. "It's not because I think they need to," he explained, "but in order not to antagonize the other rabbis here." He "converts" them in a Mexico City *mikveh* (ritual bath) run by Orthodox Jews. He only requires an immersion, dispensing with the religious instruction which ordinarily precedes a conversion. Although he is a Conservative rabbi, he expects his conversions to be "kosher" even by Orthodox standards, because he was originally ordained by Jerusalem's Orthodox rabbinate. Every couple, then, married since 1968, and every child born to those couples, is now incontestably Jewish.

•   •   •   •

Venta Prieta had noticeably changed in five years' absence. In 1975 the entire village had been east of the Mexico City–Pachuca highway. But five years later a new, California-style housing tract had sprouted to the west. Pedestrian bridges straddled the highway, connecting the two halves of the village. Nearly everyone in Venta Prieta was commuting to Pachuca, many in their own cars. There were other signs of prosperity, too: new houses of superior construction, television antennas sprouting from every roof, a few new stores. Though its streets were still unpaved, an electric substation stood at the edge of the village as a reminder of how far it had already come. Young people were attending high school in Pachuca, and sometimes higher education in Mexico City. Many Jews were working as accountants or in other professions, for industry or government agencies.

The Jewish population had grown to 155, including a few who had moved to Mexico City, Israel, or the United States, and the village as a whole to approximately four thousand. The Jewish community was prosperous. "We have the highest standard of living in the old part of Venta Prieta," one Jew boasted. "We're not rich, but we have good food and good clothes. We go to movies and entertain ourselves. We all have televisions, and most of us cars. We take vacations at the beach. We live a good life."

The community's president in 1980 was Saúl Gonzalez Olvera, a Pachuca tax official. He was hospitable but reserved, clearly tired of being treated as a curiosity. He allowed photographs of their Passover seder (but not their synagogue) as a courtesy to Rabbi Lerer, who had arranged an introduction. In return he asked, as friendly banter but with barely disguised bitterness, "If I come to New York next year can I photograph *your* seder?"

Another Venta Prietan explained their reserve more bluntly: "Who wants to live in a zoo?"

Gonzalez Olvera lives a few blocks from the synagogue, in a rambling brick home behind a patio full of parakeets. His family showed none of Saúl's reserve. His wife, Margarita Marron de Gonzalez, served soft drinks and commanded her two sons to entertain their guest until she could finish her household duties. Twelve-year-old Marcos excitedly interrupted his Bar Mitzvah studies to put an Israeli record on the phonograph. But David, an athletic eighteen-year-old, was more interested in the teenage girls calling to him from the front gate. When Margarita returned and saw him outside, she shrugged her shoulders and apologized. *"Las muchachas,"* she explained. "The girls. What can I do?"

Like other Venta Prietans, Margarita preferred discussing their present rather than their past. She complained about what she considers their shabby treatment by other Mexican Jews. The real reason for it, she said, is rarely reported: "The whole problem is money. We are not rich enough for them." One hears this over and over again in Venta Prieta. Another Jew said, "It's because we have no money to give them. If we had money you'd see how fast they'd come to us." Even Rabbi Lerer, who predicts their rapid upward mobility, agrees: "You'll see. When they're rich the Jews of Mexico City will be glad to accept them."

On the afternoon before Passover, the community busily prepared for the seder. Unlike wealthier synagogues it hires no employees; the entire congregation pitched in. Women spent the afternoon cooking at home and removing traces of leaven. Later they drifted into *el club*, arranged the tables, brought chairs from their homes, and set out matzo, fruit, bitter herbs, hard-cooked eggs, wine, and grape juice for the children. As the sun went down they paused to light candles. The eldest woman cupped her hands in front of her while reading the blessings in halting, deliberate Hebrew, syllable by syllable, prompted by Margarita. None of the other women cupped their hands. The younger generation is gradually abandoning those practices which are out of line with mainstream Judaism.

As the women bustled around the room, another prominent Venta Prietan wandered in: Benjamin Bolde, a veterinarian in his late thirties. Benjamin is the first "outside" Jew to have married into the community. Raised in Pachuca and educated in a Mexico City Jewish school, he married a Venta Prietan girl in 1976 and moved into the village. On the ground floor of his house, directly across from the synagogue, is a small stationery store run by his elderly father, born in Minsk. Benjamin speaks of Venta Prieta as a paradise. "I came here looking for a girl to marry," he joked. "I thought that if I got a girl from a small town it would be like a wife in the old way. And you know what? I was right."

His wife, occupied with their babies in another corner of the room, overheard and rolled her eyes. Benjamin laughed. "No, she's not as crazy about living here as I am. She was living in Rochester, New York, and was visiting her family on holiday. We met, fell in love, got married, and I talked her into coming home. In Venta Prieta I live like a king. I don't have as much money as if I stayed in Mexico City, but I am richer. You know why? Because I made my money there and I spend it here, where things are cheaper. I have a better life than I did there. There is no smog, no traffic, no noise. My father lives with me, and my father-in-law is across the street. Everyone here is one family, one community. They honor me by accepting me as one of them. Yes, it is a little like a *shtetl* in the old country."

Benjamin is proud of his new neighbors, and compares them favorably with Mexico City's Jews. "They are better Jews than I am," he said. "I go to synagogue more than I used to in Mexico City. There it was only for Rosh Hashanah and Yom Kippur, but here I go every week with the rest of them. And when they go to synagogue they go to read the holy books. In Mexico City everyone talks about business, the price of this and the price of that. There is a real Jewish feeling here."

Proudly he added, "You know we have eight people living in Israel now. Two have married Israeli girls. They had to convert, but only in the *mikveh*—the same as Rabbi Lerer makes us do. Rabbi Lerer told us it is not for him that he asks us to do this, but in case one of the rabbis in Mexico City challenges our marriages."

Before the seder Benjamin walked to the far, hidden side of the synagogue. Nestled into a corner of the courtyard was a small construction site. "We are building our own *mikveh*," Benjamin said, "so we won't have to use the Orthodox one in Mexico City. We are proud people. We don't like having to ask them for anything. Now Rabbi Lerer can come here to make his conversions. It will be finished in about two weeks."

Passover began with evening prayers in the synagogue. The service was familiar from Patai's description—less changed, apparently, in the sixteen years since his second visit than in the same length of time between his two. It was led by Saúl's son David, with his father's assistance. Since the community has no rabbi (or, as Saúl puts it with a laugh, "We have *many* rabbis"), each family takes a week in charge of the synagogue: holding the keys, running the services, and supplying oil for the Eternal Lamp.

David read the service in rapid-fire Spanish, slowing only slightly for the familiar Hebrew blessings. Only a few copies of the

Spanish-Hebrew prayer book—the same one used in Patai's day—
were available, so most of the congregation listened in silence as he
hurried through the prayers. They rose and sat according to his
instructions. David paused frequently to consult with his father over
what to do next. Through it all, people kept drifting in. Half-empty
at the start, the fifty-four-seat synagogue was standing-room-only for
the concluding songs. That was the high point for most of the
congregation. Afterward, the crowd adjourned to *el club* for the seder.
More than eighty people crowded into the room. There were not
enough chairs, so some men stood.

The seder began with the reading of the *Haggadah* (Passover
prayer book), recalling the events of more than three-thousand years
ago when Moses led the Israelites out of Egypt. This Passover they
were trying out a new *Haggadah:* an illustrated, tri-lingual (Spanish,
Hebrew, and English) volume printed by Rabbi Lerer for his own
congregation. The service followed the familiar order: the four cups of
wine, the four questions, the hard-boiled eggs dipped in salt water,
and the bitter herbs eaten between two pieces of matzo. But for a
visitor the words took on new meaning.

"Why is this night different from all other nights?"

"Because *we* were once slaves to Pharaoh in Egypt. Had the
Lord not brought us out, our children and grandchildren would still
be slaves to a Pharaoh in an Egypt."

When the "evil son" asked, "What does this service mean *to
you?*" a cardinal lesson of Judaism was repeated, as it was that night in
Jewish homes around the world:

"*To you* and not *to him.* By this expression he excludes himself
from the community. So tell him, 'This is on account of what the
Lord did *for me* when I came out of Egypt.' *For me,* and not *for him.*
For had he been there, he would not have been redeemed."

The seder soon disintegrated, as do all eventually, into the
merrymaking at the heart of the ritual. Restless children were let
outside to play. Shy teenagers fled to a corner to flirt. The familiar
songs were sung heartily if not always tunefully. Dinner, an eclectic
mélange of potato *latkes* and guacamole salad, was consumed *con
mucho gusto.* It was an evening of heartfelt conviviality. Several of
those present, asked to explain it, independently hit on a single word:
unidad (unity). It was a family celebration, by a community which
was truly a single family, and which felt part of a larger family. It was

an outpouring of joy in being Jewish—and in being Jewish together.

As the community ate and sang and laughed, Saúl Gonzalez Olvera took his guest aside and waved his arm toward the festivities. "Look at this," he said. "We are as good Jews as anybody. We will not go to the rabbis in Mexico City on our hands and knees, begging them to accept us. If they accept us, fine. If they don't, also fine. We know who we are."

Back in Mexico City, Rabbi Lerer agreed. "It makes me crazy whenever I see one of those articles criticizing them," he said. "They are such sincere people. What makes somebody want to write such things? You know what they said when I offered to convert them, to come at no charge and give them the same conversion I give to other Mexican converts? They told me, 'For us to be converted means a falsification of our identity. How much more can you prove you're a Jew than we can?' I don't care where they came from. When a group of people wants to live as Jews—and you and I don't know what it is to sacrifice to be a Jew, to live as Jews in an ocean of Catholicism—why shouldn't I accept them? They are paying a price for their identity."

CHAPTER TWO

The Not-So-Secret Jews of Portugal

"Yes, I am a Jew," admitted the man in the cafe. "In a few minutes I must go home to light the Sabbath lamp. No, you may not come with me. I'm sorry."

The cafe was in Belmonte, a picturesque village on a mountaintop in northeast Portugal. The conversation took place on a Friday afternoon, shortly before the start of the Sabbath. Belmonte is known in that part of Portugal as a "Jewish town," and its many Jews were preparing their homes for what they call "the holy night of the Lord." The women were pouring olive oil into Sabbath lamps, winding fresh wicks from seven strands of linen, and cooking meatless meals to eat warm that night and cold the next day. The men were winding up their week's activities, hurrying to make it home by sundown. Some, already finished, were drinking beer in local cafes. The entire town took on an air of anticipation, as do all Jewish neighborhoods at the end of the week.

But this "holy night of the Lord" was unlike any other Jewish Sabbath. The "Jew" in the cafe had been baptized a Catholic. He was married in Belmonte's Catholic church. When he dies, they will hold his funeral there. He is not circumcised. He eats pork. And he keeps his religion absolutely private. Not a single non-Jew has ever seen the lamp-lighting ceremony which takes place in his home every Friday night. Nor have they seen him fast on Yom Kippur or eat unleavened bread on Passover. Along with hundreds of others in Belmonte, he is a Marrano—one of the last surviving secret Jews.

It is hard to believe that Marranos still exist, hundreds of years after they were driven underground by the Inquisition. It was considered a miracle when they were discovered early this century. No one had suspected that thousands of Marranos were still practicing a rudimental Judaism in the remote towns and villages of northeast Portugal, long after the entire episode had been relegated to history books.

The discovery thrilled the entire Jewish world. Funds poured in from other countries to help the Marranos return to mainstream Judaism. A magnificent synagogue was built in Oporto, northern Portugal's largest city. Marrano children learned to read Hebrew and sing Jewish songs. Men of all ages were circumcised. Public congregations were opened in the provinces, and young Marranos were trained in an Oporto yeshiva to be their leaders. At the height of this "renaissance" Marranos from thirty-four different villages were said to be participating.

It was to be shortlived. The Marrano renaissance mysteriously vanished as suddenly as it had begun. No one is sure exactly why. War, anti-Semitism, political repression, and economic upheaval all played a role. The Marranos themselves seem to have been of two minds about it—as if, after hiding so long, they were blinded by the light of day and returned to their shadows.

Today, not a single public Jewish community remains in northern Portugal. Oporto's synagogue stands empty, a stark and pathetic monument to the shattered dreams of its creators. Services were held only once in recent memory, when an Israeli ship docked in Oporto during the High Holy days of 1976 and the captain ordered his sailors into town to help Oporto's few foreign-born Jews make a *minyan* (quorum) for Yom Kippur. In the villages Marranos did not survive disclosure of their secret. Of the thirty-four villages in which they had been found, only one still has an active community: Belmonte, where the Marranos regrouped as a semi-secret cult.

Secrecy has become the essence of their Judaism. But the "secret" has changed: it is no longer their identities but their rituals which are closed to outsiders. Any schoolchild in Belmonte can take a stranger in hand and point out who is Jewish and who is not. Yet the Marranos conceal their ceremonies from prying eyes, as though it were a sin to let a non-Jew see them. Only a handful of "outside" Jews have been allowed to witness their secret rites. It is through their eyes that we are permitted a glimpse of this remarkable sect.

* * * * *

The first of these, in 1917, was an itinerant mining engineer named Samuel Schwarz who had recently settled in Portugal. At that time secret Jews were considered a thing of the distant past. All the Marranos of Spain and Portugal were assumed to have been either killed, exiled, or genuinely converted long before. And, in fact, exactly that had occurred in Spain and most of Portugal. Schwarz's announcement that it had not occurred in all of Portugal was electrifying. "The existence of secret Jews in the full tide of the twentieth century in a republican country of Europe may appear incredible," he wrote. "Nevertheless—as it has been my good fortune to discover—secret Jews are still to be found in Portugal."[1]

Schwarz, a Jewish-history buff, was well-versed in the episode of the Portuguese Marranos, whose ancestors had been forced to convert to Christianity in 1497. The vast majority of the converts were recent arrivals from Spain, where Judaism had been outlawed five years before. At least one hundred thousand Jews fled to still-tolerant Portugal in 1492. Of those, sixty-eight thousand are said to have crossed the border at three northeastern stations leading directly into the mountainous region where the Marranos were discovered this century.[2]

The persecutions lost little time in following them across the border. Four years later, Portugal's newly crowned King Manuel asked Ferdinand and Isabella of Spain for their daughter's hand in marriage. They accepted on one condition: that Manuel eliminate Jews from Portugal as they had already done from Spain. Manuel agreed reluctantly, not really wanting to lose these immigrants who had already contributed so greatly to the Portuguese economy. He hit on an ingenious solution: ridding Portugal of "Jews" by converting them to Christianity.

On the first day of Passover 1497, thousands of Jews who had gathered in Lisbon for transportation out of the country were, instead, herded together and doused with water. This was their "baptism." As Christians, it became illegal for them to practice Judaism. By the end of that year Ferdinand and Isabella's condition had been met through the rest of the country, at least in name. There were no more Jews in Portugal. Only "New Christians."

The insult marrano (swine) was never actually used in Portugal. This Spanish word passed into English as the generic term for a secret Jew, usually in Spain and Portugal but also in other countries where the phenomenon has occurred (see Chapter IV). In Portugal, the converts and their descendants were properly known as *cristãos novos* (new christians). Some more erudite writers, including many New Christians themselves, preferred such euphemisms as *homens de negócios* (men of affairs) or *gente da naçao* (People of the Nation). It was rarely necessary to spell out which nation. In common parlance they were—and still are—simply *judeus*—Jews.[3]

Not even King Manuel believed that dousing Jews with water would turn them into good Christians. Declaring that his interest was in saving future generations for the cross, he offered the New Christians temporary immunity for "crimes of faith." This had the opposite of its intended effect: instead of giving Jews time to accustom themselves to Christianity, it allowed them to reorganize as a secret cult. The immunity lasted forty years, until the extent of its failure became apparent. Only then was fire brought in where water had failed. The Holy Office of the Inquisition was established in Portugal in 1536. Its first auto-da-fé (act of faith) was held four years later.

Over the next two centuries more than twenty thousand New Christians fell into the hands of the Portuguese Inquisition. An anonymous accusation by any two adults or children was sufficient to bring one before the Holy Office. Prisoners who denied their guilt were often tortured until they changed their mind; the easiest way to come out alive was to confess one's crimes—whether genuine or not. The sentencing took place at the public autos-da-fé. Those to be burned were taken to a nearby execution site; those to be spared could be sentenced to banishment, public whipping, years in the galley, or imprisonment. All their property was confiscated.

Not all New Christians were Marranos—secret Jews. Many were sincere Catholics who wished to assimilate but were not permitted to. Even those who considered themselves Jews did not always practice Judaism in secret. The number of those who observed any sort of Jewish rituals grew smaller and smaller in time. And those rituals grew farther and farther from standard Judaism.

It would be a mistake to view Marranos as some sort of organized conspiracy, secretly practicing Orthodox Judaism in clandestine synagogues. Twisted by secrecy and stunted by ignorance, the religion of the Marranos soon bore scant resemblance to Judaism as elsewhere known. For many, it was little more than a psychological disposition to think of themselves as Jews. The first Jewish custom to disappear (or nearly so) was circumcision; a male New Christian could scarcely afford to be found without a foreskin. Kosher meat-slaughtering was nearly as difficult to hide. Dietary laws grew distorted. Hebrew books were discarded, and many Jewish holidays were forgotten. Before long the secret religion of the Marranos was reduced to a few oddly misshapen ceremonies and prayers for Yom Kippur, Passover, and the Sabbath, the same ones discovered in northeast Portugal this century. These, performed by rote, were ill-understood and confused with Christian concepts.

The richest and most educated New Christians, with the most property to be confiscated, were singled out for persecution by the avaricious Holy Office. Other wealthy Marranos, or those with business connections abroad, fled to Jewish communities in Holland, Turkey, Italy, North Africa, and the New World. Still others sought safety in the isolated towns and villages of the northeast. These provinces provided a disproportionate share of victims to the Inquisition, whose depredations have been blamed for the region's decay. Nevertheless, it was only in these mountains that history passed the Marranos by, and eventually forgot them.

The last Marrano was burned in Portugal in 1760, and the Inquisition was officially abolished in 1821. Foreign Jews began settling in Lisbon in the early 1800s. By the turn of this century the Portuguese capital had four hundred Jewish residents with their own school, a kosher restaurant, and plans for a grand synagogue which would be completed a few years later. They generally ignored the hints and rumors of Marranos surviving in the countryside: two villagers had come to Lisbon from the far northeast in 1819 to find out the date of Yom Kippur that year; a Portuguese consul dying in England in 1885 had asked to be buried in a Jewish cemetery; in 1903, a description of contemporary Marrano rituals had been published in London. Few people paid attention.

Schwarz had traveled widely in Spain before settling in Portugal in 1915. He had searched that country for living traces of Judaism with no success, and was convinced that no such survivals remained in Spain. His observations in Lisbon and Oporto convinced him that the same was true in the coastal cities of Portugal. Although *judeu* was a common insult and many families bore such names as Levy, Cohen, and Maimon, all were good Catholics.

That such was not the case in the rural northeast, Schwarz discovered on a mining expedition to the Serra da Estrela, a formidable mountain range separating Belmonte from the rest of Portugal.[4] While visiting Belmonte to buy supplies, he was warned away from one merchant by a malicious competitor who said, "It is enough for me to tell you he is a Jew." As Schwarz relates: "It was indeed enough." Memories of similar boycotts against the Jews of his native Poland spurred the engineer into investigating further. He began by befriending the merchant he had been warned away from. Unfortunately, this man was not fully trusted by other Marranos because he had married a Catholic girl. His introduction, "He is one of us," was unconvincing. The Marrano women, especially, were skeptical of Schwarz's claim to be a Jew. Largely illiterate, these women were the bedrock of the cult. They had never heard of Jews outside Portugal. They knew no Hebrew, and refused to believe that such a language existed.

Finally, one old woman devised a novel test of Schwarz's sincerity. "Since you claim to have different prayers from ours," she told him, "at least recite for us a Jewish prayer in that Hebrew language you assure us is used by other Jews." Schwarz naturally chose the *Shema*, the Jewish confession of faith which he was sure would have survived if any prayer had. The women were unfamiliar with the prayer. But at the word *Adonai* (My Lord), they all touched their fingers to their eyelids. The old woman turned to the others and said, "He is a Jew, for he has uttered the name *Adonai*." This was their "password": their secret name for God.

From that moment, Schwarz enjoyed access to Marrano communities throughout Portugal. In the following years he sought out Marranos and studied their traditions, ceremonies, and prayers. He discovered manuscripts of Marrano prayers which had been transcribed in the early 1800s, when it was no longer dangerous to possess such clear-cut evidence of being a Jew. In turn, he told the Marranos about the Jewish religion, about Jews in other countries, and about Zionism, which excited even those Marranos who no longer practiced their religion. His book, *The New Christians in Portugal in the 20th Century*,[5] published in 1925, spread that excitement abroad. Foreign Jews and journalists visited Portugal, and were introduced to Marranos by Schwarz. It was his spadework which prepared the ground for one of the most disappointing chapters of modern Jewish history.

●　●　●　●

Any tour of Marrano country begins in Oporto. Cherished by

wine-lovers as the home of port, this ancient city commands a
spectacular site on the banks of the Douro River, two hundred miles
up the coast from Lisbon. It once contained a large Jewish population
whose only trace survives in a few obscure street names in the old part
of town: *Rua da Monte dos Judeus* (Jews' Mountain Street), and
Escadas da Esnoga (Stairs of the Synagogue). Oporto's modern Jewish
community is not much more visible. But the synagogue was listed in
the telephone book and easily found. It sits on a prosperous, tree-
lined boulevard where the Jewish presence was otherwise hinted at
only by swastikas painted on nearby buildings. Swastikas recently
painted on the synagogue itself—with the slogan "Death to the
Jews"—had been scrubbed off. Though clean and well-kept, the
synagogue was closed. The only sign of life was a swarm of cats in the
garden, bristling at the presence of rare intruders on what they
obviously considered their turf. On the way out the gate, an elderly
Portuguese woman approached. Oblivious of the Hebrew letters
above her she asked if the large white building was a church. She was
directed farther down the street.

One set of synagogue keys is held by Amílcar Paulo, an
Oporto public-relations man, journalist, and ethnologist who has
succeeded Schwarz as the foremost student of Marranos. Paulo is a
short, nervous man who has been recording Marrano practices for
more than thirty years. He has published numerous books, articles,
and monographs on Marranos and Jews, collected Marrano artifacts,
and compiled a comprehensive library on the subject. He is also
devoted to Oporto's synagogue—more so, perhaps, than are its Jews.
Paulo, born to a rural Marrano family, practices no religion and
considers himself neither Jewish nor Christian.

Paulo's synagogue tour was a melancholy affair. The building
was more lifeless within than it was outside, without even cats to
enliven it. Paulo explained that it is now used only for special
occasions. Only three Jewish families remain in Oporto. The parents
are old and their children have moved away, married non-Jews, or are
apathetic. A non-religious Jew in Oporto also contributes to the
synagogue, but never visits it. Among the former Marranos, only one
still shows any interest.

On its walls are two plaques which recall better days. One
honors a Shanghai philanthropist, Elly Kadoorie, after whom the
synagogue was named because he and his family donated most of the

money to build it. The other honors a second man who played a role in its founding. It reads: "This plaque is erected by the Portuguese Marranos Committee of London in honor of Captain Artur Carlos de Barros Basto, as tribute for the historic services he rendered as Leader of the Jewish Redemption in Portugal, and in the establishment of this synagogue, with which his name will be associated for all time." Although the synagogue is named after Kadoorie, it is the memory of Barros Basto—one of modern Judaism's unsung heroes—which truly haunts it.

Barros Basto was born in 1887 to a mixed family of New and Old Christians. His parents separated while he was young, and Artur went to live with his Old Christian mother in Oporto. But his holidays were spent with his father's family in a small town not far away. There, his grandfather would open an old illustrated Bible and tell him, "We are Jews."[6] His grandfather died when Artur was ten, but not before teaching the boy to say to himself before entering a church:

"In this house I enter, I adore neither the wood nor the stone but one God who governs all the world:

"*Adonai*, my God, in my thoughts [touching his brow];

"*Adonai*, my God, on my lips [touching his lips];

"*Adonai*, my God, in my heart [touching his chest]."[7] When performed rapidly, the gesture resembled the sign of the cross made by all Catholics entering church.

In his early twenties Barros Basto began to frequent the Lisbon synagogue. It was an era of intellectual ferment in Portugal, and the young man was also caught up in other movements of the day, political and philosophical. In 1910, during a premature revolutionary outbreak in Oporto, Barros Basto hoisted the republican flag over City Hall and was carried through the streets by an enthusiastic throng. After the revolution succeeded he founded the Oryamita Institute in Oporto, dedicated to the theosophic ideas of Helena Blavatsky and Rudolph Steiner. He published various pamphlets, magazines, and even a novel based on those ideas under the Hebrew pseudonym Abraham Israel Ben-Rosh. Later, when he actually converted to Judaism, he continued using that nom de plume. Nor was Barros Basto's enthusiasm confined to religious or revolutionary activities; among other things he eventually founded the Portuguese Boy Scouts. Historian Cecil Roth described him after a visit in 1930 as "overflowing with energy and life," having a personality "more magnetic than perhaps any other with which I have come in contact."[8] His activities were interrupted by World War I, during which Barros Basto served with distinction and reached the rank of captain in the Portuguese Expeditionary Force. During the war he continued his theosophic reading. While in Paris he visited several synagogues.

After the war and subsequent death of his mother, Barros Basto followed his Jewish inclination to its logical conclusion. He went to Tangiers to be circumcised, and on his return married the daughter of a prominent Jewish family in Lisbon. Back in Oporto, where he served as governor of a military prison, he organized a congregation out of the various foreign Jews who had settled there. "Of this congregation," a Jewish diplomat later reported, "he is President, Chazan, Treasurer, Secretary and General Fairy God-mother."[9]

The diplomat who made that remark was Lucien Wolf, a noted journalist for the Times of London who had won fame organizing refugee relief for the League of Nations. In 1926, after Schwarz published his discoveries and Lisbon's Jews appealed for aid, Wolf was dispatched to Portugal by Jewish organizations in London and Paris. The Lisbon community had proposed setting up a boarding school for Marrano children. But Wolf, after speaking with everyone involved, including the president and prime minister of Portugal, was "not very much impressed by this scheme."[10] Lisbon was too far from Marrano centers, he said, and the plan would be too expensive for the small number of children it would help. Instead, he suggested a mission for Marrano adults in Oporto. "For me the great attraction of Oporto is that it is the seat of a small Jewish community which is presided over and managed by the one Marrano who in the last 150 years has re-entered the Synagogue. . . . As an ex-Marrano himself he knows the Marrano psychology better than anyone else in the Portuguese Jewish community."[11]

Wolf went on to outline the basic elements of his proposal: giving public lectures in Marrano villages, distributing publications explaining Jewish history and rituals, building a synagogue in Oporto, and hiring a foreign rabbi who could supplement his income by giving English or German lessons. Later, a school for Marrano children might be possible. But, ever the diplomat, Wolf added a prescient warning: "Whatever is done, it must not take the form of a noisy and aggressive propaganda. In the eyes of the Church the great bulk of the Marranos are still its baptized children, and anything in the shape of an offensive propaganda for converting them to Judaism would be bitterly resented."[12]

The dramatic renaissance of the following years would closely follow Wolf's predictions. Unfortunately, so would the backlash.

The "redemption" began without delay. Barros Basto converted his first Marranos in Oporto, later that year and in early 1927. The following autumn he made his first foray to the isolated towns and villages of the northeast, where most Marranos lived. In the city of Bragança in the extreme northeast, Barros Basto overcame the fears of leading Jewish families by appearing at their doors in full military dress and announcing to their servants that a Jewish captain from Oporto wished to speak with them. "The elderly women wept with joy mixed with fear," he later wrote. "It is a stupid fear, but, nevertheless, it is still strong."[13]

For the next decade and more, Barros Basto was a whirlwind of activity. In addition to running Oporto's synagogue and military prison, he toured the towns and villages of the northeast, leading prayer meetings and organizing the Marranos. Rented synagogues were opened in Bragança and two other towns, Covilhã and Pinhel. In smaller villages, less formal groups were formed and arrangements were made for them to attend services in the larger towns. In this way, Belmonte's Marranos were considered members of the synagogue at Covilhã, seventeen miles down the highway. Barros Basto also published a newspaper, *Ha-Lapid* (The Torch). He translated Sephardic prayers into Portuguese, and issued pamphlets on Jewish doctrine and culture. Ironically, some of those writings had originally been compiled to instruct Marranos fleeing Portugal three hundred years before.

After organizing adult Marranos, Barros Basto felt ready to educate their children. In 1929 he brought five teenage boys to Oporto for instruction in traditional Judaism. This modest start grew into the *Rosh Pinah* Jewish Theological Seminary, a yeshiva which educated ninety Marrano youths over the next decade. Barros Basto and other teachers instructed the boys in Hebrew, Portuguese, French, and social service, as well as Jewish history, theology, apologetics, homiletics, and ceremonial liturgy.

Barros Basto's most ambitious project was a grand synagogue in Oporto, large enough to accommodate the multitudes of Marranos he anticipated would return to Judaism. Undaunted by lack of funds, he bought land in a new neighborhood of Oporto. The cornerstone was laid in 1929, but little more than the foundation was laid before he ran out of money. The half-built synagogue stood exposed to the elements until 1933, when Elly Kadoorie came for a visit. The persuasive Barros Basto ended his interview 4,700 pounds sterling wealthier than he began it. The synagogue was renamed the Kadoorie Synagogue of Oporto.

Its dedication in 1938 was Barros Basto's finest moment. Jewish leaders from around the world gathered to honor him. Three hundred people crowded into the chapel. A Torah scroll which had been used in Oporto prior to the expulsion was donated. "It has probably never happened," wrote the secretary of London's Portuguese Marranos Committee, "that *one* man should have conceived the idea of building a house of worship in a place and at a time when there was practically no Jewish community there; it has certainly never happened that any such idea has been carried out by that same man."[14]

Such romantic views of the Marrano renaissance were widely held at the time. They were overdrawn. Oporto's Jewish community still consisted largely of foreign Jews. The cautious Marranos remained in their villages, taking a longer view of events—which would turn out to be justified. In retrospect, the glowing words of the London secretary reek with irony. There was certainly no Jewish community in Oporto to justify such a magnificent synagogue. After its dedication it would never again come so close to being filled.

A number of Marranos also came to the dedication. Dressed in pointed caps, fur-lined capes, and their finest village costumes, these weather-beaten peasants contrasted sharply with the cosmopolitan Jews who had gathered there. One group, arriving while the service was already in progress, stood shyly outside so as not to interrupt it— even though the synagogue had been built with such as them in mind.[15] The Marranos, in fact, never felt comfortable with the movement which had been launched in their name. The rigor of traditional Judaism was as foreign to them as the Jews who adhered to it. It was only the infectious enthusiasm of Barros Basto which brought them up from underground. When he succumbed, so did they.

Barros Basto had done his best to avoid trouble. Following Wolf's advice he discouraged unnecessary publicity. "I don't proselytize among believers who practice with conviction another religion than mine," he told one journalist. "I only want to guide those who, groping in shadows and fear, attempt to return to the faith of their fathers."[16] Even when announcing Yom Kippur services in the press, according to one assistant, "every word of these advertisements was carefully chosen for the purpose of . . . avoiding any discrepancy with followers of other rites."[17]

Nevertheless, a backlash began from the start. Marranos who opened a synagogue in Pinhel were boycotted by local Catholics.[18] Their synagogue was attacked during an Easter procession. Catholic women in Bragança asked the governor to close the synagogue there.[19] The author of a book about Marrano customs in Covilhã was ostracized by his neighbors.[20] Barros Basto himself came under attack in the Portuguese press. One Catholic newspaper accused him of being "more philosophic and pantheistic than religious and Jewish, aggravated by having been a revolutionary." His assistants were accused of "democratic" and "Masonic" connections. The Jewish refugees from Hitler were charged with "corrupting the atmosphere with their moral miseries." The entire movement was attacked as a "de-Christianization." One editorial charged: "With outside money they built synagogues and teaching establishments called 'seminaries,' to feed this Jewish propaganda in the centers in which the descendants of the ancient New Christians live, jeopardizing the religious peace and moral unity of the Portuguese nation."[21]

Nor did all the movement's problems come from without; the Oporto synagogue was racked by dissension. The prominent Cassuto family, Sephardic refugees from Hamburg, Germany, who had been assisting Barros Basto since their arrival, angrily quit the congregation in 1935. Leon Cassuto had taken over Barros Basto's duties as president of the congregation, and his son Alfonso had taught in the *Rosh Pinah* yeshiva. The cause of their feud with Barros Basto is not known.

Another dissenting voice, this one more revealing, was heard in a letter printed in London's *Jewish Chronicle* just two days before the synagogue was dedicated in 1938. It was written by one of Barros Basto's earliest backers, Mordechai Van Son, the founder and president of the Dutch Pro-Marranos Committee. The Dutch committee had ceased its efforts abruptly in 1935. Since then, Van Son had been distributing circulars and writing letters against his former colleagues in London and Oporto. His letter, in the midst of those euphoric days, painted a very different picture of the Marrano renaissance than readers of the *Chronicle* were accustomed to. Its thrust was that the renaissance was such a failure that the synagogue should be sold and the proceeds returned to the Kadoorie family.

"There are, in Oporto, only a very few Marranos," Van Son wrote, "and those who do live there have long since refused to have anything to do with the Community—as have also the dozens of Jewish families from Poland and Germany which have settled in Oporto during the last few years." Van Son singled out the yeshiva for attack, charging that "during the last seven years, not a single [student] has become, even in the slightest degree, a truly religious Jew, let alone a Rabbi, fit to act as a teacher in Israel. On the contrary, some of them have become more like anti-Semites than anything else as a result of their sojourn at the Yeshiva." He added that Oporto's community had no rabbi, no qualified teachers, no kosher slaughtering, no Jewish cemetery, no religious instruction for the children, and couldn't even raise a *minyan* for the Sabbath. "The entire Community consists of no more than four or five families, among which there is only one Marrano. . . . It is for these fifteen or so people composing the community that a Synagogue has been built, providing seating accommodations for at least 500 persons!"[22]

The campaign against Barros Basto grew, with tacit government support. He was finally forced out of the army on charges of "immorality."[23] His fall brought the movement to a standstill. Amidst the upheavals of World War II the Marranos' plight went unheeded by world Jewry, which was preoccupied with more important tragedies.

Barros Basto spent his final years in solitude, a beaten man. He published occasional issues of *Ha-Lapid* until 1956. He still received visitors from abroad, with whom he reminisced. He often prayed, but usually alone. Most of Oporto's Jews left for America or Israel after the war, and the synagogue was rarely opened. He died in 1961.

Nearly two decades later, Amílcar Paulo unlocked the door to Barros Basto's second-floor office in the synagogue. Yellowing letters, files, and other papers dating to the 1920s and '30s cluttered its tables and shelves—a gold mine for some future researcher eager to fill the still-gaping holes in the history of this episode. Until that happens, Paulo is one of the few people familiar with those events.

"Barros Basto was a great man," he said, "but the newspapers and priests waged a terrible campaign against him. They said he was lying to the poor people of Bragança, Pinhel, and the other towns. They said he was depriving them of the truth of the Catholic religion. There were two reasons: because he was a republican, and because of anti-Semitism.

"Finally, one priest accused him of being a homosexual. They denounced him to the Court of Justice in Oporto. It was never proven, but there was never a formal acquittal, either. In all the time since he became a Jew he had never been promoted in the army. Now he was forced to retire on a small pension. In his last few years he was a sad man. He used to sit in his office and cry.

"After that the synagogues closed. Only a few of his former students ever came back. Most of them married Catholic girls and their children were brought up as Catholics. The people were afraid of the Salazar government, and of the Germans, too. There was a lot of Nazi propaganda in Portugal.

"After the war came the economic crisis. You couldn't make a living in those villages anymore. Everyone left for France or Brazil. Catholics, Jews, everybody. Today, except in Belmonte, there are just a few old Marranos left, who know they are the last.

"Barros Basto's closest assistant married a Catholic girl, who tried to stop him from going to the synagogue. She said it was the devil's work. He tried to prevent his daughter from being baptized, so she could choose her religion for herself when she grew up. But his wife secretly baptized her and brought her to first communion. After that he became discouraged and never returned to the synagogue.

"Barros Basto's own daughter married a Catholic, too. Her son—Barros Basto's grandson—was raised without any religion. But he is sympathetic to Jews, and interested in Jewish things. So is his mother. Both of them still visit the synagogue. She is very angry at the way the world treated her father."

. . . .

The road to Bragança is a roller-coaster of a highway, winding along the tops of ridges and plunging deep into valleys and canyons. At first the landscape is lush and fertile, painted in primary colors. Green hillsides are marked by red-roofed villages, golden swathes of wheat, and sparkling blue reservoirs. Later, the road climbs into the mountains and the land grows dry and scrubby. Olive trees replace the pines. The villages grow poor and scrubby, too. These are the villages which harbor descendants of Marranos. Today, the Marranos are just a historical curiosity, a ghost of their former selves. But the hill country of northeast Portugal is full of such ghosts. With Paulo's aid they are easily found.

Forty miles before Bragança lies one of the poorest of these villages, Rebordelo. It straddles the highway alongside a hill, with dirt streets branching up and down. A single Marrano still lives in Rebordelo: Moisés Abraão Gaspar. He is not hard to find. There is only one "Moses Abraham" in Rebordelo, if not in all of northern Portugal. He is not hard to find for another reason, too. Portugal's Catholics are extremely devout, and the landscape is littered with roadside crosses. Jewish symbols are understandably rare. But in front of Moisés's house on the outskirts of Rebordelo stands a stone gatepost carved with a Star of David.

"My father Alfredo was a Jew," Moisés explained. And you, Moisés? "The same."

It was Alfredo Gaspar who carved the stone gatepost in 1931, during the Marrano renaissance. He had visited Barros Basto in Oporto a few years before, and showed him his most treasured possession: a leather-bound manuscript already more than one hundred years old, entitled *Book of Prayers to the Almighty and Most High God.* It contained seventy-two pages of Marrano prayers, with a register in the back listing family deaths. The latest entry was for 1848. Barros Basto reprinted the entire book in three issues of *Ha-Lapid* in 1928.[24]

Alfredo named his son "Moses Abraham" in the same exuberant year that he carved the gatepost. A few years later, apparently subdued by the turn of events, he named his second son Francisco.

Moisés married a Catholic girl and does not practice any

Marrano customs. But he is proud of being "Jewish" and still guards the prayer book jealously. He also owns an outdated Jewish calendar illustrated with pictures of Jerusalem. It is printed in Hebrew and Spanish, neither of which Moisés can read. For that matter, he is illiterate in Portuguese, too. When he brought out the ancient prayer book, he handed it to his wife to read aloud.

His oldest son, twenty-year-old Manuel António, pointed to the pictures on the calendar and said he wanted to go there. He asked if he could find work in Israel. Told he could work on a kibbutz, he asked what that was. He said he had never heard of such a thing.

Bragança, the district capital, is only a short drive from Rebordelo. It is a small, prosperous city in the far northeastern corner of Portugal, hiking distance from Spain to either the north or east. A walled old city and an eight-hundred-year-old castle crown the hilltop on the city's edge, reminders of its central role in Portuguese history. The House of Bragança was Portugal's ruling family for hundreds of years, until the republican revolution in which Barros Basto took part.

Bragança's Jews have a long history, too. Their presence is recorded as early as the year 1250, when nineteen of them were accused of usury. After the exodus from Spain their population multiplied, and Bragança became a prime feeding-ground for the Inquisition. The city itself provided eight hundred victims, and the surrounding district another nine hundred. A single auto-da-fé in 1718 included more than fifty residents of Bragança. The city was also the birthplace of one of Amsterdam's leading philosophers: Isaac (Baltasar) Oróbio de Castro.

More recently, Bragança played a leading role in Barros Basto's Marrano renaissance. The first stirrings of revival were felt there even before the arrival of Barros Basto, in 1921. They began, in fact, with a non-Jew: a scholarly, freethinking abbot in the nearby parish of Baçal, Francisco Manuel Alves. The abbot of Baçal was compiling a comprehensive history of the Bragança area, a work which would eventually fill eleven volumes. The fifth volume was entitled "The Jews of the District of Bragança." It consisted primarily of a list of Bragança's 1,705 victims of the autos-da-fé. The abbot prefaced the volume with a lengthy defense of Judaism and a harsh attack on the Inquisition. He dedicated it to his three closest friends, including a bank director named José Montanha who had funded the publication of his writings. In a letter to Montanha he expressed his dismay over the atrocities performed in the name of Christianity: "Oh, José, the study of this question has me in such a state that . . . I am sorry I am not Jewish."[25]

Word of the abbot's introduction leaked out before publication. The entire edition was destroyed; only a few copies have survived. It was not finally published until 1926, with the offending preface replaced by a banal profession of tolerance for all faiths. Recently it has been reprinted with the original introduction.

But when the Marrano renaissance reached Bragança, its leader would be none other than José Montanha. The bank director visited Barros Basto in Oporto in February 1927. That autumn he greeted Barros Basto at the train station at the start of the captain's historic visit to Bragança. On that day and the next, Montanha and six other men were circumcised there. Public Jewish services were held in Bragança for the first time in more than four hundred years. Montanha was elected the new congregation's first president.

The following spring, Barros Basto returned to open a synagogue on the Rua das Combatentes da Grande Guerra. The synagogue was named Sha'arei Pidyon (Gates of Redemption). Its members included doctors, laborers, soldiers, and clerks. Politically well-connected, they were able to have a plaque placed on a major street indicating it as the birthplace of Oróbio de Castro. But other Marranos, including the wealthiest Marrano family, continued to practice Judaism in secret while publicly attending church.

For several years Bragança even had its own rabbi, Jacob Shababo. Rabbi Shababo was born in Palestine, later lived in Brazil, and briefly taught at the yeshiva in Oporto. He was sent to Bragança in the early 1930s to lead the synagogue and take over a Hebrew school founded by a Rosh Pinah graduate. As Lucien Wolf had suggested, he supplemented his income by teaching languages on the side. Rabbi Shababo often drew large crowds for Sabbath prayers. As many as forty to fifty Bragançans would show up, some of them Marranos and others simply curious. This is what caused Bragança's Catholic women to complain to the governor. Young men who studied French with the rabbi were staying afterward and being seduced into Judaism, they claimed. Their request for his expulsion was denied.

The good ladies needn't have bothered. Rabbi Shababo fell

victim to the feuding between Barros Basto and Van Son. A few years later, after the Dutch committee withdrew its support, the rabbi left Bragança. After the fall of Barros Basto, the synagogue was shut down altogether. Montanha was fired as bank director, and his chief deputy lost his job in the mayor's office. Since then, all but one of the Marranos who took part in the renaissance have either passed away or emigrated. Only one man in Bragança still speaks openly of being Jewish, a shoemaker who studied at the *Rosh Pinah* yeshiva in 1930–31, and who was circumcised there at the age of fourteen.

João Baptista dos Santos has a tiny shoe-repair shop on the *Rua das Combatentes da Grande Guerra*, a few doors down from where the synagogue used to be. He is now a wizened old man in his sixties. Every day he recites the Marrano prayers he learned from his parents, sings the Jewish songs he was taught at the yeshiva, and teaches them all to his children. Squatting on his stool with a shoe punch in one hand and a leather strap in the other, João sang the Hebrew song *Eliahu Ha-Navi* (Elijah the Prophet). Then he reached for his ten-year-old daughter's hand and asked her to join him in *Ha-Tikvah*, the national anthem of Israel. She turned away and blushed as João proceeded to sing it alone. The girl is shy, he apologized, but knows *Ha-Tikvah* in both Hebrew and Portuguese.

João no longer allows himself to be photographed. After his picture appeared in an Oporto newspaper in 1978, in a series of articles by Amílcar Paulo on "Secret Jews in Portugal," he was the subject of malicious gossip. Threats were made on his life. His business was boycotted. "I am a poor man with eight children to feed," he said, "not like those rich Jews who are ashamed to say what they are." Indeed, there are others in Bragança who still practice the Marrano rites in secret. Amílcar Paulo has met a few old women who still light Sabbath lamps. But they no longer gather for Passover or Yom Kippur. Outside of Belmonte, not enough Marranos remain interested.

The village of Belmonte, whose name means "beautiful mountain," is perched on a hilltop one hundred fifty miles south of Bragança, commanding the countryside for miles around. Its dramatic skyline is dominated by a fourteenth-century castle, a nineteenth-century parish church, and a twentieth-century watertower—the same mixture of modern and medieval which dominates the town's mentality. Belmonte is the only place in Portugal where the ancient division between Old and New Christian remains a central fact of life. Of Belmonte's approximately four thousand residents, five to six hundred are New Christians. That is their own estimate. Belmonte's Old Christians are as likely as not to shrug their shoulders and say, "Oh, every other house is Jewish."

A stranger in Belmonte notices few overt signs of Marranos. Swastikas are found among the political graffiti scrawled on village walls, but the graffiti is left over from an election several years before. Residents assured a visitor that they have nothing to do with Belmonte's own Jews. The Marrano presence is more subtle than that. A local guide is required to discern it. The patroness of one cafe was pleased to oblige by identifying the "Jews" among her patrons. She pointed out about half her customers.

Belmonte's Old Christians speak proudly of their well-known neighbors. They are the village's claim to fame. Even the parish priest takes pride in them, making the strange boast that more Jews attend his church than any other in Portugal. But Marranos will not discuss their secret lives, and the gentiles know only what they see with their own eyes—in other words, very little. In the cafe, no two Old Christians agreed about what takes place in private. The Marranos smiled and listened quietly to the debate.

On Friday evening Belmonte was peaceful, though not remarkably more so than other Portuguese villages. Nothing indicated that the men drinking beer in cafes had just returned from a secret religious ceremony. Nothing marked the men discussing politics on streetcorners as different from men discussing politics in other villages except, perhaps, that all had put on their "Sunday best" for the occasion. But the town's only discotheque was nearly empty. One of its few customers apologized to the stranger who had wandered in. "We have many Jews in Belmonte," he explained, "so on Friday nights most of us go to other towns for something to do. You should come back tomorrow. That's our big night."

Old and New Christians alike claim they can distinguish each other by appearance alone. "It's not just that we know which families are Jewish," said one young Catholic. "It's a look in their faces, the way they dress, the way they walk." At first glance, a stranger is tempted to agree. Several Marranos have a remarkable "Jewish" look, as though they could have stepped out of a Brooklyn *shul*. But objective observers remain skeptical. "It is certain that they do not constitute a distinct anthropological type in northern Portugal," writes Amílcar Paulo.[26]

Belmonte's Marranos are mostly prosperous, members of the middle class. They are known as hard-working and conscientious, devoted to their families. Some are craftsmen, others are salesmen or petty merchants; nearly all work at some sort of business. According to some Old Christians, however, they refuse to make any sales after dark. Many work in the garment industry, as do Jews in other parts of the world. Two have opened a small clothing factory, easily identifiable by the anti-Jewish slogans scrawled on its walls. None farm.

The Marranos still attend church alongside their Catholic neighbors. Belmonte's parish priest explained that he sees them for baptisms, weddings, and funerals—and occasionally to light a candle for a saint. But they never take communion, he added. An earlier priest tried to bar them from church, but the Marranos insisted on attending. The current priest, who has mended relations with his wayward parishioners and is respected by them, explains that his predecessor wanted the Marranos to build a synagogue where they could be real Jews. He refused to baptize them for the same reason. But the Marranos reacted angrily. The current priest shrugged his shoulders. "They are strange Jews," he mused. "Going to church is part of their religion."

Lighting the Sabbath lamp is the quintessential Marrano ritual. After sundown Friday night, the family gathers for a brief ceremony. Women cover their heads with napkins or white cloths resembling Jewish prayer shawls. The lamps are made from tin by trusted craftsmen, and the wicks from seven strands of pure linen. An old Marrano woman spins each strand from the whitest flax she can find, and blesses each one individually. Before they are lit, curtains are drawn and the lamps sometimes hidden in pots. A blessing is recited which resembles the blessing recited by other Jewish families around the world: "Blessed be my God, my Lord, my *Adonai*, who ordains us and commands us with his blessed and most holy commandments to kindle this holy wick. . . ."[27]

Marrano men are allowed to work on Saturdays, except during the months preceding Passover and Yom Kippur. Those Sabbaths are observed scrupulously. It was on one of those weekends in 1918 that Samuel Schwarz, on a return visit to Belmonte, observed the following incident:

"We sat at the *table d'hôte* of the little village hotel. A Marrano merchant was discussing the sale of his wares with an out-of-town buyer. It was Friday evening and night fell without a bargain being reached. After dinner the buyer, seeing nothing further of our Marrano, decided to accept his price. He sought out the merchant, who to his surprise refused to conclude the deal. The next day, Saturday, spurred by the necessity of leaving the town, he again approached the merchant, who remained obdurate, even when in desperation he raised his bid. To every plea the merchant simply responded, 'Come tonight.' The buyer began to doubt the merchant's good faith and to suspect he did not actually possess the merchandise in question. However, his curiosity and determination impelled him, on Saturday night, to visit the merchant again. His suspicions were set at rest on receiving the goods, but his stupefaction was considerable when the merchant insisted on accepting the first and lower price they had agreed upon. . . .

"It remained for me to explain to the buyer that the merchant had acted in accordance with his Jewish faith, which prohibited him not only from doing business on the Sabbath but from profiting by any advantage the Sabbatical rest might accidentally yield." [28]

Yom Kippur is the holiest day of the Marrano year, as it is for all Jews. They call it the *Dia Grande* (Great Day) or *Dia Puro* (Pure Day), an apparent corruption of the Hebrew *kippur* (atonement). All Marranos fast on Yom Kippur. Even those who have left the community close their shops and take the day off. Those who are more religious gather five times to pray. They calculate its date from the moon itself, since they long ago lost the lunar Jewish calendar. They celebrate it on the eleventh day after the new moon of September, one day later than other Jews—a practice which apparently began in more dangerous times in order to avoid suspicion.

Their other holiday is Passover. Preparations begin a month in advance when Marranos observe a "Fast of Esther," a vestige of the holiday of Purim. In the intervening weeks they abstain from pork and observe the Sabbath meticulously. If a Marrano is traveling that month and cannot avoid eating pork, he is barred from the Passover meals. He must sit apart, eat from a separate plate, and may not sleep with his wife during Passover week. Nor may he eat any *pão santo* (holy bread), the unleavened bread of Passover.

Baking the *pão santo* is a ceremony of its own. It does not take place until the third day of Passover, discreetly postponed as was Yom Kippur. No bread at all is eaten on the first two. On the morning of the third the Marranos throw little balls of dough into the oven and wait for them to explode; the explosions are taken as good omens. When baked, the bread is holy and may not be thrown away. Uneaten portions are kept for the following year; what can't be preserved is burned. Marrano girls are sometimes given pieces as wedding presents and keep them in small boxes for the rest of their lives. But for all its sanctity, *pão santo* is a thick, tasteless, often undercooked, and barely digestible little cake, according to the few foreign Jews who have been allowed to sample it. That may be what makes it holy. When offered modern matzo Marranos have refused. Those "crackers" are too tasty for Passover, they say.[29]

The Marrano Passover begins on the fourteenth day after the new moon in April. Throughout the week Marranos go out on picnics to pray. The most important gathering takes place on the final morning, when they gather on the banks of the Rio Zezere. Prayers and hymns are recited, including a special "Water Prayer" that recounts the story of Moses parting the Red Sea. When they reach the words: "Then came Moses with his lifted staff to beat on the salty sea," the chanters strike the water with olive branches and repeat the next line in unison: "The sea opens in a dozen roads—my people will pass in safety."[30] The olive branches are saved for the following year, when they are used to light the ovens for baking *pão santo*.

This prayer, like all their prayers, is entirely in Portuguese. Only a few Hebrew words have survived among them. *Adonai*, of course, is their secret name for God. *Goyo*, from the Hebrew *goy*, still refers to a non-Jew. *Entrefada*, from the Hebrew *trefa*, means impure, or not kosher. Some of their prayers contain words which are indecipherable in either Hebrew or Portuguese. And in one prayer an entire sentence of Hebrew is preserved, though completely garbled. The Marranos pronounce it, *"Adunai Sabaat Malcolares; Cobrado."* In the original Hebrew it is *"Adonai Tzeva'ot m'lo kol ha'aretz k'vodo"* (Lord of Hosts, the whole earth is full of his glory). They recite these words mechanically, without any hint of their meaning.

In addition to their prayers, Portuguese Marranos have a small folk literature in the style of the Iberian romance. Although the great age of the romance, when such classics as *El Cid* and the *Song of Roland* were spread through Spain and Portugal by wandering minstrels, has long since passed, many of these popular epic poems are preserved in oral tradition. Marrano *romanceiros*, unlike their non-Jewish counterparts, are on biblical themes, such as Daniel in the lion's den or the sacrifice of Isaac. Similar romances, coincidentally, have been preserved by Sephardi Jews in Turkey.[31]

Belmonte's Marranos also have their own marriage and funeral rites. Each couple is married twice, first at home and then, to make it legal, in church. Non-Jewish friends are only welcome at the second ceremony. Funerals, similarly, take place in church and are followed by the Jewish seven days of mourning at home. On the eighth day, again on the thirtieth day, and every three months thereafter until a year of mourning has passed, the relatives fast. There is no Jewish cemetery. Marranos leave this world as they entered it: as Christians, buried under crosses in Belmonte's only burial ground.

Few foreigners gain entrée to these secrets. Marranos are still as suspicious as ever. They have been misled in the past, they say, by foreigners posing as Jews. The most persistent visitors are still screened as Samuel Schwarz was. Old women ask them to recite Jewish prayers, and wait to hear the secret name of God. Amílcar Paulo had to pass such a test, as have others whom he introduced to them.

Most visitors do not get even that far. An eager American writer was told by one Marrano that if he ever returned to Belmonte he would be welcome—as an old friend—in his home for the Sabbath. But not on this visit, added the Marrano; we are still strangers. "It's not because I don't believe you," he reassured the American. "You do look Jewish."

.   .   .   .

Back in Oporto, a surprise dinner guest appeared at the home of Amílcar Paulo: Professor Herman Salomon of Albany, New York. Salomon is a vocal proponent of what might be called the "revisionist" school of Marrano history. He and other historians deny that secret Jews ever existed. Few, if any, New Christians practiced Judaism, they claim, and the Inquisition was a colossal hoax bent on destroying the former Jews for social and economic—not religious—reasons.

The Jewishness of Marranos has been debated since the days of the Inquisition. Rabbis in other countries were often called on to decide whether or not Marranos were Jews. Their decision had legal ramifications. Was a Marrano eligible to inherit the property of his Jewish father? Was a Marrano's widow, who fled the peninsula and returned to Judaism elsewhere, required to obtain her brother-in-law's release in order to remarry, as the widow of a Jew was? Was wine prepared by a Marrano kosher? Following criteria established by Jewish law, the rabbis tried to distinguish between New Christians who voluntarily practiced Catholicism and those who did it against their will. Sympathetic at first, the rabbinical consensus turned against Marranos—who were behaving, charged the rabbis, as though what began as rape turned out to be a pleasurable experience.

Today this debate is confined to historians. On one side are revisionists such as Herman Salomon, who share the rabbis' perception. They claim, in the words of Benzion Netanyahu, that "the overwhelming majority of the Marranos . . . were not Jews, but . . . Christians."[32] In their view, the Inquisition was an attempt to eliminate the New Christians as a social class which dominated the Portuguese economy. Those New Christians who fled to other countries did so out of fear. Whatever Jewish rituals any New Christians may have observed, claim revisionists, grew as a response to their persecution.

On the other side are scholars who disagree with the rabbis' perception of what a Jew is. Writes Gerson D. Cohen: "The historian is not at liberty to restrict his definition of Jewishness to one laid down by rabbis or their adherents. Granted that the Marranos created a new kind of Jewish religion for themselves, they still have to be considered a Jewish phenomenon, for they often lived, suffered, and died as Jews."[33] The living Marranos of Belmonte and other villages are often cited in support of this view. Their stunted religion has been called a "potential" Judaism, only fulfilled when Marranos fled Portugal and reentered Judaism elsewhere. But for the pathetic remnant of Marranos who never left Portugal, it was the only Judaism they had. It was their Judaism, and they knew of no other. To this day there are Marranos who believe it is the outside Jews whose religion is impure.

Although they are on opposite sides of this controversy,

Herman Salomon and Amílcar Paulo remain good friends. Salomon is a frequent visitor to the Paulo home. On this particular evening, all fervor was set aside and Marranos were discussed dispassionately over dinner. But, as on all his visits, Salomon ate only the soup course. He ignored the *tripas a moda do Porto* (Oporto-style tripe) and other local specialties prepared by Paulo's wife for their other American guest, who freely indulged in everything set before him. Salomon peered at him quizzically. "You don't keep kosher?" Salomon asked. "What's the point in being Jewish if you don't keep kosher?"

Later, Paulo took exception to that remark. "For Herman," he said, "Judaism is only a religion. I do not agree. If it were only a religion there would have been no Marranos, no Zionism, and no Israel."

But Paulo does not consider himself a Jew. Since he is descended from Marranos, why not? If he believes that Judaism is more than a religion, why doesn't he qualify as a Jew?

"Circumcision," he replied, "is the bare minimum of being Jewish. I am not circumcised." Paulo paused for a moment. "Nevertheless, I have a Jewish heart."

Indeed he has. Paulo is obsessed with things Jewish. He denies with equal vehemence that he is a Christian, practically taking offense at the suggestion. His home is cluttered with Jewish artifacts and souvenirs from several trips to Israel. He listens to Jewish records; his walls are covered with Jewish art. He is the founder and president of the Institute for Portuguese-Israeli Cultural Relations, which is seeking to have the Oporto synagogue named a cultural landmark and reopened as a Marrano museum and archive. In addition to his many works on ethnography and Marranos, Paulo is the author of a small book entitled *Israel: Young Nation of an Ancient People.* So many foreign Jews visit his home that his neighbors teasingly call it "the Jewish guest house."

Paulo is not alone in this feeling. Many Marranos who have abandoned the secret cult say they feel a kinship with the Jewish people. Moisés Gaspar is one, Barros Basto's grandson another. Back in 1926, Lucien Wolf reported a widespread interest in Judaism among educated Marranos who no longer believed in any religion. "I am not and probably never will become a believer," one high government official told him, "but every day I feel more profoundly a compassionate and intimate sympathy, an intense solidarity, with the Jewish race."[34]

This feeling has survived in Portugal longer than the Jewish religion. Judaism has not really existed there (except in the new Lisbon community) for hundreds of years. The religion of the Marranos is no more than a fossil. But the Jewish people live on in Portugal; arguments to the contrary can convince only on paper. The proof still lives in the villages of the northeast. There, for nearly five hundred years, Marranos have struggled to live and die as Jews, if in little more than name alone. Only for those who believe with Professor Salomon that being Jewish is no more than keeping kosher are there no secret Jews in Portugal.

CHAPTER THREE

The Chuetas of Majorca:
No Longer Jews, but Still Victims
of the Inquisition

When Nicolas Aguiló was a boy on the Spanish island Majorca, his playmates suddenly turned on him. They called him a *chueta* and wouldn't play with him anymore. Nico didn't know what a Chueta was, other than a common Majorcan insult, so he asked his parents. Yes, they told him, you are a Chueta, a descendant of Jews who lived on Majorca in the Middle Ages. "At first it was a real shock," Nico recently recalled. "My friends had always spoken badly of Chuetas, and it was a shock to find out I was one." But Nico was a curious boy, and started reading up on Jews. When foreign Jews opened a synagogue on Majorca he paid them a visit. "I began to feel a stronger and stronger connection with Jewish culture and the Jewish people," he said. "One day I simply didn't feel like I was a Christian anymore."

Nicolas Aguiló is now Nissan Aguiló, an Israeli citizen. He renamed himself after the month in which he converted to Judaism, during spring 1978 when he was twenty years old. He is the first Chueta to convert back to the religion their ancestors were forced to abandon.

But are Majorca's other Chuetas proud of him? Hardly. Nico is an exception—the exception, perhaps, that proves the rule. On Majorca, unlike northern Portugal, not a trace of secret Judaism survived. Though descended from Jews, Chuetas are among the most pious Catholics on the island.

Chuetas are descended from Majorcan Marranos who were discovered practicing Judaism secretly in the late 1600s, more than two hundred years after *their* ancestors had been forced to convert to Christianity. The fifteen surnames of those Marrano families were posted on a church wall and never forgotten. Ever since, anyone on Majorca with one of those names has been branded a Chueta. Until recently that was enough to make one a second-class citizen. Chuetas now enjoy equal rights, but many Majorcans still think of them as "Jews."

It is not always Jews, after all, who determine who is or is not Jewish. Often it is their enemies—a species Jews never seem to run out of—who decide. Like the many devout German Christians who woke up as "Jews" one morning in 1933—as though Judaism had somehow been inherited in their blood cells (see Chapter VII)— anyone on Majorca with a "Jewish" name was discriminated against. Not Chuetas but other Majorcans refused to forget which families were descended from Marranos. Other Majorcans refused to marry or even go to school with them. And because of those other Majorcans, hundreds of years later one Chueta—Nico Aguiló—decided to become a Jew by belief, not just by insult.

. . . .

As it has been since the Middle Ages, the *Carrer de l'Argenteria* (Street of Silversmiths) in Palma, the major city of Majorca, is lined with jewelry shops. To most tourists scouring it for a bargain, there is nothing else unusual about the street. Its erratic sidewalks and overhanging balconies are little different from the other narrow, winding lanes of old Palma. Nor is it as overcrowded and frenetic as it used to be, bustling with activity, contrasting vividly with Majorca's otherwise leisurely pace of life. "What can they be doing there," asked a Spanish writer early this century, "so many people gathered together in these boxes; poking their noses out of the little windows and furtively watching the passers-by; amusing them- selves with their lacemaking; working on little wheels with pincers; pulling out drawers full of precious stones and putting them in the presses?"[1]

The proprietors of the jewelry stores are famous for standing in their doorways, hawking their wares to passing shoppers. They are quick to engage a visitor in conversation, hoping for a sale. But there is one subject they do not like to discuss: Chuetas. They may say they know nothing, that Chuetas are no different from anyone else, or that they have no time to waste on such matters. "I am a Catholic," one young jewelry dealer recently told a reporter from *The New York*

Times. "My nose is the same as your nose. I am white and you are white."[2]

The *Carrer de l'Argenteria* is the main street of a Palma neighborhood called the *Call Menor.* Even most Majorcans mistakenly assume that this name comes from the Spanish word *calle,* meaning "street." Actually, it comes from the Hebrew word *kahal,* meaning "assembly." The *Call Menor* (little assembly) was formerly one of two Jewish ghettoes in Palma. (There has been no *Call Major* since the Middle Ages.) Its huge Church of Santa Eulalia used to be a synagogue. Nearby, a socket of one of the gates which used to seal off the ghetto can still be found.

There are no longer any Jews in the *Call,* but it is still thought of as Palma's Jewish neighborhood. Even some visiting Jews have made this mistake. A century ago, one tourist wrote back to England that "a stranger strolling unawares down this street might easily imagine himself in the Jodenstraat of Amsterdam, the Judengasse of Frankfort-on-Main, the Rue des Rosiers, Paris, or the purlieus of our humbler London brethren."[3]

The residents of the *Call* (with a few recent exceptions) are Chuetas, not Jews. Each bears one of their fifteen surnames: Aguiló, Bonnin, Cortès, Forteza, Fuster, Martí, Miró, Picó, Piña, Pomar, Segura, Taronjí, Valentí, Valleriola, and Valls. On the Spanish mainland these are ordinary names, with no special implications. But on Majorca they have been "Jewish" names since the late seventeenth century, when their bearers were convicted of worshipping the wrong God.

In the Middle Ages, Majorca's Jews had been among the most prosperous in Spain, which is to say the entire world. First under Moslem and then under Christian rule, Jews helped make Palma one of the Mediterranean's greatest seaports. They enjoyed complete autonomy within their walled ghetto, dominating the island's commerce and culture. Their mapmakers in particular were renowned as the best in the world. One of them, Abraham Cresques, is remembered as the "father of modern cartography" for adding Marco Polo's discoveries to existing maps, a breakthrough said to have inspired Columbus.

Their prosperity came to an end—as for all Majorcans—in the fourteenth century. Taxes and plague reduced the island to poverty. As usual, Jews were made the scapegoat. In midsummer 1391, during a wave of anti-Jewish riots throughout Spain, thousands of Majorcan peasants gathered outside Palma's walls, seeking revenge for the loss of their lands. Most of the island's nobility and wealthy merchants, including about eight hundred Jews, took refuge in a castle above the city. The mob spent its fury on those left behind: sacking the ghetto and killing three hundred Jews. The remainder of the ghetto's residents—excluding those who had escaped to the castle—were forced to convert to Catholicism.

After the riot, Palma's ghetto was shared by two groups: the unconverted Jews who had taken refuge in the castle, and the *conversos* who had not. By Spanish law, *conversos* were forbidden to relapse to Judaism. Other regulations encouraged the yet-unconverted Jews to become *conversos*. Jews were not only forbidden to wear expensive clothes, but selling food or giving medicine to Christians, even eating or drinking with them, was illegal. These side-by-side communities lasted only until the next riot, in 1435, when the Jews were accused of mocking Christianity by crucifying a slave on Good Friday. They fled to the mountains, but were pulled from their hiding places and given a choice between death and baptism. All chose the latter. Judaism was declared illegal on Majorca more than half a century earlier than in the rest of Spain.

Little actually changed. The ex-Jews, now all *conversos*, simply reorganized as a guild. Palma's Jewish community became known as the "New Brotherhood of St. Michael the Archangel." *Conversos* continued to live in the same neighborhoods, attend segregated schools and houses of worship, and dominate formerly Jewish professions such as foreign trade and metal-working. Other Majorcans still called them Jews. Many continued to practice Judaism in secret.

To root them out, the Holy Office of the Inquisition set up shop in Majorca in the late 1400s. Its first action was to issue an edict of amnesty. Hundreds of self-confessed secret Jews turned themselves in under this and a second, succeeding edict. Hundreds more who didn't were tried and convicted. Inquisition procedure left little room for innocence. A *converso* who confessed his crimes would be "reconciled" to the faith at a public auto-da-fé and given minor punishments, such as wearing a penitential robe called a *sanbenito* with his name and offense written on it. Second offenders, or those who for some other reason were judged impenitent, would be "relaxed" to civil authorities for capital punishment. To be "relaxed" became a euphemism for being burned at the stake. Few of those "relaxed" were actually burned in person; most had already escaped the island and were only burned in effigy. And most of those burned in person were executed before being put to the flames; few were actually burned alive. That distinction was reserved for a small but distinguished minority of impenitent Jews.

After an initial burst of energy in the late fifteenth and early sixteenth centuries, Majorca's Inquisition grew dormant. It still rooted out a "Lutheran heretic" or two, but ignored the *conversos*. Not a single Majorcan was burned as a Jew for nearly one hundred fifty years, either in person or in effigy. Only rarely was one even brought to the attention of the Holy Office. But this changed rapidly in the 1670s, beginning with a series of apparently unconnected events. Serving girls reported seeing strange ceremonies in *converso* homes. Travelers to Italy reported that Italian Jews knew about Marranos on Majorca, even providing their names and addresses. Finally, a Jewish teenager from North Africa was arrested when his boat stopped in Palma on its way to Italy, because he had been born and baptized in Madrid before fleeing Spain. When he refused to repent, the boy was burned alive in January 1675.

The sight of a boy being burned alive—for the first time in living memory—spurred the Inquisition into further action. Acting on information already received, it arrested six *conversos* in Palma. Their testimony led to others. Eventually more than a hundred were seized in what became known as the "conspiracy of 1678." Their confiscated property was the largest sum seized in the entire history of the Spanish Inquisition. The following year, all were publicly "reconciled" to the faith in five autos-da-fé.

But while still in prison, the conspirators hatched a plot to escape Majorca. For nearly a decade they sneaked off in small groups so as not to arouse attention. The gradual exodus was interrupted in 1688. One young *converso*, angered by their attempt to prevent his marriage to a non-Jewish girl, informed on the others. The remaining conspirators hurriedly made arrangements to flee en masse.

On the night of March 7, small groups of women and children casually left their homes in the *Call Menor* for what seemed like an evening stroll. After dark they joined their husbands outside the city walls, and boarded an English ship with a sympathetic captain. But as luck would have it, a sudden storm prevented them from setting sail. After six hours on board they returned to their homes. Officers of the Inquisition were waiting for them.

Their trials lasted three years, ending in four autos-da-fé in the spring of 1691. Of the eighty-six arrested, thirty-seven were burned. Most renounced Judaism and were mercifully garrotted to death first. Only three remained impenitent, including their reputed "rabbi." Thirty thousand Majorcans watched as these martyrs faced the flames alive, on a hilltop outside town. Palma was so crowded for the occasion that the British ambassador to Spain complained that he couldn't even find a decent room. All that were available were "very ill accommodations," he wrote to his father, "by reason of the concourse of people which are here; for Tuesday last there were burnt here twenty-seven Jews and heretics, and tomorrow I shall see executed about twenty more; and Tuesday next, if I stay here so long, is to be another *Fiesta*, for so they entitle a day dedicated to so execrable an act."[4]

The ashes were barely cold when Majorca's chief inquisitor decided that the executions should never be forgotten. In 1693 he ordered that all *sanbenitos* worn in the autos-da-fé of 1679 and 1691 should be displayed in Palma's Dominican church. Portraits of the condemned were later hung alongside them. Fading names were restored. The *sanbenitos* remained on the walls until 1820, when they were burned in a popular uprising against the Inquisition. But it was too late to help those Majorcans who bore one of the fifteen surnames written on them. They were already branded as Chuetas.

The word *chueta* is not actually pronounced that way on Majorca; it is the Spanish spelling of the Mallorquin word *xueta*, or *xuetó*, meaning "little Jew"—literally, "Jew-ette." (Mallorquin is the local dialect of Catalan, the language of northeastern Spain including the Balearic Islands, of which Majorca is one.) Such diminutives were once common in Catalan and not, by themselves, necessarily intended as insults; similarly, a Moslem was formerly called a *moreto* (little Moor). But on Majorca it is popularly believed that *xueta* is derived, rather, from *xuia*, local slang for "bacon," and applied to the island's ex-Jews in the same way *marrano* was on the mainland. Majorcans freely interchange the words *xueta, jueu,* and *hebreu;* in their eyes, all mean the same.[5]

Chuetas themselves do not use those names. They refer to

each other, in Mallorquin, as *d'es carrer*—"those of the street." That name refers to the *Carrer de l'Argenteria,* but it includes all Chuetas— even those whose families have not lived on "the street" for generations.

Discrimination against Chuetas was at first legal. Chuetas were barred from schools and the University of Palma, forbidden to serve in the army or hold public office, and prevented from joining social clubs or professional guilds. They could not become priests without leaving the island. But after a century as pariahs, Chuetas appealed to the Spanish crown. They protested that they were faithful Catholics, loyal citizens, and paid their taxes on time. King Carlos III responded in their favor, issuing three proclamations in the 1780s which Chuetas consider an "emancipation proclamation." One ordered that the gates of the ghetto be torn down, that Chuetas be allowed to live anywhere on the island, and that it be a crime to call them Jews, Hebrews, or Chuetas. The second allowed them to serve in the armed forces or hold public office. The third allowed them to work at any trade they wanted.

But it took more than the force of law to wipe out the island's deep-rooted prejudice. The king's decrees had little effect on everyday Majorcan reality. The university and the clergy both continued to exclude Chuetas. Palma's tailor guild, rather than admit one (as ordered by a civil court), declared it would rather disband. Even Palma's civil authorities complained that the decrees were opposed to Majorcan tradition.

Only the island's intelligentsia accepted Chuetas as equals. Majorcans who took part in the mid-nineteenth century Catalan *Renaixença,* or literary renaissance, included numerous poets and writers with such names as Cortès, Taronjí, and Fuster. The common people were less open-minded; twice that century the *Call* was sacked by angry mobs. The French writer George Sand, who wintered on Majorca in 1838 with her tubercular lover Fréderic Chopin, noted of Chuetas: "When one . . . observes the relentless hatred by which the unhappy Jews [sic] are still pursued in Majorca, even after twelve to fifteen generations of conversion to Christianity, it is hard to believe that the spirit of the Inquisition had died out so entirely."[6]

Schools, churches, and the clergy have gradually opened to Chuetas this century. When a Chueta priest delivered a sermon in Palma's cathedral for the first time in the 1930s, it was a celebration all Chuetas turned out for. Social barriers persisted longer. A Majorcan who freely did business with Chuetas would not think of having one to his house for dinner. Intermarriage spelled disgrace for a Majorcan family, and even now is discouraged. One elderly Chueta recently recalled from his childhood that "we were someplace between the horse and the dog on the social scale."[7]

The Catalan writer Gaziel, editor of a Barcelona daily, tells of an incident which occurred to him in the 1920s. He had rented a summer home on the island and gone fishing with Majorcans he befriended there. On one trip he noticed that his companions sat down to eat in two separate groups. Since his was larger, he asked his fellows to call the others over. To his surprise, no one made a move. Finally, one of his companions shrugged his shoulders and explained, "They sit apart because they are Chuetas." What surprised Gaziel most, he later recalled, was that this man was a socialist.[8]

Majorca's post-war tourist boom delivered the *coup de grâce* to any lingering discrimination. On an island now dominated by outsiders, Chuetas have become a native ethnic group. They are not the only one; Palma's fishing families and the island's old nobility also remain distinct. An American anthropologist who recently studied Chuetas, Kenneth Moore of Notre Dame University, reports that most Majorcans describe the differences as psychological. He quotes a Mallorquin proverb: *Es xueta, fa xuetadas*—"Is a Chueta, acts like one."[9]

How do Chuetas act? Most Majorcans describe them as conservative, traditional, and genuinely—if ostentatiously—pious. Chuetas are famous on Majorca for the giant crosses dangling from their necks, and the extra-loud voices they pray in. Some used to kneel *on top* of the church pews so everyone could see them praying. Chuetas are also said to be overly defensive and insecure, sensitive to social slights. Chueta women are reputed to be beautiful and self-sacrificing, the men ugly but "sensual." Traditional anti-Semitic adjectives also find their way into Chueta stereotypes: greedy, miserly, large-nosed, round-shouldered, and timid (except in business, where they are said to be ruthless). But other reputed Chueta characteristics are not found in Jewish stereotypes elsewhere: large ears and a singsong tone of voice. One Majorcan novelist recently described Chuetas as "traditionalists and *enragé* Catholics, because Majorca and the Church had given it to them like no one else. More intelligent and cultivated than average on the island, almost all well-to-do, it would be difficult to sort out the obscure reasons for such masochism." [10]

Chuetas dismiss these descriptions as envy. "What do we care?" one told the English poet Robert Graves, who lives on the island. "Our success is due to three qualities which we have learned to cultivate: intelligence, sobriety, and strict honesty." [11]

There are now some ten to fifteen thousand Chuetas on Majorca. Only a minority still lives in the *Call*. Many left for the smaller towns and villages around the island and, since World War II, for newer neighborhoods on the outskirts of Palma. Most are middle-class tradesmen or businessmen. They still dominate the island's metal trade as they have since they were Jews. But few are now silversmiths; most shops on the *Carrer de l'Argenteria* house either goldsmiths or retail jewelers. Many Chuetas are now plumbers, apparently because—surmises Robert Graves—indoor plumbing was introduced to Majorca around the same time that silver chain purses went out of style. Others are bartenders, shoemakers, garage owners, carpenters, hoteliers, movie distributors, food wholesalers, grain and nut merchants, mechanics, moneylenders, perfumers, tailors, doctors, and so on. They also predominate among the island's musicians, especially pianists and violinists. For some reason, Majorca's trumpeters and drummers are almost entirely non-Chueta.

Many Majorcans predict the final assimilation of Chuetas within another generation or two. "When we started selling sun and water it was finished," gloated one Chueta. [12] Not only Jews but Protestants, Moslems, Hindus, Buddhists, and foreigners of every imaginable persuasion now visit the island. A kosher hotel appeals to the Jewish tourist trade, and a small synagogue accommodates retired English Jews. In addition to tourists, workers from all over Spain have moved to Majorca permanently. They freely intermarry with both Chuetas and non-Chuetas; the distinction is meaningless to anyone from off the island. "My generation," says Nico Aguiló, who grew up in the Palma of the 1960s and '70s, "has no real problems. It's nothing at all like it used to be, even for my father's generation."

•   •   •   •

Nico Aguiló is a quiet, self-possessed young man whose serious demeanor belies his youth. His smiles are rare enough to be eloquent, as are his words. His eyes never flinch from a direct gaze as he speaks of his decision to become a Jew. "I was already religious," he explains. "I believed in God before I believed in Judaism. But every time I take another look at the history of the Chuetas I become more and more convinced that he exists. That Chuetas remained separate for more than five hundred years cannot be mere coincidence."

Although Nico, as he still likes to be called, is the only Chueta who has formally converted to Judaism, he is only one of many who in the last few decades have taken an interest in their Jewish roots. It is a small movement of perhaps a few dozen people, involved for different reasons and to varying degrees. But it has been blown out of proportion by misleading headlines in the foreign press, and by the misperceptions of well-intentioned outsiders.

This modest revival began in the 1950s when a Chueta named Cayetano Martí-Valls decided to become a Jew, after having a mystical experience on the site of an ancient synagogue. Knowing no Jews, he taught himself Hebrew and educated himself in Judaism. He also formed a Chueta study group which met in his library to discuss Jewish history and religion. In his spare time he painted, mostly on religious subjects. Later, after a bad eye forced him to retire as a plasterer, he taught painting and worked with local youths, especially young Chuetas.

Martí-Valls also wrote letters about religion to celebrities around the world, such as David Ben-Gurion and Queen Elizabeth of England. One such letter to Ben-Gurion was picked up by the press in 1956, and led to the confusion which has plagued the revival ever since. "We have heard," wrote Martí-Valls, "that after two thousand years the Jewish state has been re-created. We are several thousand men, women, and children, the remnants of Spanish Jewry. The cruel Inquisition forced our ancestors to deny their religion and accept the Catholic faith. We appeal to you as the head of the Israeli government to help us return to the faith of our fathers, to our people, and to our homeland. Regretfully, we know very little of Jewishness, and therefore urge you to supply us with books on Judaism in the Spanish language. . . ."[13]

Martí-Valls's letter was misinterpreted to mean that thousands of secret Jews wanted to come out of hiding on Majorca. It drew headlines from Tel Aviv to New York. But when news of the letter filtered back to Majorca, the reaction was less than overwhelming.

Commented one Chueta to Robert Graves: "Who knows what some imbeciles will write in a moment of enthusiasm?"[14]

Other misunderstandings followed. In 1960, Israeli newspapers reported that a "Marrano" from Majorca named Isabel Muñoz had come to Israel and "returned" to Judaism. Muñoz was reassuming her secret family name of Yemin-Oz, added the accounts, and would soon return to Majorca to open a synagogue for "the so-called 'Chuetas.'"[15] Anyone familiar with Chuetas would have realized that "Muñoz" was not a Chueta name, but no one bothered to point it out at the time. Muñoz did eventually return to Majorca, where she was committed to an institution for the mentally ill.

Among Israelis inspired by those romantic accounts was a retired professor in Jerusalem, Israel Ben-Zeev. Formerly a professor of Semitic languages at universities in Cairo and Frankfurt, Ben-Zeev had recently founded the World Union for the Propagation of Judaism, to counteract the inroads made by Christian missions to the Jews. On the lookout for potential converts, he dispatched an assistant to Majorca in 1963.

The assistant returned with two Majorcans: Daniel Crespi and his son Raphael. The Crespis arrived in Tel Aviv, converted to Judaism, and at a press conference were introduced to journalists as "former Majorcan Marranos."[16] "Crespi" was not a Chueta name, either, but again no one pointed it out. The Crespis told Israeli journalists that a group of Marranos had been arrested in Palma for trying to organize a synagogue. Only the *Jewish Chronicle* bothered to confirm their story with a correspondent on Majorca. He reported that it was "absolutely without foundation. . . . There is evidence of an apparent 'return' to Judaism on the part of some Marranos, but their number does not run into more than double figures."[17]

Two years later, Ben-Zeev flew off to Majorca in person. He had struck a deal with Israeli authorities to finance Chueta immigration. Under this agreement, Chuetas would be admitted to Israel as temporary residents, pending their conversion to Judaism, rather than as Jews under the Law of Return. Ben-Zeev spent three months on Majorca, but could not find any Chuetas who wanted to emigrate. Explained one Chueta to Robert Graves: "Why should we want to leave Majorca? We have been here many centuries longer than the noble families themselves. This is our home."[18]

Nevertheless, Ben-Zeev found four families who were willing

to leave. None were Chuetas, a fact of which he neglected to inform the Israeli press. One family was not even Majorcan but recent immigrants from southern Spain. Ben-Zeev told them they were descended from Jews because their name was García—one of the most common Spanish surnames. The immigrants accepted his offer for mostly economic reasons: it included free transportation and promises of good jobs and housing.

The twenty-four Majorcans arrived by boat on May 30, 1966. They were welcomed in Haifa by a brass band and schoolchildren bearing flowers. Ben-Zeev and immigration officials were on hand to accompany them to new apartments in Nes Ziona, a Tel Aviv suburb. Journalists, told that they were descendants of Spanish Marranos who survived on Majorca under the name "Chuetas," waxed enthusiastic. The Israeli press dubbed them the "Inquisition migrants." One French magazine reported that "after six centuries of secret fidelity to Judaism, the survivors of the autos-da-fé discovered the path of Zion."[19] Before long, embarrassed newspapers had to report that the immigrants were not really secret Jews. Nor did many of them want to become Jews. But not even the press found out then that the Majorcans were not even Chuetas. That fact was not unearthed until the 1970s, by Kenneth Moore.

Though unwilling to adopt the local religion, the immigrants showed how quickly they could pick up some other native customs. After only three days in Israel they staged a sit-down strike. They complained that they had not received jobs in their trades as Ben-Zeev had promised, but instead were sent out as day-laborers, clearing stones for a new forest. The next day they demonstrated in front of the Spanish consulate in Jerusalem. Ben-Zeev told reporters that the local labor exchange had made a "tragic error."[20]

Reacting quickly, immigration authorities found the workers better jobs. One was hired as a carpenter, another as a plasterer, and four others as construction workers. Each family received an outright grant of 100 Israeli pounds (then worth $33). But they were still unhappy. Three families returned to Majorca in mid-July. The fourth, an elderly couple who were the only ones actually claiming to be descendants of Jews—though not actually Chuetas—stayed long enough to convert to Judaism. They returned to Majorca in September.

Ben-Zeev stopped talking to the press. Other Israelis were less reticent. The independent daily *Ha'aretz* called for disciplining the responsible officials in the immigration ministry.

To this day, an unrepentant Ben-Zeev still calls the immigrants "Chuetas." In a recent interview, he blamed the fiasco on Christian missionaries. "Four hundred years as Catholics in Spain had changed their mentality," he complained. "I explained to them that to be a Jew and a Christian is not possible. But then the missionaries came and told them not to become Jews."

That episode discredited the Chueta "revival" in the public eye, but really had nothing to do with it. Back in Palma, Martí-Valls and his followers were unaffected by the sensational stories in the foreign press. They continued to pass around Jewish reading materials, holding occasional prayer meetings. They eventually crossed paths with Majorca's growing colony of foreign Jews. Several Chuetas attended the Jews' informal services. When the foreigners opened a synagogue in 1971, a few Chuetas were allowed to participate without actually converting to Judaism. It is hard to say how many Chuetas were involved. As many as thirty-five to forty met in Martí-Valls's study group, but not all were believers in Judaism.

Nico Aguiló is the only Chueta who has taken the formal step of converting to Judaism. Nico grew up in one of Palma's new suburbs, one generation removed from the *Call.* As a teenager he began spending two or three afternoons a week with Martí-Valls. By the time he was sixteen, he was a full-fledged member of the Palma synagogue. He continued to practice Judaism during a twenty-month stint in the Spanish army. After his discharge in 1977 he moved to Israel, studied Hebrew on an Orthodox kibbutz, converted to Judaism, and changed his name to Nissan. He later studied in a Jerusalem yeshiva and served in the Israeli army.

"There are other Chuetas who also feel a connection with Jewish culture and the Jewish people," Nico recently explained, "but mostly they are not religious, as I am. They are not willing to go through circumcision, conversion, and all the praying." One family, which is as religious as he, cannot move to Israel for personal reasons, Nico added. Not even Martí-Valls has formally converted. "Cayetano is not a Jew according to Jewish law," said Nico, "but he feels he is a Jew. He has a Jewish soul."

* * * *

In 1942, Nazi "racial experts" investigated a rumor that Chuetas were in league with the "international Jewish conspiracy." They asked the island's archbishop for a list of all Majorcans with "Jewish blood."

Chuetas, of course, are not the only Majorcans at least partially descended from Jews. Their fifteen surnames are only the names of those convicted in 1679 and 1691. Most of the island's Jewish population had already been absorbed by Majorca's Catholics. Fortunately for the Chuetas, the names of those other Jews became available shortly before the war. In 1936, a Columbia University doctoral student named Baruch Braunstein published a landmark study of Majorca's Inquisition. In an appendix he listed every *converso* ever "reconciled" or "relaxed" on the island. For the first time in hundreds of years, Majorcans could see for themselves what a small percentage of the island's converted Jews had become Chuetas.

Majorca's archbishop sidestepped the Nazi request. After consulting a few Chuetas and local historians, he listed every surname on Braunstein's list. Using those names he calculated that thirty-five percent of Majorca's population—about one hundred thousand people—was descended from Jews. No action was taken against Chuetas during the war.

It is not Jewish descent, after all, which preserves whatever Jewishness Chuetas may possess. "Jewish blood" has nothing to do with it. Chuetas are "Jews" only in the eyes of other Majorcans, and kept that way by ostracism alone.

The story of the Nazi request was only recently told, in a book called *The Descendants of the Converted Jews of Majorca: Four Words of Truth*. It was written by an elderly Chueta named Miguel Forteza who had lived off the island for ten years. On his return in the 1960s, he was appalled at the prejudice which remained. Seeking to discredit it, his book came to similar—if more modest—conclusions to the archbishop's: computing that eighteen percent of Majorca's population was descended from Jews. Since Forteza also questioned whether the fifteen Chueta surnames had ever belonged exclusively to Jews, he concluded that Chuetas were no more "Jewish" than other Majorcans. His conclusions aroused the anger of non-Chuetas who felt impugned by the possibility of Jewish descent, and sparked a bitter debate in the Palma press. It is hard for a non-Majorcan to understand their concern. Being a Jew has nothing to do with blood. For that matter, neither does being a Majorcan: the people of

Majorca are a crossbreed of all the waves of immigration which swept through the island region over thousands of years.

Recently, the debate over Chueta "Jewishness" entered the academic arena. Kenneth Moore writes: "To deny that there is anything Jewish about the Chuetas is preposterous. They retain a sense of Jewishness from their past, and on the whole tend to be sympathetic to the problems of Jews on a world-wide scale."[21]

But another professor, Thomas F. Glick of Boston University, denies even that much Jewish identity to Chuetas. He says it was the segregated Majorcan social structure which made Chuetas *appear* to be Jewish. "The case of the Chuetas," he writes, "raises the paradoxical question: is it possible to be both Jewish and not Jewish at the same time?"[22]

Perhaps the final word should be given to Nico Aguiló. "For five hundred years," he says, "we had no opportunity to say whether or not we wanted to be Jews. We were just told that we were. Now, for the first time, we are given the freedom to decide. I decided to be a Jew. So far I am the only one to go all the way. But I expect—I hope—there will be others who will follow me."

CHAPTER FOUR

The Moslem Marranos of Mashhad

An elderly Jerusalem shopkeeper leaned over his counter, as though sharing a confidence. "We have a different tradition," he explained, "even from other Iranian Jews. We don't think the same way and we don't live the same way."

In Tel Aviv, a London-born importer echoed his words. "No, we don't mix much," he said. "When we go someplace new we like to go together. Even in your New York. There is an apartment house in Queens where everyone is Mashhadi, and a building on Fifth Avenue where all the Mashhadis sell carpets."

On an upper floor of that building in the carpet district of lower Fifth Avenue, a young rug dealer born and raised in the United States leaned against a pile of carpets taller than himself. "When I marry," he said in an unaccented English, "I'll marry a Mashhadi girl. No, I don't have anyone in mind. If I can't find one here I'll look in Tel Aviv."

And a few blocks uptown on 47th Street, a Teheran-born diamond dealer sat in his heavily guarded cubicle. "It's not because other Jews aren't good enough for us," he explained, "or because we don't like them. We Mashhadis just don't feel comfortable around anyone else. We know each other. It's because of our experience together."

Our experience together. The Jews from Mashhad, the major city of eastern Iran, have shared an experience which belongs to no others in the world. They were Marranos, secret Jews. But unlike the original Marranos of Spain and Portugal, who lost touch with the Jewish world, Mashhad's Moslem Marranos survived as Jews. They practiced Orthodox Judaism in secret until they could do it openly again. Also unlike the original Marranos, this story did not occur in the distant past. The Jews of Mashhad were forced to become Moslems in 1839. They remained secret Jews well into this century. Many ex-Marranos are alive today.

"Yes, I was a good Moslem," laughed one elderly New Yorker. "I was the smartest boy in class, and the teacher always asked me to lead the prayers to Mecca. But after school I went home to study Hebrew and read the Torah."

Spain and Portugal are only the most famous countries in which Jews were forced to convert but continued practicing Judaism in secret. In Mashhad, too, "converted" Jews continued to pray in underground synagogues, teach their children in hidden classrooms, and only marry among themselves. And from Mashhad, as from Spain and Portugal, secret Jews fled to other places where they could practice their religion openly. Like the exiles from Spain and Portugal, Mashhad's refugees remained separate wherever they went. They founded their own synagogues and kept in close contact with Mashhadis in other cities, forming a Mashhadi diaspora-within-the-Diaspora. Like the similar diaspora of Sephadi Jews, it outlived the home community. Only a handful of Jews live in Mashhad today, but some ten thousand Mashhadis keep its memory alive around the world.

These Mashhadis may be the most clannish Jews in the world. Though geographically dispersed they are a single community. They often keep in closer touch with the friends and relatives they left behind than with the people they have chosen to live among. They almost never marry outside their community, even non-Mashhadi Jews. Young Mashhadis who may never have lived in Mashhad, or even seen Iran, sometimes travel halfway around the world to find a Mashhadi spouse. As of this writing, their largest communities are in Tel Aviv, New York, Teheran, Milan, Jerusalem, London, and Hamburg. Mashhadis are constantly on the move, seeking new cities, new countries, new markets for their goods.

But for some reason, their romantic story is hardly known to other Jews. Jewish communities are often unaware that former Marranos live among them. Schoolchildren who study Spanish and Portuguese Marranos never hear a word about these more recent—and more successful—secret Jews, whose history reads like a tale from the Arabian Nights. Articles in English about Mashhad's Marranos are few and far between. Even many Jews well-versed in Jewish history have never heard of them.

*   *   *   *

Mashhad is the capital of Khorasan Province in the northeast corner of Iran, near the borders of Russia and Afghanistan. It is the holiest city in Iran, the burial place of Imam Riza. Shi'ite Moslems, the majority of Iranians, trace their schism with Islam's dominant Sunni branch back to the prophet Mohammed himself, and count a succession of twelve *imams* who inherited his mantle of leadership. The first was the prophet's son-in-law Ali, and the second his grandson Hussein. Both are buried in Iraq. Riza, the eighth *imam*, is the only one buried in Iran. The magnificent mosque over his tomb in Mashhad is visited by pilgrims from all over the Shi'ite world, not just from Iran but from Yemen, Iraq, India, Afghanistan, and Pakistan as well. Pilgrims to Mashhad, in fact, have always been the majority of visitors to Iran—even before the recent revolution cut off non-religious tourism.

Shi'ites were famous for their intolerance long before the Ayatollah Khomeini. They consider non-Moslems to be "unclean," and have carried anti-Jewish laws to heights of absurdity undreamed of outside Iran. In the seventeenth century Jews were not even allowed to go outside in the rain, for fear of contaminating rainwater which might then touch a Moslem. Jews had to wear different clothes, live in smaller houses, and walk through smaller doors than Moslems. They had to salute every Moslem they saw, and could not raise their voices in anger against one. They were only allowed to ride donkeys, not horses, and even then had to ride sidesaddle. They were not allowed to be rich. And, for a long time, they were not allowed to live in the holy city of Mashhad.

Even today non-Moslems feel a sense of exclusion in Mashhad. The city is no longer off limits to them, but it is still palpably hostile. Non-Moslems may not enter Riza's shrine, nor even photograph it from afar. They approach the mosque at their own risk; "infidels" are often assaulted or abused in the neighborhood around it. They are refused lodging in pilgrims' hostels, and sometimes even haircuts by fanatic barbers.

Jews were not allowed to live in Mashhad until the early 1700s. The Iranian ruler Nadir Shah (1736–47) made Mashhad his capital while trying to expand his empire to the east. Nadir was a friend to Jews throughout Iran, and abolished many anti-Jewish restrictions. When he moved to Mashhad he brought a number of Jewish families with him. As Mashhad was an important crossroads on the caravan routes of Central Asia, these merchants soon grew rich. But Jews were never more than barely tolerated there, and even that for only a century. Jewish life in Mashhad officially came to an end on March 26, 1839: a day remembered by Mashhadi Jews as *Allah Da'ad*—"God has given."[1]

It was a Shi'ite day of mourning: the Tenth of Muharram, the holiest day of the Shi'ite year. The Tenth of Muharram is a day of fasting and self-flagellation commemorating the death of Hussein, the second *imam*. On that day in 1839, as Mashhadis tell the story, a Jewish woman asked a Moslem doctor to treat her hand. In line with the current state of medical science the doctor advised her to wash it in the blood of a newly killed dog. The woman hired a local boy to kill a dog for her, but had an argument over how much to pay him. The boy ran away and cried out that the Jews had killed a dog and called it "Hussein" to mock the Moslems on their holy day. His slander was heard by thousands of fasting Moslems in the Imam Riza Mosque. The mourners poured out of the mosque and stormed the nearby Jewish quarter. They broke into homes, stole property, destroyed books and religious articles, and burned the synagogue. They killed thirty-two Jews and gave the rest a now-familiar ultimatum: conversion or death. All chose to become Moslems.

Like the New Christians of Spain and Portugal, Mashhad's forced converts were not immediately accepted by their neighbors. A converted Jew became known as a *jadid al-Islam*, or "new Moslem." The Jadidis continued to live together in the old Jewish quarter. They attended a separate mosque named the Mosque Jadid al-Islam. They continued to use the Oriental Hebrew script, even when writing Persian. A high priest of the Riza shrine, or *mujtahid*, was assigned to them in a dual role: religious instructor and inquisitor. The *mujtahid* taught the ex-Jews the precepts of Islam, gave them Moslem names, and judged their disputes according to Moslem law. He tried to arrange marriages between Jadidis and other Moslems. At the same time he watched for their mosque attendance and listened for their recitation of the Moslem confession of faith: "There is no God but God and Mohammed is his prophet."

At first, the Jadidis were too frightened to become a community of underground Jews. Some accepted Islam and became sincere converts. Others prayed alone in secret. But before long a few old men began meeting on Friday nights for Jewish prayers, after finishing their Moslem ones. Soon they were studying Torah and observing Jewish holidays. The clandestine synagogue moved frequently; each week its location would be spread by word of mouth a few days in advance. It was not long before the Jadidis were able to resume complete Jewish lives in secret.

They were aided by Iranian architecture. Houses in Iran were built around private courtyards, with windows facing inward instead of out toward the street. In Mashhad's old Jewish quarter the houses presented a united—and windowless—wall to the rest of the city. Inside they were connected by internal doors. The Jadidis could gather for secret meetings or distribute kosher meat without ever going outside. Also aiding them, ironically, was a peculiarity of Shi'ite law. It was considered improper in Iran for a stranger to enter a house where women were present. When Jadidis met secretly, they stationed women to sit by the doors and forestall unexpected visitors.

Most of what we know about secret Jewish life in Mashhad comes from folk tales, passed down from generation to generation.[2] According to these tales, Jewish shopkeepers who could not close completely on Saturdays tried not to make any sales. They quoted ridiculous prices, or said that an item was out of stock. Sometimes they simply left their shops in the hands of young children who were not allowed to make any sales.

Jewish customs were only partially observed. Extra wheat was stockpiled for Passover, and matzo secretly baked. Jadidis continued to buy bread in the market but did not eat it. Yom Kippur was also observed, but not Sukkot, because a *sukkah* (ceremonial hut) would have given them away. Circumcision, which is also practiced by Moslems but not until an older age, was carried out on the Jewish date: eight days after birth. Curious Moslems were told it was done for the health of the baby. Secret Jewish names were given at the ceremony. Mezuzahs were explained as protection from the evil eye. Jewish courts were convened in secret. Kosher slaughtering was performed at night and the meat carried from house to house. Meanwhile, Mashhadi women continued to buy non-kosher meat in the market, but fed it to their dogs. Jewish pets were said to be the fattest in Mashhad.

Gallows humor aside, the threat of discovery was real. Mashhad's "old Moslems" never quite knew what to make of the Jadidis. They sent spies to see if Jadidis were fasting on Yom Kippur, and checked corpses for Jewish burial shrouds. Some Jadidis who were sincere converts are thought to have informed on the others. Not long after *Allah Da'ad,* one kosher slaughterer, caught in the act, was slaughtered himself. More often, disclosure was prevented by well-placed bribes. Local officials were paid off until World War II.

A few years after *Allah Da'ad,* Arminius Vámbéry, an eccentric Hungarian linguist who roamed about Asia in the guise of a dervish, visited Mashhad. There, he ran into a Jewish merchant he had earlier encountered in Afghanistan. When he hailed him as "Jew," the merchant ran up and protested. "For God's sake," the merchant told him, "do not call me a Jew here. Beyond these walls I belong to my nation, but here I must play the Moslem."[3]

The Jadidis joined other Moslems in pilgrimages to Mecca and Karbala (a Shi'ite shrine in Iraq). They took extraordinary precautions to conceal that they were Jews. Some stories tell of Mashhadis who brought tiny prayer shawls and *tefillin* to Mecca, a city ordinarily closed to non-Moslems, and secretly prayed there with them. When they returned to Mashhad the pilgrims received the honorific titles *hajji* and *karbalai.* Some Jewish *hajjis* were honored with positions in the Imam Riza Mosque: doorkeeper, lamp-lighter, and even muezzin, calling Mashhad's Moslems to prayer. The shrine's high priests never fully trusted them, it was said, but were scared to denounce them because they would be admitting that Riza's shrine had been defiled.

Children were initially expected to learn about Judaism by watching their elders. They were told the story of *Allah Da'ad* and instructed to pass it on to their own children. There was no formal Jewish education in Mashhad for twenty years after the conversion. But when an entire generation grew up without knowing Hebrew, the Jadidis started a secret school. Every afternoon, after studying Koran in a Moslem school, the boys came home to study Torah in a basement. Girls had to pick up what they could from older relatives. Children under eleven years old were left out completely; they could not be trusted to keep the secret from their Moslem playmates. Only after 1910, when national education reform gave Iranian schoolchildren their first summer vacation, were small children enrolled in a secret Jewish "summer school."

Jadidis were rarely forced to marry Moslems. They evaded the efforts of the *mujtahid* by arranging marriages at a very early age, even earlier than usual in Iran: when girls were four to six years old, and boys not much older. Couples were only allowed a few face-to-face meetings before their marriage, which took place when the girl was nine or ten. First the *mujtahid* performed the Moslem ceremony, and then the Jewish rite was held in secret, followed by a feast. Two marriage contracts were drawn up: a public Moslem contract in Persian, and a secret Jewish *ketubah* in Hebrew. But even on the Persian contract witnesses signed in Hebrew script, which remained the alphabet of the "new Moslems."

Their funerals were also double. After listening to Moslem prayers during the day, Jadidis recited kaddish in their homes at night. They sewed Jewish burial shrouds whenever they could without being caught. The first Jadidis were buried in Mashhad's Moslem cemetery, but later the influence of Jewish *hajjis* won them their own burial ground, which is still used. Tombstones were inscribed in both Persian and Hebrew. On them, names were followed by the words *jadid al-Islam.*

．　．　．　．

One of the few Jewish books which survived *Allah Da'ad* was a handsome prayer book bound in red leather. Two months after the massacre, the prayer book's owner, whose name was Samuel, wrote a brief account in its flyleaf. He concluded with these words of despair: "Now we have no hope other than the grace of the Almighty, the coming of the Messiah, or the arrival of the British, who will keep us alive, treat us compassionately, and save us from this exile in Ishmael."[4]

The arrival of the British? No, that is not the usual messianic prayer of persecuted Jews. But in Mashhad it was, perhaps, the most realistic. Mashhad and its Jews were pawns in the big-power politics of the day: the "Great Game" between England and Russia for control of Central Asia. In the early 1800s the Russian and British empires were both expanding: Russia from the north and the British up from India. Iran was allied with Russia, and the British feared a combined attack on India. They sent out diplomatic missions to win the support of local potentates, and employed a network of local agents as their eyes and ears. These agents were drawn chiefly from the area's disaffected minorities: Jews and Sufis, equally despised by the Shi'ites. This, in fact, was an underlying cause of the massacre of *Allah Da'ad.* Much of this background has only recently been pieced together from

British archives and other sources by Azariah Levy, a Mashhadi in Jerusalem.

Three times in the late 1830s, the Iranian Shah Mohammed led his troops into Afghanistan and attacked Herat, just over the border from Mashhad. Three times he was beaten back. The third time, in the winter of 1838–39, he was forced to lift his siege of Herat when British gunboats bombarded the Persian Gulf port of Bushire. A mob in Bushire retaliated by attacking a Jewish banker holding British funds.

When the shah retreated from Herat in 1839, he passed through Mashhad on March 1. Many soldiers deserted there, adding to that city's already volatile atmosphere. It grew worse on March 21, the Spring Equinox and Persian New Year, usually a time of festivity, but which the shah declared would be a day of mourning that year because of his defeat. Five days later, while Mashhad was still inflamed by deserters, came the Tenth of Muharram—*Allah Da'ad*. . . .

After the tragedy, Mashhad's Jews continued to work for the British. Two were hanged as British spies: one in Afghanistan and the other, whose family was rewarded with a British pension, in Bukhara. The leader of the Jadidis in Mashhad, Mullah Mehdi, was a virtual clearinghouse for British messages and travelers. "There are few Englishmen who have been in Khorasan who have not had cause to be grateful for his service," wrote one.[5] Mehdi even corresponded with the English philanthropist Moses Montefiore, whose fame spread in the East as the "rich Jew in London who will save the Jews."[6]

Two other Mashhadis also distinguished themselves as British agents: Mullah Ibrahim Nathan and his brother Mullah Musa. The brothers worked for the British throughout the East, wandering from city to city, delivering messages and gathering information. They guided British envoys on their travels, loaned them money without security, and smuggled messages and supplies to British prisoners. When British troops were routed from Afghanistan, the brothers had to abandon their property and retreat with them to India. There, they were repaid and awarded pensions. Musa died soon after arriving in Bombay, but Ibrahim sent for his family and went into the textile-importing business. Other Mashhadis continued to work as British agents until the late 1940s, when the British were expelled from India and Pakistan.[7]

Why were the Jadidis so eager to help the British? Partly because of their suffering under Moslem rule, and partly because they had heard how well Jews were treated in England. One young Mashhadi explained his motives eloquently as he refused to accept interest from a British officer borrowing money from him. "We know that the English are everywhere kind to the Jews," he told him, "and we have heard that your people are striving to collect together our scattered race, to restore them to their kingdom."[8]

. . . .

The Mashhadi diaspora began immediately after *Allah Da'ad*. Jadidis who fled Mashhad continued to trade with their friends and relatives who had stayed behind. Their ordeal produced a sense of solidarity, and they trusted each other to a degree few other merchants achieved. Before long they built a lucrative commercial network throughout the East. Mashhadis moved north to the oases of Merv and Ashkhabad; northeast to the fabled bazaars of Bukhara and Samarkand; west to Teheran, Baghdad, Beirut, and Istanbul; east to Herat, Kabul, and Peshawar; and southeast as far as Bombay and Calcutta. They dealt mostly in carpets and furs, along with precious stones, silks, clothing, spices, and other Oriental goods.

Inside Iran, Mashhadis passed as Moslems among Moslems and Jews among Jews. Freed from anti-Jewish restrictions by their "conversion," they became the wealthiest Jews in that country. They could circulate as they wished, they did not have to wear special clothes or pay special taxes, and they could trade in every marketplace—including those from which other Jews were barred. They used their wealth to aid poorer Jews in other cities. As recently as the 1930s, when the shah went on an inspection tour of Iran, Mashhadis bought new clothes for the poor Jewish children of Isfahan and Yezd.

Outside Iran, Mashhadis lived openly as Jews. They built their own synagogues and remained separate from the larger Jewish community. Even where tolerated, however, they remained wary. In Merv, just over the Russian border, one British traveler reported in the 1880s that the Mashhadis "live in dread, and meet for prayer in a cellar which is surrounded by a high wall. There is no Ark in the synagogue, and the scrolls of the Law are kept in a separate room, which can be entered only through a secret door. The Jedids have a dejected appearance and fear everybody."[9]

One of their communities was founded for not economic, but religious reasons: Jerusalem's. The Jewish *hajjis* had long been detouring through the Holy City on their way back from Mecca, leaving other pilgrims in Alexandria and taking a boat to Jaffa. In Jerusalem they prayed at both Moslem and Jewish holy places: the Dome of the Rock and the Western Wall. These *hajjis* brought back news to Mashhad of Palestine's growing Jewish settlement. In the 1890s a few began returning to Mashhad only long enough to pick up their families and bring them back to Jerusalem. They joined the new Jewish colonies outside Jerusalem's wall—on the fringe of the Bukharan Quarter founded by other immigrants from Central Asia— and built the kind of houses they were used to in Mashhad, with large courtyards and windows facing in instead of out toward the street.

Mashhadis entered Palestine as Jadidis, professing Islam and with Moslem names on their passports. Only after completing immigration formalities did they apply to change back to their secret Hebrew names—to the consternation of Jerusalem authorities. They built two synagogues in the Bukharan Quarter which are still in use today, and their own cemetery on the Mount of Olives. Those synagogues must be the only ones in the world named after Moslem *hajjis*: Hajji Adoniyahu Ha-Cohen and Hajji Ezekiel Ha-Levy.

This created quite a stir in Jerusalem. Moslem *hajjis* becoming Jews and founding synagogues was not an everyday occurrence. Jerusalem's chief rabbis went to investigate. They pronounced the Jadidis genuine Jews, and did not require them to "convert" back to Judaism.

The turning point in the Mashhadi diaspora was the Russian Revolution. Mashhadi communities in Russian Turkestan—Bukhara, Merv, Ashkhabad, and Samarkand—had been their largest. Suddenly, these independent businessmen found themselves with no role to play in the new Soviet order. Labeled "bourgeoisie," many had their shops looted during the Civil War. Judaism and Zionism were suppressed shortly afterward. Mashhadis joined the general Jewish exodus from Soviet Central Asia. Many returned to Mashhad but paused only briefly before moving on, unwilling to revert to the double life still led there. They went on to build Mashhadi communities in major world commercial centers: Teheran, Istanbul,

Bombay, and London. Applying methods learned on Central Asia's trade routes, they grew even wealthier than before. Settling in close-knit colonies and specializing in the same merchandise—carpets, furs, textiles, and precious stones—they imported goods from their relatives back home and sold them to wealthy Western consumers.

In Bombay and Calcutta, refugees reinforced the small Mashhadi colony founded by Ibrahim Nathan. They were closely associated with India's prosperous Arab Jews, called "Baghdadis" (see Chapter X). These Baghdadis ran commercial empires stretching from London to China. Ibrahim Nathan's oldest son, in fact, had to miss his father's funeral in 1868 because he was working for a Baghdadi firm in Shanghai.

Bombay became a refuge and way station for Mashhadis fleeing anti-Semitism in Russia, Iran, Afghanistan, and Pakistan. Many years later, in the early 1950s, one Mashhadi merchant described his remarkable family history to a Jewish Agency fund-raiser visiting Bombay. The merchant's grandfather had fled Mashhad for Samarkand in the nineteenth century. After the Russian Revolution the family fled to Kabul. After anti-Zionist riots in Afghanistan they fled to Peshawar in what was still British India. But after India divided along religious lines and Peshawar became part of Moslem Pakistan, the merchant's family continued south to Bombay. He was, at the time of the interview, preparing for a "final" move to Israel.[10]

In London, Mashhadis founded one of their richest and most influential communities. There, too, they had their own synagogue and kept to themselves. Although more than a hundred lived in London by the 1930s, hardly any other London Jews knew they were there. Today it is an aging community; most of the younger Mashhadis left for New York after World War II.

Meanwhile, their situation began to improve back in Mashhad. Constitutional reforms in the early years of this century allowed the Jadidis to relax their precautions. They moved their schoolroom up from the basement around 1910, and began revealing their secret to younger children. In 1925 a new shah was crowned: Riza Shah Pahlavi, father of the shah who was recently deposed. Riza Shah awarded new rights to Iranian Jews; both he and his son remained popular among Jews even after other Iranians turned against them. Jews enjoyed the Pahlavis' protection and later benefitted from the son's close relations with Israel.

Nevertheless, Jadidis could not yet return to Judaism publicly in Mashhad. Five hundred miles from the shah's residence in Teheran, that holy city remained a virtual theocracy. Most day-to-day power was in the hands of Shi'ite mullahs, in whose eyes it was still a crime for a Moslem to become a Jew.

Mashhad's Jews could only gradually allow their secret to become an open one. They protected it by paying off Moslem officials. Wealthier Jadidis left their old quarter near the Riza Mosque and started a new, more public Jewish neighborhood across town. But when French philanthropists in the *Alliance Israélite Universelle* tried to open a Jewish school in Mashhad, as they had done in other Iranian cities, the Jews declined. That would be *too* public. Similarly, Zionist fund-raisers were asked not to enter Mashhad; Jadidis agreed to raise funds themselves and turn them over quietly in a nearby village. But this delicate arrangement only lasted until World War II. At the end of the war, in 1946, Mashhad's long-tormented Jewish community suffered its final indignity—in the form of that ancient Jewish nemesis, the "blood libel."

The accusation that Jews use the blood of a gentile during Passover is no longer a strictly European obsession. After persisting there plague-like since the Middle Ages, simmering dormantly only to erupt in violent epidemics, the libel was carried to the East by Christian missionaries. In the notorious Damascus Affair of 1840, the disappearance of a Franciscan monk brought down the wrath of Syria on its Jews. Thereafter the blood libel infected the Moslem world, too, causing several attacks in nineteenth-century Iran which drew on that country's deep reservoir of anti-Semitism.

The seeds of Mashhad's 1946 outbreak had been planted by Nazi propagandists before the war, when Iran had been a German ally and a center of German influence. Two German teachers had opened a technical institute in Mashhad in 1938, and their students scrawled anti-Jewish slogans on walls around the city. Iran was divided under Soviet and British occupation in 1941. Mashhad fell into the Russian sector. As always in that country, the power of the mullahs increased as central authority weakened. Soviet troops were not withdrawn until a few days before Passover in 1946.

Passover happened to coincide with another Shi'ite day of mourning that year, commemorating the death of Imam Riza's sister Fatima. Aware of their vulnerability, Mashhad's Jewish elders warned the community not to provoke any Moslems. But just before Passover Moslem boys were caught harassing women on the streets of the Jewish quarter and scolded. Some Mashhadis believe the boys had been sent there by older Moslems to instigate a riot.

A crowd gathered to defend the boys, and a rumor spread that their blood had been taken for baking matzo. The next day a larger mob attacked the quarter. Houses and synagogues were robbed and burned, Jews were beaten and stabbed on the street, and old women and children assaulted in their homes. Escape was prevented by the mob outside. Mashhad's police could not protect them, and, according to one eyewitness, even the army had to be "bribed for every bullet." Wealthier Jews across town appealed through the Russian and British consulates until Moslem leaders were finally induced to help. One Moslem elder announced to the mob: "These Jews are *jadid al-Islam* who have lived among us for years, and we never saw anything evil among them."[11] The elder also wrote a pamphlet defending the Jews, which was dropped over the city from government planes.

That was the last straw for Mashhad's Jews. More than a century after they had been forced to become Jadidis they gave up on that city. Over the next few years, more than two thousand left, mostly going to Teheran and Tel Aviv. No more than a dozen families were left by the mid-1950s; by the 1970s perhaps half that many remained, none of whom still lived in the old Jewish quarter. A few were fabulously wealthy, reported visitors, but because of longstanding Shi'ite prejudice still lived as though they were poor. The old cemetery was maintained by contributions from Teheran. A small synagogue was kept up, but used only when there were visitors to help make a *minyan*.

Teheran became the new mecca for Mashhadis, until the shah was overthrown in 1979. It was a boom town for all Iranian Jews, who were members of that country's entrepreneurial class which soaked up most of its oil income. Some two to three thousand Mashhadis lived in Teheran before the revolution. They supported six synagogues of their own: a grand central synagogue in a wealthy suburb and smaller ones in older neighborhoods of the city. Mashhadis had a formal organization of elders which raised funds for the synagogues, charity, and Israel. No poor Mashhadi needed to turn outside the community for aid.

All this ended with the revolution. Along with other businessmen in Teheran, many Mashhadis were wiped out. Those who could, left. The new refugees joined other Mashhadis in Tel Aviv, Hamburg, Milan, and New York. Others are still exploring new markets in places like Tokyo, Miami, and Durban, South Africa.

New York has succeeded Teheran as their most prosperous community. Most Mashhadis are importers of carpets or other Oriental goods. Nearly all their businesses are concentrated in a few blocks of midtown Manhattan. A few work in the diamond industry on 47th Street. Very few New Yorkers are aware that ex-Marranos live among them. Even Jewish social workers who deal with the new Iranian immigrants know nothing of the Mashhadis, who rarely seek aid outside their own community. Few know they are renting the basement of a Kew Gardens synagogue for a house of worship, or raising funds to build one of their own.

Milan's community is the youngest and, along with New York's, the fastest growing. The Mashhadis who began moving to Italy in the 1960s all settled in Milan. Why Milan and not, say, Rome? "There is no one in Rome," a "Milani" answered. "Why should I go there?"

About half of all Mashhadis now live in Israel, some five to six thousand. They are generally less well-off than their brethren overseas; many went to Israel because they could not afford to go elsewhere. Most Israeli Mashhadis live in or near Tel Aviv, that country's commercial center. In addition to the two old synagogues in Jerusalem, they now have four in Tel Aviv and one each in the nearby cities of Herzliya and B'nei Brak. There is a friendly rivalry between Jerusalem's older community and the more prosperous one in Tel Aviv. "Their new synagogue is like a discotheque," sneered one Jerusalemite. Replied a Tel Avivi, "Jerusalem is full of stubborn old men who like to make trouble."

Mashhadis in each city have an organization to run their synagogues and old-age homes, collect donations from overseas Mashhadis, distribute charity, offer interest-free loans to young couples, and throw an occasional party. In earlier days they also ran Hebrew classes for new immigrants. The presidents from each city meet once a month to coordinate activities. They are famous for disagreeing with each other. "Our people in other countries complain," said one Israeli Mashhadi. "They ask us, 'Why can't you get together and collect money from us all at once?'"

Every Saturday night in Tel Aviv, young Mashhadis hang out American-style in what they call the "Persian corner" of Atarim Square, in the fashionable hotel district. If a foreign Mashhadi is visiting, that's where he'll go to meet his Israeli counterparts— especially of the opposite sex. One Mashhadi who lives nearby estimated that eighty percent of Mashhadi couples meet there.

It is in Israel where Mashhadi separatism is breaking down most quickly. Young Mashhadis there are increasingly marrying non-Mashhadis—especially Western Jews, whom they consider upwardly mobile. Explained one Israeli, "We go to high school and join the army and do everything other Israelis do. So our young people feel, why should they have to marry a Mashhadi girl? But they usually regret it. With us the family is still very strong. We respect our old people." It is still rare, however, for a Mashhadi to marry another Eastern Jew. They consider themselves an Oriental elite. They particularly shun other Iranians. Back in Iran, said one, when they were still *jadid al-Islam*, other Iranian Jews refused to marry *them*.

*   *   *   *

The "Jewishness" of Mashhadis has never been in doubt. Unlike the Marranos of Spain and Portugal, rabbis never insisted that Mashhadis convert back to Judaism when they "returned." They had never left it. But their experience as Marranos gave Mashhadis a different, more casual attitude toward religion than most other Orthodox Jews. They are more interested in the spirit than the letter of the law.

"We had great leaders," explained one Mashhadi, "but no great rabbis. We had no place to study. Anyone who knew how to translate from Hebrew to Persian we called a rabbi. One thing we all knew was *shechitah* [kosher slaughtering], because we all had to do it at home. We still know it today because we travel so much. No matter where we are we can buy a chicken and make kosher meat, even if there are no other Jews around."

Jerusalem rabbis who investigated Mashhadis at the beginning of this century, when they showed up as Moslems and suddenly became Jews, already complained of their lax observance. The rabbis found that Mashhadi women did not know how to use a ritual bath. As secret Jews they had no *mikveh*. Instead of completely immersing themselves after their menstrual periods as directed by Jewish law, they only poured water on themselves. An Ashkenazi rabbi in Jerusalem had to publish a pamphlet in Persian for them, explaining the proper use of a *mikveh*. [12]

Mashhadis still have no rabbis of their own. In Jerusalem weekly sermons are delivered by a visiting Ashkenazi rabbi. In Kew Gardens the synagogue's Orthodox rabbi had to ask Mashhadis to stop arriving by car on Saturday mornings; driving on the Sabbath is forbidden to the Orthodox. More Orthodox young Mashhadis in New York and Israel prefer to pray with non-Mashhadi congregations. But most Mashhadis are devout Jews, with a basic, ingrained belief in God. Their observance may waver, but not their faith. That, they say, is what kept them Jewish.

Sermons in their Kew Gardens synagogue are often delivered by a young Mashhadi who is not a trained rabbi but an inspirational speaker. It is his job to teach young Mashhadis about their past. "When you are attacked," he tells his congregation, "the most important thing to do is find out what kind of enemy you are facing. Usually they are only concerned with your life, and that is straightforward. But sometimes they want your soul, and they don't care about your life. This is how it was in Mashhad."

CHAPTER FIVE

The Dönmeh of Turkey: *Wife-Swapping Moslems Waiting for a Jewish Messiah*

Not long after World War I, European diplomats faced one of the most bewildering dilemmas in the annals of Jewish identity. It occurred when the Ottoman Empire was carved into the new nations of Greece and Turkey. The two states agreed on a population exchange to transfer their peoples to match the new borders. Although Greeks and Turks had lived side-by-side—if not exactly peacefully—in all parts of the old empire, the idea of the modern nation-state was to give each people its own homeland. In 1922–24, more than a million Greeks moved to what was now Greece and three hundred fifty thousand Turks to Turkey.[1]

In the Treaty of Lausanne, endorsed by most European powers in 1923, the two nations agreed to define identity according to religion. Greeks and Turks were not allowed to decide what they were themselves. With only a few exceptions, Moslems had to move to Turkey and Orthodox Christians to Greece. Jews, wherever they happened to live, were allowed to stay there. It became one of those occasions when the question "Who is a Jew?" was of more than academic interest.

The city most affected by the population exchange was the old Turkish commercial center, Salonica (now Thessaloníki, Greece). It was perhaps the most Jewish city in the world. For centuries, until it was captured by Greece in 1912, more Jews had lived in Salonica than Greeks and Turks combined. It was the capital of Sephardi Jewry and, in more prosperous times, of the entire Jewish world. Jewish merchants had run the great trading houses, Jewish scholars headed the city's academies, and Jewish longshoremen controlled Salonica's docks. Only Christians rested on Sundays and only Moslems on Fridays, but the entire city shut down each Saturday: Moslems, Christians, and Jews strolled down the waterfront calling out, "*Shabbat shalom*," to each other as they passed on the esplanade. The commercial lingua franca of the city was neither Greek nor Turkish but Ladino, the Judeo-Spanish dialect brought by refugees from the Inquisition four hundred years before. It had been spoken ever since in Salonica, where the majority of Jews were of Spanish or Portuguese origin.

A group of ten to fifteen thousand Moslems in Salonica, known as Dönmeh, tried to circumvent the population exchange. They said they were not really Turks, but Jews who only practiced the Moslem religion.

Their appeal was denied. The Greek government did not dispute their contention, but simply pointed to the Treaty of Lausanne which defined Turks by religion, not ethnic origin.

At about the same time, a few Dönmeh asked Salonica's rabbis to accept them back into Judaism. They claimed they were really secret Jews. For the last two hundred forty years, they said, they had only pretended to be Moslems.

The rabbis, too, denied their appeal. But, like the Greeks, they did not dispute the Dönmeh's strange contention. Their refusal was based on even odder grounds: that Dönmeh were "bastards" (in Hebrew: *mamzerim*; for a precise definition of this term see Chapter VII). They held annual orgies where they slept with each other's spouses, charged the rabbis, and could not be sure who their fathers were. As the Bible says, "A 'bastard' shall not enter into the assembly of the Lord, even unto the tenth generation."[2]

The Dönmeh had no alternative but to leave Salonica. Some went to Bulgaria and other Balkan states, where they were thought of as Turks. A few are said to have gone to Western Europe, Palestine, or America, where they may have become Jews. The vast majority joined Salonica's other Moslems in the exodus to Turkey. There, the Dönmeh settled in three cities: Izmir (formerly Smyrna), Edirne (formerly Adrianople), and Istanbul (formerly Constantinople). Most continued to live together in their own neighborhoods. Some—no one knows how many—continued practicing their strange secret cult. To this day, a few aging Moslems in those cities may still be praying to the God of the Jews—and waiting for the return of his "Messiah," Shabbatai Zevi.

•   •   •   •

The word *dönmeh* means "convert" in Turkish, but only Salonica's Turks used that name for the sect. Jews preferred to call them *minim*, a Hebrew word meaning "heretics." The Dönmeh themselves used neither of those terms, preferring another Hebrew word: *ma'aminim*, meaning "believers." This terminology was an accurate reflection of each group's perspective.

In this day and age, what the Dönmeh believed in can only be described as incredible: that a seventeenth-century false Messiah named Shabbatai Zevi was the redeemer of Israel, that the path of redemption lay in pretending to be a Moslem, and that Shabbatai's appearance had invalidated old concepts of law and morality—what once was prohibited was now permitted. The story of the Dönmeh may be the most bizarre in the annals of Judaism. That voluntary Marranos lived a licentious double life as Jews and Moslems, in a major European city in our own time, challenges our credulity. Only by suspending our rational instincts can we comprehend their faith in a false Messiah otherwise discredited hundreds of years before.

Mysticism and messianism used to be the neglected stepchildren of Jewish studies. Until recently modern Jews preferred to ignore that "dark side" of their heritage. Jewish historians, schooled in nineteenth-century rationalism, dismissed it as the superstition of a misguided few. All this has radically changed in the last few decades. Led by the remarkable Gershom Scholem, who virtually "invented" kabbalah (Jewish mysticism) as a field for scientific research, contemporary scholars are reevaluating its place in Jewish history. Long-neglected writings have been brought to light and maligned philosophies have been rehabilitated. The messianic movement of Shabbatai Zevi is now recognized for its enormous impact on Judaism. It is considered, in Scholem's own words, "one of the most important phenomena of Jewish history and of the history of religions."[3]

Shabbatai Zevi was born in Smyrna, on the Aegean coast of Turkey, in 1626. The first half of his life was spent in solitude and continence, apparently because of an unpleasant experience with masturbation at the age of fifteen. (He was later divorced by his first two wives because he refused to consummate those marriages.) He was a brilliant student, and was ordained a rabbi at the age of eighteen. Shortly afterward he began to study kabbalah, as did many young rabbis of the day. But Shabbatai stood out from other young kabbalists by virtue of his periods of "illumination," as his followers later called them. At odd intervals he would be filled with an ecstatic, inexplicable joy, when he would perform strange acts which often violated Jewish law.

Professor Scholem has reexamined Shabbatai's behavior in the light of modern psychology. He finds unmistakable evidence that Shabbatai suffered from a disease his contemporaries could not have recognized: manic-depression. Shabbatai's "illuminations" were merely the manic phases of a personality cycle which also included periods of deep, unrelieved melancholy, when he was tormented by demonic, often erotic, anxieties.

In his early years Shabbatai only hinted he might be the Messiah. He was dismissed as a crackpot, and his eccentricities rewarded with excommunication by several Jewish communities. It was not until shortly before his thirty-ninth birthday, when he joined forces with an ascetic Palestinian rabbi named Nathan of Gaza, that Shabbatai was taken seriously. Nathan became his leading prophet, reinterpreting popular kabbalistic doctrines to fit Shabbatai's symptoms. He declared that Shabbatai's soul was waging a battle for freedom from the forces of evil. In his states of "illumination" Shabbatai was prevailing; in his "days of darkness" he was not. Nathan compared the "Messiah" to Job, who also fell under the influence of Satan before returning to divine favor. But unlike Job's, Shabbatai's battle would decide the future of all mankind. A new age was dawning.

Nathan's teachings touched a chord of longing among Jews everywhere. Rich and poor alike flocked to Shabbatai's banner for a year-long revel in 1665–66. Pious Jews danced in the streets of Amsterdam. Jewish gamblers in London and Hamburg offered ten-to-one odds that Shabbatai would rule the world within two years. Polish villagers packed their belongings for a trip to Jerusalem, expecting to ride there on the backs of clouds. Shabbatai's "believers" clashed with "infidels" in the streets of Constantinople, easily carrying the day. Iranian Jews abandoned their homes to live in the fields, dressed in sackcloth and ashes. Even in far-off Yemen Jews ceased all business, gave their money to charity, and put on their best clothes for the trip to Jerusalem. In Salonica, perhaps the world's largest Jewish community, seven to eight hundred girls were married off early in order to speed the redemption. Salonica's richest merchants gave away their belongings, touching off an economic crisis from which the city never fully recovered.

Shabbatai himself spent much of that time in prison. He was arrested on his way to Constantinople to assume the sultan's throne, just eight months after he and Nathan had declared his mission. Although treason was ordinarily a capital crime, the unusual nature of Shabbatai's "troopless rebellion" apparently spared his neck. For seven months in the spring and summer of 1666, Shabbatai "reigned" from various Turkish cells. Jailers were bribed to give him the run of the prisons, which came to resemble palaces more than jails. Visitors came by the thousands to pray at his feet. During his manic phases Shabbatai continued to flout Jewish law, reviving the ancient temple sacrifices on Passover and transforming two of Judaism's most sacred fasts (the Seventeenth of Tammuz and the Ninth of Ab) into feasts. Debauchery with female visitors was rumored to be frequent; as the Messiah, Shabbatai abandoned his earlier modesty.

That September, Shabbatai was brought before the sultan in Adrianople for a final disposition of his case. Thousands of believers followed, expecting to see the sultan turn over the throne. They were cruelly disappointed. Shabbatai was allowed to live only by agreeing to convert. The "Messiah" became a Moslem.

His apostasy threw Shabbatai's followers into turmoil. Most admitted their error and returned to more traditional forms of Judaism. But a surprisingly large number was unable to. Their messianic experience had been so profound—actually living and behaving as though the Messiah had already arrived—that even his conversion to Islam could be rationalized.

Their rationalization: a doctrine of *necessary* apostasy: that the Messiah had to descend into the deepest realms of evil in order to return and redeem the entire world. This doctrine had a personal appeal for many believers, who were themselves born as or descended from Marranos in Spain and Portugal. For them it was no sin to pretend to follow another religion. But believers were divided on this doctrine's implications, splitting into two main camps. The "moderates" held that it was only necessary for the Messiah himself to convert. The "radicals" argued that his followers should become Moslems, too. The moderate camp survived within the framework of Judaism as a secret cult (whose extent is only now becoming apparent) for about one hundred fifty years. But the less numerous radicals were the movement's elite.

The converts did not consider themselves essentially different from the believers who remained "Jewish." What mattered most was their inner reality. In their hearts they all remained Jews, who followed a new and higher law introduced by Shabbatai Zevi. This "higher law" is the key to their theology, which was based on the idea of *two* Torahs—two sets of laws. They considered traditional Jewish law just an "earthly" Torah which was only valid until the coming of the Messiah. Shabbatai had replaced it with a higher "spiritual" Torah.

Paradoxically, these two Torahs were considered one and the same. The new spiritual Torah was the previously hidden inner meaning of the earthly Torah. In effect it was the *idea* of law without any specific *laws*. As Shabbatians explained it, in their rewritten version of the Jewish credo *Ani Ma'amin* (I Believe): "I believe with perfect faith that this Torah cannot be exchanged and there will be no other Torah; only the commandments have been abolished. . . ."[4]

Until Shabbatai returned and inaugurated the messianic age, this new spiritual Torah had to be practiced in secret. This became one of their principal tenets. Unmarried believers were not even told about some rituals, such as the "extinguishing of the lights." One young Dönmeh who tried to penetrate his sect's mysteries early this century was told, "Get married and you'll find out."[5]

Shabbatai himself spent the rest of his life oscillating between Judaism and Islam. At times he seemed a genuine Moslem; at other times he was caught practicing Judaism—or various other rituals of his own devising. The Turks ignored his obvious lapses because of his success as a missionary. He stayed in Adrianople with his followers for six years, until a series of impossible-to-ignore heresies (including one evening spent with wine, women, and several leading followers, all wearing Jewish skullcaps), forced the Turks to banish him in 1672. He died in exile four years later, at a Turkish fortress in Albania. Believers were seen making pilgrimages to his grave up until the twentieth century.

During his lifetime the apostate Messiah had only convinced a few hundred of his followers into becoming Moslems with him. The largest conversion did not take place until after his death. In 1683, two to three hundred families converted en masse in Salonica. The sect eventually converged in that city and they became known as the Dönmeh.

•　•　•　•

More than two hundred years later, in 1898, a learned British Jew who visited Salonica was surprised to find followers of Shabbatai Zevi still living there. "I saw them smoking outside their open shops on Saturday," wrote Elkan Adler, the son of England's chief rabbi, "but was assured that they were crypto-Jews, and practice all they can of Judaism at home. . . . I spoke to one of them in Hebrew and he evidently understood, though he protested he was a Turk."[6]

Actually, it is not very likely that the shopkeeper had any idea what Adler said to him. By the turn of this century the Dönmeh knew no Hebrew other than a few secret prayers they recited by rote. Nor could they be said to be "crypto-Jews," since their religion was a repudiation of Judaism. Adler was correct only in a broader sense: even at that late date the Dönmeh were a far cry from what they seemed on the surface.

Some ten thousand Dönmeh lived in Salonica, about half the city's Turkish population (Turks were Salonica's third largest ethnic group, after Jews and Greeks). They were Moslems on the surface but lived apart from the city's other Turks, occupying several all-Dönmeh neighborhoods. They did not marry non-Dönmeh. No one else in Salonica knew quite what they were up to. Wild rumors floated through the city, but little solid information. Not until the last years of the nineteenth century, as a few young Dönmeh began to reject their traditions, did any of their prayers, beliefs, or rituals begin to emerge. These confirmed the most scandalous of the rumors.

A number of their once-secret manuscripts have come to light this century, along with other sources of information. Still, even today, very little about the Dönmeh can be said with certainty. "The sources about this sect—especially for the years 1760–1960—are frequently contradictory," warns Professor Scholem. "Even the Dönmeh's own memories (as far as one can judge from what they said, at least) are often muddled and full of holes."[7] The following description of Dönmeh life, then, compiled from diverse sources, is offered with that caveat.

Within the confines of their own community, it is now known, the Dönmeh were never Moslems. If not exactly Jews, either, their religion was completely derived from Jewish tradition. Among themselves they spoke Ladino until the late nineteenth century. They used secret Jewish names which they only rarely confided to outsiders. Their prayers, recited in Hebrew and Ladino, were the same ones said by Salonica's Jews—with key words and phrases changed. The Dönmeh even had secret courts to resolve disputes according to Jewish law. Rabbis were consulted on their most ticklish legal problems, since the Dönmeh themselves preferred the study of mystical over legal literature. Clandestine relations with Jewish rabbis were not broken off until the 1860s.

But Dönmeh parted company with Salonica's Jews when it came to actual practices. They feasted on Jewish fast days, as had Shabbatai Zevi, and ate forbidden foods as part of their ritual. They also invented a new calendar of holidays, based mostly on events in Shabbatai's life. Youngsters were initiated into the secret cult in a ceremony paralleling the Bar Mitzvah rite.

The climax of their yearly cycle came on the twenty-second day of the month of Adar: the "Sheep Night." Dönmeh couples gathered privately for a feast of mutton, a meat which Dönmeh ate only during their rituals. A sheep was specially slaughtered for the occasion, and the meat distributed to each couple. "Praised be he who permits the forbidden," they prayed.[8] At the end of the feast came their notorious "extinguishing of the lights." Each husband and wife paired off with another. "The heroines of this night," according to one Dönmeh, "were those who knew how to prolong the love which the Sheep Night procured for them."[9] Children born of these unions were considered blessed.

Actually, there was no single Dönmeh religion. This tiny sect was subdivided into three smaller sub-sects. Each one lived apart, had its own secret synagogue and private cemetery, and observed separate rituals (all three practiced the Sheep Night, with some variations). They were strictly endogamous, only marrying within their tiny sub-sect. Each, too, was differently coiffured: the Dönmeh held a monopoly on Salonica's barbers and used it to make sure each sub-sect was instantly identifiable.

The largest sub-sect, with about four thousand members at the turn of this century, was called the Jacobites. (Each sub-sect had several nicknames; those given here are the most frequently used.) They shaved their heads but not their beards. Jacobites were followers of Shabbatai's brother-in-law Jacob Querido, a leader of the mass apostasy in 1683. His sister (Shabbatai's fifth wife and widow) had declared him the "mystical vessel in which the soul of Shabbatai had taken up its abode." Querido went on a pilgrimage to Mecca with several supporters in 1689, and died on his way back the following year. For more than two centuries afterward his believers could be seen on Saturdays at Salonica's waterfront, scanning the horizon for the return of his ship. Jacobites lived in their own closed-off quarter of northwestern Salonica. Most were in the middle or lower-middle class, often working as scribes or other kinds of government officials. They were subdivided into rich and poor classes—each of which only married within its own sub-sub-sect! Many became involved in local politics, later spearheading the Dönmeh assimilation movement.

The second largest sub-sect, with some thirty-five hundred members, was the Koniosos. They shaved neither their heads nor their beards. The Koniosos believed in another Dönmeh prophet, Baruchya Russo (in Turkish: Osman Baba). In the early 1700s Baruchya had declared himself the new messiah, a reincarnation of Shabbatai. He was the most radical Dönmeh theologian, declaring that many of Judaism's most heinous sins were not only permitted but actually commanded by the new "spiritual" Torah. Most of these sins were various forms of incest, whose sanctity Baruchya proclaimed. Koniosos were the poorest and least educated Dönmeh, mostly workers and artisans. It was this sub-sect which was said to provide Salonica's barbers. Later, after the emigration to Turkey, it transplanted itself more successfully than the other two groups.

The smallest sub-sect, with some twenty-five hundred members, was known as the Izmirlis, after Shabbatai's home town of Smyrna. They shaved their beards but not their heads. Izmirlis claimed to follow Shabbatai's original, unadulterated teachings. Their leading theologian was the last of the great Dönmeh prophets: Judah Levi Tovah (in Turkish: Dervish Effendi), who lived in the late eighteenth and early nineteenth centuries. He was a prolific writer of songs and homilies praising the joys of "the forbidden," i.e., their orgiastic rituals. Izmirlis shared a quarter in northeastern Salonica with the Koniosos. Many were merchants or, later, professionals; one writer described them as "hosiers, haberdashers, and hardware dealers."[10] They were the most educated of the three sub-sects, and, with the Jacobites, played a leading role in the Dönmeh "enlightenment" of the late nineteenth and twentieth centuries.

Each sub-sect was organized separately, with its own community council to run its affairs. The councils taxed each member according to his means, arranged for visits to the sick, gave charity to the poor (there were no Dönmeh beggars), maintained their cemeteries, paid taxes to the city, and paid the ransom which enabled young Dönmeh to evade army service. Separate three-man religious courts oversaw the spiritual side of their lives, running their synagogues and deciding disputes. Each court was separate, and rarely conferred with the others. One was said to have excommunicated a member of its sub-sect for consulting the court of another, though it later relented and took him back with the payment of a fine. The synagogues were located in the center of each neighborhood. They housed each sub-sect's library and contained a large room for prayers and other ceremonies, including the Sheep Night.

In the late 1800s, life in Salonica began to change. Modern European culture seeped into the Ottoman Empire. The empire had long been in decline and with it Salonica and its Jews; once envied by less fortunate Jews around the world, Salonica's were now their poor cousins. The first Western-style school in Salonica was opened in 1873 by Jewish philanthropists in the *Alliance Israélite Universelle.* Salonica's other residents soon joined the rush toward European culture. Young Dönmeh were in the vanguard. They studied French and other secular subjects with teachers from Western Europe, and turned their secret synagogues into lecture halls for discussions of political and literary subjects.

It was a revolutionary age in Salonica, and Dönmeh were in the vanguard of that, too. In the first decade of this century they flocked to a revolutionary society centered in that city: the Committee for Union and Progress, better known to the rest of the world as the "Young Turks." Dönmeh were well-represented at all levels of the Young Turks. In later years Moslem reactionaries were heard to blame the 1908 revolution on Dönmeh and other "non-Turkish" minorities.

After the successful Young Turk revolution, a few Dönmeh began moving to Istanbul. Many rose to high positions: cabinet ministers, parliamentary deputies, college administrators, and newspaper editors. The most renowned was Djavid Bey, a talented economist in the Young Turks' inner circle who became their finance minister. Djavid Bey is best remembered as the founder of the first native Ottoman bank. Back in Salonica he had been a leading member of the Koniosos, and said to have been a direct descendant of

Baruchya Russo. Djavid Bey was hanged in the 1920s because he was viewed as a threat to power.

When Salonica was captured by Greece in 1912, during the First Balkan War, Dönmeh emigration to Turkey multiplied. Five years later, the city was devastated by fire. Half of Salonica was levelled, including twenty thousand homes, eight schools, and thirty synagogues. The accumulated wealth of both Jews and Dönmeh was destroyed overnight. At least one Dönmeh synagogue burned down, along with its library of priceless manuscripts. Only one non-Dönmeh, a Jewish scholar, had been admitted to it before the fire. He was there only long enough to jot down the titles of some writings. His list of prayers, mystical texts, and "songs in bad taste" has tantalized historians ever since.[11]

After World War I and the subsequent war between Greece and Turkey, Salonica was flooded by Greek refugees. The Dönmeh exodus resumed, primarily to Istanbul but also to Izmir, Edirne, Ankara, and other cities. It was forcibly completed during the population exchange of 1923–24. As it turned out, the exile was fortunate. More than ninety percent of Salonica's Jews were killed during World War II. If the Dönmeh had stayed in Salonica, they undoubtedly would have been, too.

· · · ·

Under Turkish law, the Dönmeh had always been considered Moslems, with the same rights and privileges as other Turks. That is one of the few unequivocal statements which can be made about their identity.

No one else in Salonica trusted them. Moslems considered the Dönmeh Jews and Jews considered them Moslems. Their neighbors nicknamed them "little carp," after that fish which shows different colors as it changes direction in the water.[12] One writer described them as combining the "flexibility of the Jew with the arrogance of the Turk."[13] But the Dönmeh themselves, at least before their "enlightenment," privately thought of themselves as Jews. Their writings leave little doubt on that score. Among them is an extended version of the Ten Commandments, which they called in Ladino *Las Diez-y-Ocho* (eighteen) *Incommendanças* (eighteen is a sacred number in Jewish mysticism). Their seventeenth *incommendança* commanded bluntly: "Do not contract alliances with Moslems, for they are an abomination and their women are reptiles. It is on this subject that it is said, 'Cursed be he who sleeps with animals.'"[14]

But their "Jewishness" grew less certain in the late nineteenth and early twentieth centuries. As Dönmeh were exposed to secular European culture they began asking the same questions secular Jews had asked before them. The great question of nineteenth-century European Jews had been how to remain Jewish in the modern world. Or, phrased differently: what did it mean to be a Jew without traditional Judaism? Different Jews had answered this question differently, some becoming atheists, some Zionists, some Reform Jews, some even Hebrew Christians. Most continued to think of themselves as Jewish even when they no longer believed in Judaism. The Dönmeh faced a similar dilemma. What, they had to decide, did it mean to be a Dönmeh without believing in Shabbatai Zevi?

Different Dönmeh solved this problem differently, as had European Jews. Politically, at least, Salonica's Dönmeh vote aligned itself with the Jewish vote. In municipal elections between the Young Turk revolution of 1908 and the fall of Salonica in 1912, the Dönmeh teamed up with local Jews to defeat Moslem candidates.[15] At least one Dönmeh turned to Zionism. A future president of Israel who visited Salonica at that time, Isaac Ben-Zvi, met a young Dönmeh named Anwar Bey who became a Zionist and moved to Palestine. He taught Turkish in a Tel Aviv high school until he was deported back to Turkey at the beginning of World War I.[16]

Dönmeh were not the only Turks rethinking their identity in that era of transition. A new Turkish nationalism was on the rise, which did not define itself by religion alone. Later, in the 1920s, secular reform in Turkey would abolish Islam as the state religion, replace Islamic law with Western legal codes, replace Arabic script with the Latin alphabet, and even ban the fez—only Western-style hats were to be worn. Such attitudes made it easier for Dönmeh to think of themselves as Turks, since they did not have to accept Islam to do so. After hundreds of years of pretending to be Turks, many genuinely began to think of themselves that way.

The change was astonishingly rapid. In the space of just one or two generations, from the 1870s until World War I, the Dönmeh transformed themselves from semi-Jewish mystics into Turkey's leading secularists. They did not, however, abandon their separate communal organizations. As with Jews, their fraternal ties outlasted their religious ones.

Secular Dönmeh no longer had any reason to think of themselves as Jewish. Over the years, while living as Moslems, the Dönmeh had drifted away from Jewish traditions. Close familiarity with Judaism had died with their great theologians of earlier times. Clandestine relations with Jewish rabbis had been cut off after they were betrayed to Turkish authorities in the 1860s. Even those Dönmeh who still prayed in Hebrew no longer understood it. This is known from their manuscripts, in which Hebrew prayers had been transcribed into phonetic spelling in order to pronounce them correctly. The most recent transcriptions (c. 1870) are full of errors, showing how little of what they were copying the scribes understood.

After World War I, history overtook what had been the leisurely process of allowing a new identity to evolve. Allied forces occupying Istanbul allowed Greek, Armenian, and eventually Jewish merchants to leave. But when some Dönmeh in that city asked to be included, claiming they were not Turks but Jews, the Allies turned down their request. Likewise did Greek authorities during the population exchange, when a few Dönmeh requested to stay in Salonica. And likewise did Salonica's rabbis, when several Dönmeh—none of whom had any relatives in Turkey—requested to return to traditional Judaism.[17]

The rabbinical ruling was no spur-of-the-moment decision. Salonica's rabbis had pondered the status of Dönmeh ever since their apostasy in 1683. At first they allowed repentant Dönmeh to return to Judaism, without even a full conversion. A few Jewish-Dönmeh marriages were held. But as rumors of their licentious ways reached the rabbis' ears, later generations of Dönmeh became suspect. They were considered "bastards" from the mid-eighteenth century on. But rabbis did not treat the Dönmeh as completely non-Jewish. They answered their queries on Jewish law, furnished them with books, and sent them fund-raisers to collect for charities in Palestine. However, they also ruled that Jews could sell them non-kosher meat as they did to other non-Jews, or hire a Dönmeh to be their "Sabbath goy" (someone who would light fires and cook meals on Saturdays, when Jews were forbidden to).[18]

The last of the Dönmeh moved to Turkey in 1923–24. Their

arrival sparked a new debate in the Turkish press. Were they really Moslems, Turks wanted to know, or were they still secret worshippers of Shabbatai Zevi? The debate raged back and forth in several newspapers, including one owned and operated by Dönmeh journalists.

In one article a renegade Dönmeh charged that his ex-comrades still practiced their secret cult. "Their origin is Jewish and their spirit is completely foreign to Moslems," he said.[19] Dönmeh journalists responded by impugning the renegade's integrity, charging that he was a spendthrift maneuvering for a diplomatic position because he had squandered all his wealth.

Another Turkish writer asked why Dönmeh still lived apart in their new homes in Turkey, if they no longer had a secret religion. The Dönmeh journalists replied that this was a "ridiculous custom" observed more out of habit than anything else.[20] Dönmeh protested that they were "Turks and Moslems in the truest sense of the words."[21] But the Dönmeh were never fully trusted by other Turks. An English visitor to Izmir reported in the late 1930s that prejudice was even stronger against them than it was against Jews.[22]

A few years later, during World War II, anti-Dönmeh prejudice was officially endorsed in a discriminatory tax policy (which turned out to be an embarrassment for Turkey when Germany lost the war). This was an emergency "capital tax," levied on property owners to control wartime inflation. The amount of the tax was not specified in the legislation, but determined in each case by commissions whose decisions could not be appealed. The actual percentage ranged anywhere from five percent to seventy-five percent. Defaulters were sentenced to forced labor. Ostensibly aimed at profiteers who were "exploiting the difficult economic situation,"[23] this tax was actually designed to extort huge sums from Turkey's non-Moslem minorities. Nearly forty percent of the total revenue was garnered from Turkish Jews, Greeks, and Armenians. Those minorities also provided nearly all the defaulters actually sentenced to labor camps. One pro-Nazi newspaper defended this policy: "These people are not foreigners, but persons whom the Ottoman Empire has left us as a heritage. They call themselves Turks but we have not yet been able to liquidate them. . . . By [their] liquidation we mean the liquidation of a mentality. If they are our subjects, let them tuck up their sleeves and swing the hoe; if they are foreigners, let them leave this country."[24]

The rate of taxation was at first determined by placing taxpayers on one of two lists: an M-list for Moslems and a G-list for non-Moslems (*gayrimüslim*). Those on the G-list were taxed at a rate at least ten times, and up to twenty-five times, as much as those on the M-list.

When foreign governments complained that this discriminated against their nationals, a separate E-list was introduced for foreigners (*ecnebi*). Except for Jewish subjects of Axis nations, who were excluded from the E-list at the request of Nazi Germany, foreigners were taken off the G-list and taxed at the same rate as Moslems.

But when it came to the Dönmeh, commissioners were stumped. Did they belong on the M-list or the G-list?

The government compromised and started a fourth list: a D-list for Dönmeh. The M-list was carefully scanned and Dönmeh were removed from it.[25] They were taxed at least twice as much as other Moslems. One wealthy Dönmeh family in Istanbul was taxed more than a million Turkish lira ($750,000).[26] Dönmeh journalist Ahmed Emin Yalman was the first to publicly oppose the capital tax; his enemies charged that he only opposed it because he was on the D-list.[27] The government closed his newspaper twice because of his opposition. The absurdity of a separate tax for Dönmeh later prompted Turkey's finance minister to comment, in an apologetic memoir, that "the hysteric trembling of Hitler captured our nervous system. We all lost the sangfroid and sense of balance which should be the main quality of a financier."[28]

Isaac Ben-Zvi visited Izmir in 1943, and was told by a Dönmeh that "Our movement is dead and exists no longer. My ancestors were Shabbatians, but I content myself with the reading of the Koran; I retain nothing of my past."[29] Nevertheless, Ben-Zvi found other evidence that some Dönmeh still gave themselves secret Jewish names, and studied Hebrew with Jewish teachers.

At the very least, some Dönmeh retain a "Jewish consciousness."[30] Even after World War II Dönmeh storekeepers in Izmir were known for giving easy credit to Jews. Some displayed Jewish heirlooms. Dönmeh women anonymously donated oil to synagogues through trusted Jewish peddlers. Some used to visit Shabbatai's birthplace in that city to light candles. The mayor of Izmir in the 1960s, Osman Kibar, was from a Dönmeh family. He was rumored to practice Shabbatian rites although he always denied it. Still, he earned a reputation for his friendly treatment of Izmir's Jews.

At least a core of active believers has survived. In the spring of 1960, reports Gershom Scholem, an associate of his in Istanbul interviewed the leader of the Koniosos in that city. It turned out that he had heard about Scholem. The leader was convinced that Scholem, too, was a secret Shabbatian. He had assumed there could be no other reason for anyone to be so interested in Shabbatai Zevi.[31]

CHAPTER SIX

Samaritans:
"Life Is Politics"

Few legends have fueled man's imagination as have the ten lost tribes of Israel. Nations and races from the Aztecs to the Zulus—including many of those in this book—have been identified as their descendants at one time or another. The lost tribes have been discovered in Japan (where priestly classes were said to have Jewish features), in Australia (where aborigines practiced circumcision), and in Peru (where imaginative explorers claimed to hear natives recite the *Shema* in Hebrew). The honor has even been claimed by the English, on the dubious grounds that they "live in a far-off isle, speak in a strange tongue, have colonies throughout the world, and yet worship the true God."[1] None of this speculation, of course, is still taken seriously. Modern historians prefer to believe that the only survivors of the ten lost tribes are located in the one place where no one bothered to look for them: the land from which they were originally expelled. There, in what is now the city of Nablus on the West Bank of the Jordan River, the tiny sect of Samaritans has survived since biblical times.

To most people the word "Samaritan" conjures up a do-gooder who helps out others in need. Few who use the term "good Samaritan," referring to the passerby in Jesus's parable who assisted a wounded stranger whom a priest and a Levite had both ignored, realize that the Samaritans of the New Testament still exist. They have lived as an independent people for more than two thousand years: as neither Moslems, Christians, nor Jews. Five hundred Samaritans survive today, sometimes called "the world's smallest ethnic group."[2] About half of them still live in Nablus; the other half lives in the Tel Aviv suburb Holon.

Samaritans can be thought of as Jewish fundamentalists. Their religion branched off from Judaism more than two thousand years ago. In many ways it resembles the ancient Jewish religion more than modern Judaism does. Samaritans believe in the first five books of the

Bible, but no others. They worship the Jewish God, revere Moses as his prophet, and literally obey the words of the Torah (with a few words changed). But their religion is not simply a petrified Judaism. Samaritans are a living people with their own history, their own diaspora, their own poets, philosophers, heroes, holocausts, and their own struggle for survival.

Five hundred members may not sound impressive for a two-thousand-year-old sect, but Samaritans do not feel on the verge of extinction. In fact they speak of this century as a renaissance, having more than tripled their population since it began. They are now experiencing what the Israeli press has dubbed (with tongue only partly in cheek) a "baby boom"[3]—although, as one Samaritan admitted, "It's not exactly as in India or China."

Samaritans are at peace today, a rare event in their history. They have mended their ancient quarrel with Jews, who now protect them from their other traditional enemy: Nablus's Arabs. They live quietly in their neighborhoods of Nablus and Holon, barely noticed except by the trickle of historians, folklorists, journalists, and the simply curious who seek them out. This changes only once a year. Every Passover the two Samaritan communities gather on a mountaintop next to Nablus, along with hundreds of non-Samaritans who come to watch, to perform the rite for which they are most famous: the sacrifice of the Paschal Lamb.

•   •   •   •

Nowhere on earth does the Bible come alive as it does each Passover on Mount Gerizim. The sacrifice of the Paschal Lamb is the one which was first performed by Moses and the Israelites in anticipation of their flight from Egypt. The book of Exodus relates how they smeared lamb's blood on their door frames so that God would know which houses to spare from the tenth plague, the death of the first-born son. In ancient Jerusalem, Jews reenacted that sacrifice every Passover. Hundreds of thousands flocked into Jerusalem each spring; a Roman governor once counted the sacrifice of a quarter of a million lambs. But for the last nineteen hundred years Jews have performed this sacrifice only symbolically, in the Passover seder. But Samaritans have continued to perform it literally—on Mount Gerizim.

The Samaritan Passover takes place on the fourteenth day of Nissan, the same date as the Jewish (although, because the two calendars are calculated differently, the two Passovers may fall as much as a month apart). By mid-day before the first night, all Samaritans are on the mountaintop. Guests and other visitors straggle in through the afternoon. Spectators have become an integral part of the ceremony—as much as they are, say, at Indian dances in the American Southwest—without detracting from its sanctity. Journalists, politicians, neighbors, friends, and tourists come by the hundreds. Samaritans clearly enjoy their moment in the limelight. Parts of the service are amplified for the crowd.

The afternoon is spent in preparation. Young men light a fire in a pit and set a barrel of water over it to boil. The men wear flowing white robes and headdresses instead of their usual street clothes. (Only priests wear robes and turbans all week; other men reserve them for Saturdays and holidays.) At twilight they gather in two groups. Priests pray by the altar while other men wait near the ovens.

Yearling lambs are chosen for their perfection. Two dozen lambs are now sacrificed each year; in previous years they needed as few as seven. As the sun begins to set, the high priest climbs the altar and reads the story of Passover from the Torah. When he reaches the verse, ". . . and the whole assembly of the congregation of Israel shall kill it at dusk,"[4] the lambs are slaughtered with a single stroke of the knife. Samaritans dip branches into the blood and anoint their door frames and their children's foreheads.

The carcasses are fleeced with steaming water, hung upside down for the blood to drain, skinned, dressed, and salted. The heads, right forelegs, entrails (except the liver), and other forbidden parts are burned on the altar. Samaritans continue to pray and sing, thanking God for their deliverance from Egypt. At about eight o'clock the lambs are spitted and placed in the ovens. The pits are covered with branches and earth. While the lambs roast, Samaritans go home to rest, visit, and gossip with their neighbors.

The men return at midnight to divide the meat. They bring back full platters to their wives and children, who gobble down the lamb quickly with matzo and bitter herbs. Leftovers, bones, and wool are immediately gathered and thrown in the still-smoldering, early-morning fire. No scrap is left un-consumed by either man or flames. After symbolically reenacting the Exodus by walking around the sacrifice grounds, the men return to their families for a full-scale feast.

Samaritans live on the mountaintop for that entire week. On the seventh day they ascend the last few hundred yards to the actual summit of Mount Gerizim. This is their actual "pilgrimage," one of three which they perform each year (the other two are on Shavuot and Sukkot). They carry with them their most ancient Torah scroll and visit their holy places—singing, praying, and voicing their absolute faith in God. Carrying staffs and dressed in white robes, they look as their ancestors, the patriarchs, must have looked thousands of years ago.

But are Samaritans really descended from Abraham, Isaac, and Jacob? Who are they, and where did they come from? Are they actually Israelites, from the ten lost tribes?

The answers, of course, depend upon whom you ask. Samaritans answer these questions differently than do Orthodox Jews. The answers of modern scholars generally differ from both—and from each other as well. Few questions of biblical history are debated more vigorously and less conclusively than the origin of the Samaritans.

The Samaritans' own chronicles record their descent from the tribes of Levi, Ephraim, and Manasseh. The two latter tribes, they claim, were never completely exiled and therefore never "lost." Samaritan priests, like Jewish kohanim, formerly traced their lineage directly to Aaron. (Their last priest died with no sons in 1624, however, and his duties were taken over by a family of Levites.) Samaritans believe that their religion is the original Israelite one, practiced in an unbroken chain since the days of Moses and Aaron. It was Mount Gerizim where the Israelites built their original shrine in Canaan, they say, and heretical Jewish priests who broke away to establish a rival shrine which eventually landed in Jerusalem, rather than the other way around.

Naturally, Jewish tradition disagrees. The Talmud describes Samaritans as "Cutheans," connecting them with a story told in II Kings 17. According to this biblical account, the Assyrians settled colonists from Cuthah and other cities in place of the ten northern tribes which they deported. These colonists were attacked by lions and feared they had offended the local god. They asked the Assyrians to return an Israelite priest to teach them the local religion, and blended his teachings with their own idol-worship to produce a semi-pagan religion. Until the era of modern Bible criticism, this story was accepted uncritically as explaining the origin of the Samaritans.

It did not stand up under critical scrutiny. There is not the slightest shred of idol-worship or any other syncretism in the Samaritan religion. During their two-thousand-year independent history, Samaritans have never compromised their rigid monotheism. Besides, it is no longer believed that all members of the ten northern tribes were deported. The archives of the Assyrian king who conquered Israel, discovered by archeologists, record that he deported only 27,290 people and "let the rest keep their property."[5] Modern estimates of ancient Israel's population range from one hundred thousand to eight-hundred thousand. The Bible itself records sixty thousand taxpayers (heads of landowning families).[6] This means that the majority of Israelites never left their homeland. The "ten lost tribes" were never completely lost.

The story of the Cutheans may actually have occurred, but there is no reason to connect them with the modern Samaritans. The Bible refers to them as *shomronim*, a word which now means "Samaritans" but then meant simply "inhabitants of Samaria." The two are not identical. The Samaritans, in the sense of a religious sect centered around Mount Gerizim, probably did not even exist at the time II Kings was written.

Samaritans themselves have never referred to themselves by that name. They prefer to call themselves *shamerim*, which means "the observant" in Samaritan Hebrew—a play on words. They consider themselves the sole observers of the true Torah in its purity.

Neither the Jewish nor the Samaritan version wins unqualified support among modern Bible scholars. Throughout this century an academic debate has raged over Samaritan origins. Most historians now agree that Samaritans are legitimate descendants from the ancient Israelites, as are most Jews. The question remains: when and why did the schism occur between these two branches of the same tree?

A few historians have taken positions near the Samaritan one: that the rift is the same one which began in early biblical times as a feud between north and south—Israel and Judah. Others have staked out territory not far from the traditional Jewish one: that the rupture occurred when the Judeans returned from the Babylonian exile and isolated themselves from those who never left the land, whom they considered to be impure (as related in the books of Ezra and Nehemiah). Still others have tied the final break to one or another milestone of Samaritan history: the building of their temple on Mount Gerizim during the era of Alexander the Great (332–323 B.C.), the destruction of that temple by the Judean warrior/priest John Hyrcanus two centuries later, or the recension of the Samaritan Torah at around the same time.

In the last few years, however, a broad consensus has begun to coalesce around a landmark book published in 1975: *Samaritans and Jews*, by R. J. Coggins. Coggins's conclusions were not particularly novel, but his analysis was so thorough and his logic so formidable that his book became the starting point for all subsequent discussions of Samaritan origins. He differed from all those views listed above, siding instead with those who believe that the Samaritan and Jewish peoples were not severed from each other until nearly the Christian era.

The religion we now know as Judaism did not exist in the days of the Second Temple, Coggins points out. The religion of the Jews then included a broad spectrum of beliefs and practices. The Samaritans, he argues, were only one of many competing sects, each one claiming to possess the "true" Israelite religion. After the destruction of the Temple in 70 A.D., the rabbi-oriented Pharisees emerged triumphant to create modern Judaism. Their main rivals, the priest-oriented Sadducees, disappeared. So did the ascetic Essenes. The "Qumran covenanters," whoever they were, left only the Dead Sea Scrolls behind. The subsequent history of another sect, the Christians, needs no retelling here. Samaritans, too, thrived for a time but eventually dwindled and nearly became extinct.

No single "schism" finally divided Samaritans from Jews, asserts Coggins. Rather, Samaritan religion gradually emerged out of the not-yet-solidified traditions of the Israelite people. Its formative period was the last three pre-Christian centuries. During this time Samaritans defined most of their basic tenets: their monotheism, their veneration of Moses, their acceptance of only the Torah, and their belief in the sanctity of Mount Gerizim. (A fifth basic belief, in a messianic figure called the *taheb* who will wreak a "Day of Vengeance and Reward," did not gain general acceptance until later.)

By New Testament times, the two communities were thoroughly estranged. "Jews have no dealings with Samaritans," reports the Gospel of John (with only some exaggeration). In fact, the story of the good Samaritan was not originally intended as a compliment to Samaritans. No Jewish listener in Jesus's day would have mistaken its message: that even such a despicable creature as a Samaritan can have a strain of goodness in him.

In Roman times, three hundred thousand Samaritans are estimated to have lived in Palestine and perhaps half that many outside it.[7] The Samaritan diaspora stretched from Sicily to Persia. The major cities of Italy and the eastern Mediterranean all contained Samaritan communities: Rome, Salonica, Constantinople, Damascus, and especially Alexandria where they numbered in the tens of thousands. They were so numerous in Constantinople that the name Samaritan became a synonym for "accountant," an occupation in which they excelled. Samaritans were also well known as sailors, merchants, bankers, and slave traders.

The Golden Age of the Samaritans came in the fourth century, when they briefly won their independence from the Byzantine Empire. A high priest named Baba Rabbah (Baba the Great) led their successful rebellion, which sparked a cultural and political renaissance. Baba organized the Samaritan nation into twelve districts, each headed by two leaders (one a priest and the other a layman) who reported to a seven-man central council (three priests and four laymen). One district leader was a poet named Amram Darah, whose hymns still comprise the core of Samaritan liturgy. Another great Samaritan poet, author of the *Memar Marqah* (Teachings of Mark), is said to have been Amram Darah's son. Among Marqah's poems is one which related the story of Baba Rabbah's circumcision, which is said to have been performed in defiance of Byzantine law. This hymn is still sung at all Samaritan circumcisions. Forty years after leading the Samaritans to independence, Baba was lured to Constantinople on the pretext of signing a peace treaty, and held there in captivity until his death.

Baba's downfall marked the onset of a Samaritan decline which lasted until this century. Repeated insurrections against Byzantine rule only ended in massacre and persecution. One sixth-century rebellion is said to have cost as many as a hundred thousand lives. Increasing numbers of Samaritans turned to Christianity. At various times the Byzantine rulers forbade Samaritans to teach or practice their religion, stripped them of nearly all legal rights, confiscated their property, and burned their synagogues. The Byzantines were followed in turn by Arab, Crusader, Egyptian, and Turkish rulers, each of whom continued to harass Samaritans in their own way. Arab caliphs suppressed their religion; Crusader kings laid waste to Nablus; Egyptian Mamelukes turned their synagogues into mosques; Ottoman Turks forbade pilgrimages to Mount Gerizim. By the twelfth century only a few thousand Samaritans remained.

Their progress toward extinction seemed inexorable. Other than a small literary revival in Damascus in the thirteenth and fourteenth centuries, their cultural activity was negligible. One by one the last outposts of their diaspora were extinguished. The last Samaritans returned to Nablus from Damascus in 1625, from Cairo in 1708, from Jaffa later that century, and finally from Gaza in 1798. Even in Nablus they nearly expired. They were often attacked by local Arabs, and many converted to Islam. Samaritans claim they can still identify Nablus Arabs of recent Samaritan origin. Reduced to poverty, they sold many of their treasured books to foreigners. Few Samaritan manuscripts remain in their own hands; most are in libraries or private collections in Europe and the United States.

By the turn of this century, the demise of the Samaritans was thought to be imminent. "The venerable but unhappy remnant," stated the authoritative *Jewish Encyclopedia* in 1905, "seems wholly occupied with the material problems of a struggle for existence, which can hardly be long continued."[8] The writers of such words, if alive today, would no doubt be pleased to swallow them. No one could have predicted the political events of this century, the new partnership between Jews and Samaritans, or the tripling of the Samaritan population. Once again, Samaritans think of themselves as a people with a future as well as a past.

* * * *

"You see the Jews as a people, but I don't. I see them as a community. The people of Israel is divided into two communities: one Jewish and the other Samaritan. We are Israelites but we are not Jews."

Speaking these words was a young Samaritan named Binyamim Tsedaka, a handsome, mustachioed young man who is the unofficial public-relations man for this tiny people—or "community," as he insists. Binyamim and his brother Yephet publish a twice-monthly Samaritan newspaper in their spare time. During the day Binyamim works for the Jewish Agency in Tel Aviv. It was at his office there that he agreed to meet a visiting writer before one of his regular trips to Nablus. Every two weeks, at least, Binyamim and Yephet visit Nablus to gather news for their next edition of *A-B: Samaritan News*.

The newspaper's name is a literal translation of the word "alphabet" (*aleph-bet* in Hebrew). It is appropriate. *A-B* must be one of the few newspapers in the world with articles in four different alphabets: Hebrew, Arabic, Latin, and Samaritan. The Samaritan alphabet is the original Hebrew one. Jews have not used the old Hebrew characters for thousands of years; the square characters we now think of as Hebrew are actually borrowed from Aramaic, the lingua franca of the ancient Near East. But Samaritans preserved the earlier Hebrew letters in their Torah scrolls and other sacred writings. *A-B* uses them for its logo and a few articles. Other articles are in modern Hebrew or Arabic, the everyday languages of Holon and Nablus. The back cover usually reprints scholarly articles on Samaritan history or religion, in English or other European languages.

The first thing Binyamim explains to a visitor is how to spell his name. It is the same as the Hebrew *Binyamin* (Benjamin), but with a final "m" instead of an "n." This is the original spelling which only Samaritans have preserved, he says. Spelled this way it means "son of days," rather than "son of the right hand." But in conversation with this affable journalist, the spelling soon becomes academic. One and all call him Benny.

Benny's office is dominated by a large photograph of a man whose name has already appeared in these pages: Israel's second president, Isaac Ben-Zvi. President Ben-Zvi devoted much of his life to the problems of Oriental Jewish communities, especially remote or unusual ones. He studied them, wrote several books about them, and worked for their immigration and integration in Israel. His former home in Jerusalem now houses an institute for the study of Oriental Jewry which bears his name. Of all the communities Ben-Zvi worked with, none interested him more or longer than the Samaritans. His relationship with them began shortly after he stepped off the boat from Russia in 1907. A chance encounter introduced him to Benny's great-grandfather Abraham.

Abraham Tsedaka had been the first Samaritan to leave Nablus at the beginning of this century. He opened a small shop in the port of Jaffa, then prospering from the early Zionist immigrants. Among them was Ben-Zvi, who was twenty-three years old at the time and looking for someone to teach him Arabic. "I went into the store," Ben-Zvi later recalled, "and immediately realized the old man sitting there was no Arab, but was also not a Jew—not Ashkenazi, not Sephardi, and not Yemenite. I started the conversation in Hebrew but he barely understood. I found out he was a Samaritan, and this is how I first met someone from this special tribe."[9]

The future president began a friendship which lasted all his life, even living with the Tsedakas for three months. He became a "good Samaritan to the Samaritans," and encouraged other Nablus families to move to Jaffa. Later, his political influence won them rights as Jews under the Law of Return, even though neither they nor Jews consider Samaritans Jewish. Today, Samaritans remember Ben-Zvi as the man who saved them from extinction.

One of the ways Ben-Zvi "saved" the Samaritans was by convincing them to allow intermarriage. For more than two thousand years they had only married among themselves. Innocuous enough in ancient times when Samaritans numbered in the hundreds of thousands, this practice had obvious drawbacks for a community of 152 individuals—their population at the beginning of this century. Not only were they "probably the most inbred population in existence,"[10] as a geneticist recently described them, but they suffered from an unusual imbalance—there were ninety-seven males and only fifty-five females. The younger generation was even more lopsided: twenty-five boys under fifteen years old and only eleven girls under twelve.

Ben-Zvi talked Samaritan elders into approving the marriage of Samaritan boys to Jewish girls. Since, unlike Jews, Samaritans inherit their religion through their *fathers,* the children of those couples would also be Samaritans. "This was the ideal marriage of Israel," Benny says. "The reunification of Samaritan and Jew. I'm proud that I've also done the same thing." Tsedaka's son (Benny's grandfather) married a Russian-born widow who agreed to live as a Samaritan. Two other Tsedaka cousins also took Jewish wives. More recently, Benny and a few other young Samaritans have, too. Their population imbalance no longer threatens Samaritan survival. "We didn't love Ben-Zvi because of the economic or political or social aid he gave us," Benny says. "What we owe him is the will of the Samaritans to survive."

The drive with Benny from Tel Aviv to Nablus lasted only an hour and a half, but seemed to pass through centuries: from multi-laned freeways to winding alleys, from modern skyscrapers to rambling courtyards, from supermarkets to the ancient bazaar. Nablus is a prosperous Arab city nestled in a valley between two biblical mountains: Gerizim to the south and Ebal to the north. It is the second largest city in the occupied West Bank, after East Jerusalem. Its Arabs are known as the West Bank's most obstreperous, an inclination which predated Israeli rule. "No town in Palestine has so bad a reputation for the ill-disposition and violence of its citizens," noted an early twentieth-century writer on Samaritans. "The town and the district have been notorious for the lawlessness which the inhabitants have shown toward the Ottoman rule."[11] As if to prove their lack of prejudice, Nablus's Arabs later proved no more favorably disposed toward succeeding British and Jordanian administrations. Today, under Israeli occupation, the city is left to go its own way until the rock-throwing and tire-burning threaten to get out of hand.

There is no love lost by Samaritans for local Arabs, for whom they voice contempt. Samaritans like to show visitors their former cemetery, destroyed during Arab attacks. "They are cowards," whispered one. "They only attacked us when they had hundreds of people, and ran away when we threw stones back at them." Samaritans were protected by Jordanian police from 1948 to 1967, but do not credit this to any benevolence on Jordan's part. "King Hussein did not protect us because he was in love with Samaritans," one explained, "but because he could point to us and say, 'Look, we have religious freedom in Jordan.'" Nevertheless, they maintain cordial relations with King Hussein. The political future of Nablus is too precarious to alienate any of the interested parties. As all Samaritans are quick to point out, their main goal is survival.

Nablus's Samaritans all live in one small, badly overcrowded neighborhood, built around their synagogue. Their rambling, Arab-style houses are divided into apartments, each shared by an entire family—from grandparents to grandchildren. Three generations may share a bedroom; young couples live with the husband's parents after they are married. Each apartment also has a guest room, which goes empty even when the family bedroom is so crowded that the oldest sons have to sleep in the hallway. Only in recent years, as the community expanded, have a few families moved out of these traditional homes and built new ones nearby.

Samaritans also have a second neighborhood in Nablus which goes empty most of the year: on top of Mount Gerizim. Every family in both Nablus and Holon has a second home on the mountaintop. These homes are used only for their annual pilgrimages, especially Passover when all Samaritans live there for the entire week. For thousands of years Samaritans lived in tents during that week, until the Israeli government financed modern houses after the Six Day War. Local Arabs viewed these houses as an Israeli settlement. When young Samaritan couples tried to move into them permanently in 1974, because of their overcrowding in Nablus, the Arab municipality shut off electricity and water to the development. Terrorists placed a bomb, which failed to go off, under the car of the Samaritan high priest. The houses are again reserved for pilgrimages, although young Samaritans often use them to get away from their crowded Nablus homes. They are guarded year-round by Israeli soldiers.

Mount Gerizim is more than just a second home to Samaritans. It is their holy mountain: even more central to their beliefs than Jerusalem is to Orthodox Jews. In their writings it is the "Chosen Place," the "Eternal Hill," the "House of God," the "Original Mountain," and the "Place of the Presence of His Majesty." Ancient Samaritans built their temples on top of it and modern Samaritans point their synagogues toward it, as do Jews toward Jerusalem and Moslems their mosques toward Mecca. Samaritans place nearly every major event in the Bible on Mount Gerizim. Even the Garden of Eden is believed to have been on this now-barren, windswept peak. Two holy sites are fenced off and identified by signs: "Rock of Isaac's Sacrifice," and "Holy of Holies." The former is a niche in a rock outcropping, and the latter is a bare, table-like platform of natural stone.

Their belief in the sanctity of Mount Gerizim divides Samaritans from Orthodox Jews more than any other. A tractate about Samaritans in the Talmud concludes with the rhetorical question, "When shall we take them back?" The answer is: "When they renounce Mount Gerizim and accept Jerusalem and the resurrection of the dead."[12] Mount Gerizim is also responsible for several of the discrepancies between the Jewish and Samaritan versions of the Torah. In the book of Deuteronomy, for example, Moses commands the Israelites to build an altar when they enter the promised land. In the Jewish version he instructs them to erect it on Mount Ebal. In the Samaritan version it is to be built on Mount Gerizim. Samaritans have even added Mount Gerizim to their version of the Ten Commandments. They count the usual commandments differently, adding up to nine. Then they add a lengthy tenth which instructs the Israelites to "erect these stones which I command thee upon Mount Gerizim and build there an altar unto the Lord thy God," and concludes with detailed directions for finding it.[13]

This visit to Nablus included a side trip to a controversial West Bank settlement: Eilon Moreh, which was later ordered dismantled by Israel's Supreme Court. Though generally discreet about their politics, Samaritans are anxious to see Nablus stay in Israeli hands. They side with Jewish nationalists who want to settle the West Bank, such as the members of *Gush Emunim* (Bloc of the Faithful) who founded Eilon Moreh. At that settlement they were welcomed as comrades-in-arms. They took pains there, however, not to express any opinions for or against. In fact, Samaritans were less sympathetic to Eilon Moreh than they are to other settlements, because of the tensions this settlement had stirred up in Nablus. Militant settlers may come and go, but Samaritans must stay and face the consequences of their actions.

Benny Tsedaka responded diplomatically to political questions. "Whatever feelings Samaritans have," he said, "we keep to ourselves."

Other Samaritans were less reticent. "The only real Jews are the ones who believe in settling Judea and Samaria," a more outspoken man from Nablus said, using the Hebrew names for the West Bank. "If they do not believe this, why do they come to the Holy Land? Why not Uganda, like Herzl?" Leaving Eilon Moreh, this Samaritan shielded his face. Well known in Nablus, he did not want to be seen visiting the settlement. "We don't let the Arabs know what our real feelings are," he confided. "When we are with them we are more Arab than they are. We only get along because we have to. We are here and they are here." Finally he asked, "Do you believe in peace? That's because you don't live here. Here we know that life is politics."

On the drive home from Nablus, Benny spoke of the two events which have most changed Samaritan lives this century. The first, he said, was the return of the Jews to Palestine. "There are still only five hundred of us," he said, "but now we feel like a very large people. The return of the Jews has made all the difference. I say this not as a foreigner but as an Israeli like all other Israelis. Maybe even more so because I never left the land. I have been in Israel for 126 generations, and my young son can already tell you that he is the 127th. We are the Israelis of the Israelis."

The second great event, Benny added, was the Israeli capture of Nablus in 1967. Before the Six Day War, the two Samaritan communities had been separated by an international border. Holon's Samaritans were only allowed to visit Nablus on Passover. Even that pilgrimage had been forbidden in the early years after 1948. Later, it was subject to Jordanian whims. Pilgrims were searched and interrogated, and military-age men sometimes refused permission to cross. Israel's victory in 1967 was celebrated with such exuberance that Samaritans now fear reprisals if Nablus returns to Arab rule. "Your rejoicing is ours," they told the assembled Israeli press on its first visit after the war. The Samaritan high priest added that just as the Lord had sent Moses to deliver his people from Egypt, he sent Moshe Dayan to save his people again.[14]

The two Samaritan communities have been close since then. "After the war," Benny recalled with a smile, "we went to Nablus to give them lessons in modern Hebrew. You should have seen all the bearded old men sitting in the classroom. It was quite a sight." The two communities have been further reunited by marriages. Other Samaritans have taken advantage of the open border to emigrate to Holon. Although living conditions have improved in Nablus, they remain vastly inferior to the Tel Aviv suburb.

Holon's advantages are obvious upon arrival. In the Samaritan neighborhood most buildings are one-story stucco duplexes with small yards and separate entrances for the two families which share them, typical Israeli housing of the 1950s. Many have washing machines, ovens, and kitchen appliances which are unheard of in Nablus. The children have separate bedrooms and many more games and toys. A basketball court stands at one edge of the neighborhood. A synagogue and nearby community center have been built with government funds.

When originally built, the Samaritan neighborhood was on the outskirts of Holon. Urban sprawl has since overtaken it. High-rise apartments—typical Israeli housing of the 1970s—tower over their modest homes. The synagogue is practically in the shadow of one high rise, to the chagrin of that building's residents—after moving in they discovered that Samaritan men gather in the synagogue at 3 A.M. every Saturday and loudly pray until dawn. The mayor of Holon asked the Samaritans to start their services later or shorten them, but the Samaritans angrily refused to change what they called their three-thousand-year-old tradition.

Benny and his wife Miriam live in a modern two-story house at the end of one Samaritan street. Their front window overlooks the basketball court, which makes one of Benny's jobs easier. He has only to step outside to fulfill his duty as sports editor of *A-B*. Each edition is enlivened with such headlines as "Cairo Slaughters Damascus," which are unnerving only until you realize it is the sports page. Samaritans name their basketball teams after cities in their former diaspora.

Over dinner, Miriam Tsedaka spoke of Samaritans from her unique perspective: as a convert to Samaritanism. She was born in Rumania to a family of non-religious Jews which moved to Israel when she was four. An outspoken and high-spirited woman, she met Benny at the Hebrew University in Jerusalem, where they were both studying. Miriam says she did not find the conversion difficult: "Adjusting to married life was much more difficult than becoming a Samaritan." Before marrying Benny, Miriam related, he told her about the Samaritan Torah and its similarity to the Jewish one. But though the two Torahs are similar, she added, life as a Samaritan is very different. "Being a Samaritan is not like being a Jew," Miriam said. "It is not enough to be born one. You must practice all the commandments and keep the laws of the Sabbath and ritual purity."

Unlike Jews, Miriam explained, Samaritans allow no "cheating" on the Sabbath. They may not turn on a hot plate Friday afternoon to keep food warm until Saturday, or hire a Sabbath *goy* to cook for them. They even pull out the plugs on their refrigerators. Samaritan laws of kosher food differ only slightly from those of Orthodox Jews. They separate milk products from meat, but do not use separate dishes for the two. It is enough for them to wait four hours after eating dairy before eating meat, and six hours after eating meat before eating dairy. Their method of ritual slaughtering is almost exactly the same as that of Orthodox Jews, but Samaritans must give the right foreleg of every slaughtered animal to their priests for its meat to be kosher. An Israeli meat-packing plant prepares meat specially for them.

Like all young Samaritans in Holon, Benny and Miriam's three children attend a public elementary school. Afterward the boys study Torah with a priest. A Samaritan boy begins reading the Torah in the Samaritan script and pronunciation at the age of four or five. When he has completed it, which can happen anywhere between the ages of six and ten, he enters the adult community in a ceremony resembling a Bar Mitzvah. He recites the "Blessing of Moses" at the end of the Torah and a "Bar Mitzvah speech" written by his teacher. From that day on he takes part in Samaritan activities as an adult.

Most difficult for a non-Samaritan wife to accustom herself to are their rules of ritual purity. Samaritans still follow the literal words of the Torah[15] which say that a woman is ritually unclean for seven days after the start of her menstrual period, for forty days after giving birth to a son, and for eighty days after giving birth to a daughter. No Samaritan may touch her during those periods. Nor may he touch her bed or anything else which she touches. If he does he becomes unclean himself. Babies who must stay with their mothers are considered unclean whenever the mothers are. Anything which they touch becomes unclean as well. In addition, men become unclean after sexual activity or any nocturnal emission. In the morning they must pray in a special hall outside the synagogue and wash their entire bodies. They may not raise their voices or touch holy articles until the sun goes down.

These laws do not create problems just for the Jewish girls who have converted, but for all Samaritans, especially in Holon. Back in Nablus, complain some Samaritans, everyone lived together and one woman could take care of the family while another was unclean. But in Holon, where they live in nuclear families, their family lives are being disrupted one week of every month. Unclean women often go hungry because they do not want to "contaminate" their kitchens. Dishes pile up under their beds. Their babies crawl around and touch the furniture. The entire family gets irritable. Even worse, Samaritan women often endanger their health by taking pills to postpone or eliminate their menstrual periods.[16]

Israeli psychologists who have studied Samaritans add other, more deep-seated problems to that list: sexual frustration and lack of privacy. Samaritans are extraordinarily open about their sex lives. All sexual activity is public knowledge because of the man's need to purify himself in the morning. Sexual awareness begins especially early in Nablus, where entire families share a bedroom. "What actually is considered by us as early sexual arousal is considered by them as part of their daily life," the psychologists write.[17]

But premarital sex is strictly forbidden. Both men and women are chaste until marriage. The result: a sexual paradox, in which Samaritans are obsessed by sex but unable to fulfill their desires. This has led to a variety of psychosomatic symptoms, including menstrual irregularities, dizziness, lack of appetite, or "tired blood." Many Samaritan women find marriage traumatic; new brides frequently fall ill. Men often suffer from insomnia, headaches, or tics. These symptoms, which would be considered unhealthy elsewhere, have become normal Samaritan behavior. They are a legacy of their culture, conclude the psychologists.

Despite these hardships, few Samaritans abandon their faith. Benny estimates that only two percent of the community has "dropped out" in the last thirty years. Half were expelled for violating the Ten Commandments (i.e., adultery), and the others left voluntarily. They continued to think of themselves as Samaritans, Benny added, but could not live as Samaritans outside the community.

There are no "secular" Samaritans, either. "We have one hundred percent synagogue attendance," Benny said. "If someone doesn't show up we all run to his house to find out what's wrong." Nevertheless, one family is considered marginal. They join in the public rituals, but other Samaritans suspect them of not observing the Sabbath or laws of purity in their homes. Their sons have married Jewish girls because other Samaritans would not allow them to marry their daughters.

Even before the end of dinner, the sound of a basketball game begins to come through the Tsedakas' window. Like most Israelis, young Samaritans are sports-crazy. They play basketball almost every evening in an informal league with teams named after six cities where Samaritans once lived: Cairo, Damascus, Gaza, Alexandria, Caesarea, and Castra Samaritorum, an all-Samaritan outpost on Mount

Carmel in Roman times. The sports page of *A-B* includes articles on Samaritan history in those cities.

Samaritan adults are sports fans, too. Benny's speech is laced with sports metaphors. He resorted to one in a recent interview on Israeli radio, when the interviewer came to the question he considered crucial. "Benny Tsedaka," he exclaimed. "What can it mean to be a Samaritan today, in modern Israel? How does this express itself?" Benny's reply: "To be a Samaritan is to be an Israelite first of all, and not an Englishman, Frenchman, or American. It is to let your uniqueness take first place in your league, and then to worry about the rest of the teams. That is to say: to watch out for your identity above all else."[18]

·   ·   ·   ·

In 1841, the story is told, Nablus's Arabs were gearing up for one of their periodic attacks on the Samaritans. Under the pretext that Samaritans are not a "people of the book" (in Islamic law, special protection is afforded to those who believe in the Scriptures which predate the Koran), they stole Samaritan property and threatened to kill the sect's remaining members. The frightened Samaritans appealed for support to their age-old rivals: Jewish rabbis. The chief rabbi of Jerusalem came to their aid by issuing a certificate which reversed long-established rulings of Jewish law. It declared that the Samaritans are "a branch of the children of Israel who acknowledge the truth of the Torah,"[19] and are entitled to the same protection as Jews. The Samaritans were harmed no more that year.

The rabbi had worded that certificate carefully. He stopped short of declaring that Samaritans are Jews. Samaritans themselves, for altogether different reasons, agree. Only in the last few years have the opinions of a few non-Orthodox Jews begun to differ. Israeli law concurs with them.

Samaritans differentiate themselves from Jews for semantic reasons. The word "Jew," they point out, comes from "Judean"; it only refers to those whose ancestors lived in the southern kingdom, Judah. Since Samaritans claim descent from those tribes which settled in the northern part of Canaan, they do not consider themselves "Jews." But they do consider themselves members of the same people as the Jews. When Benny Tsedaka said, "We are Israelites but we are not Jews," he echoed an attitude thousands of years old. In the first century A.D. the Jewish historian Josephus Flavius was already explaining to Romans: "Samaritans profess to be Hebrews, but not Judeans."[20]

Today, however, the word "Jew" has a broader significance on all but Samaritan lips. It is generally used synonymously with "Israelite" and "Hebrew." If the ten lost tribes were to reappear tomorrow, the rabbis would accept them as Jews. In fact they have already done so: in the case of the Falashas, whom the rabbis have labelled as the lost tribe of Dan (see Chapter VIII).

The official attitude of Orthodox Judaism still views Samaritans as idol-worshippers and Cutheans. Orthodox rabbis are not swayed by modern scholarship, which holds Samaritans to be descended from the Israelites, or even by their own eyes, which show that Samaritans do not worship idols. They were not always so inflexible. Samaritans were only gradually written out of the Jewish people, a process which has been reconstructed from the Talmud and other historical materials.

In New Testament times the Samaritans were thought of as semi-*goyim*. On the lips of Jews the name "Samaritan" was an epithet—hurled at Jesus, among others. On the other hand, Jews were still allowed to eat Samaritan meat, drink Samaritan wine, stay in a Samaritan home, and be circumcised by a Samaritan. "Every commandment which the Samaritans keep," declared one second-century rabbi, "they are more scrupulous in observing than Jews."[21] But Samaritan meat, wine, hospitality, circumcision, and wives were forbidden one by one during the years that the Talmud was being compiled. Finally, Samaritans were excommunicated altogether. Declared the rabbis: "Let no Jew eat of one morsel of anything that is a Samaritan's, let no Samaritan become a proselyte, and allow them not to have part in the resurrection of the dead."[22]

The Samaritans, it was reported, were puzzled by this change of heart. "Your fathers had intercourse with us," one asked a rabbi. "Why do you not do the same?" The rabbi replied, "Your fathers did not corrupt their ways, but you have corrupted your ways."[23] Actually, it was not Samaritans but Jews who had changed.

Until this century it made little practical difference whether or not Samaritans were Jews. But, as Benny Tsedaka pointed out, the rules were rewritten when the Jews returned to Palestine. To Zionist pioneers busy building and defending a nation, it made little difference whether Samaritans were Judeans, Israelites, Cutheans, or whatever. Those who cast their lot with the Jews were treated as brethren. From the first days of the Jewish state, Israeli Samaritans have enjoyed the legal rights and obligations of Jews. They credit this to the influence of Ben-Zvi.

Although it was Foreign Minister Moshe Sharett who declared in 1949 that Samaritans "are like all the Jews who come from Arab countries,"[24] Samaritans believe that Ben-Zvi was behind it. Subsequently, Samaritans received immigration privileges as Jews under the Law of Return. On Israeli identity cards they are identified as Jews.

In 1953, the year after Ben-Zvi became president, Israel negotiated the agreement with Jordan which allowed Israeli Samaritans to renew their pilgrimages to Mount Gerizim. Also that year, Samaritans were *required* to serve in the army (although, in fact, they had been serving voluntarily since its founding). In 1954, the Samaritans moved into their neighborhood in Holon, built with government funds; they had previously been scattered among Jaffa, Tel Aviv, and Ramat Gan. The following year, when Tel Aviv's burial society refused to allow Samaritans into its Jewish cemetery, Ben-Zvi again defended them. In a letter to the Minister of Religious Affairs, he quoted the 1841 certificate and declared: "The Samaritans see themselves as complete Israelis, not only in citizenship but in their spiritual relationship to the rest of Israel. . . . I think it is a sin to tell them to look for a burial place alongside Christians."[25] (Samaritans were eventually granted their own cemetery.) The Israeli government also financed the Samaritan synagogue in Holon, which opened in 1963. Ben-Zvi died that same year. His death was mourned by Samaritans as though he were a Samaritan himself.

Only concerning religious matters are Samaritans not considered Jewish by Israeli law. In Israel, "religious matters" include marriage and divorce, which are regulated by religious authorities. Samaritan marriages and divorces are performed by their own priests. They are recognized as valid by the Israeli government even when the bride is Jewish, although the marriage and divorce of Jews is legally supposed to be a monopoly of the Orthodox rabbinate. The only legal problem was threatened in 1976, when a Jewish-Samaritan couple was divorced. The wife sued in an Israeli court for alimony, which the

Samaritan priest forbade the husband from paying. A showdown was averted when the court rejected her suit.

Samaritans, in turn, are loyal citizens of Israel. They are proud to pay taxes, serve in the army, and perform other civic duties on an equal basis with Jews. But they resist complete integration. They remain Samaritans first and Israelis second. Insists Benny Tsedaka: "We have a natural citizenship, which does not depend on external matters. We have an 'Israelite' citizenship."

CHAPTER SEVEN

The Split Identity of the Karaites

Among the ungodly ironies of World War II was the German obsession with Jewish identity. The Nazis approached their "Final Solution" as meticulously as they did their war. Just one month after Hitler gained undisputed power in 1933 his government issued its first definition of a Jew: anyone with at least one Jewish grandparent. This was superseded two years later by the Nuremberg Laws, which established precise categories of Jews and *mischlinge* (mixed race). A "Jew" had at least three Jewish grandparents (unless he belonged to a synagogue, in which case he needed only two), a "first-degree *mischling*" had two Jewish grandparents, and a "second-degree *mischling*" had one Jewish grandparent. A "German" could have no more than one Jewish great-grandparent.

The Ministry of the Interior was charged with determining who fit which category in Germany. In occupied territories, that task fell to a variety of German and local agencies. Confirmed anti-Semites immersed themselves in Jewish studies in order to decide whom to murder.

Among the few who benefited from this flurry of activity was a small sect called the Karaites. At first glance, the "Karaite problem" would not seem so large as to warrant all the effort that went into solving it. At the start of the war only eighteen Karaites lived in Germany, two hundred fifty in France, twelve hundred in Poland (including Lithuania), and nine to ten thousand in the Soviet Union (two-thirds of them in the Crimea). These Karaites practiced a truncated form of Judaism, accepting the entire Bible (not just the first five books as do the Samaritans), but rejecting the Talmud and other rabbinical writings. They spoke a Tatar dialect, and claimed to be descended from Tatar tribes who had adopted their Jewish-like religion. Therefore, they claimed, they were racially non-Jewish and exempt from the Final Solution.

In pre-war Poland, historians had been debating this very subject. Most non-Karaite scholars held a different perspective.

Karaites were Jews, they said, who followed a heresy which had branched off from Orthodox Judaism a thousand years before. They spoke a Tatar dialect for the simple reason that they emigrated from the Crimea, where everyone spoke Tatar.

A paper war over the fate of Karaites was waged in all parts of Nazi-occupied Europe. Letters, articles, petitions, and heated memoranda crisscrossed the continent. Expeditions were dispatched from Germany and Italy to eastern Karaite communities. Legal battles were waged in Germany, occupied Poland and Russia, and both Vichy and occupied France. Theorists of anti-Semitism were enlisted on both sides. Jewish scholars were even consulted. Ultimately, the Nazis decided that Karaites were not Jews. Nearly all of Europe's ten to twelve thousand Karaites survived the Holocaust.

But not all the world's Karaites lived in Europe, spoke Tatar, or claimed to be descended from Crimean tribesmen. A few thousand also lived in Egypt, Turkey, and Iraq. *They* never claimed to be anything other than Jews. A few years later most emigrated to Israel along with other Middle Eastern Jews. Only tiny communities are left in Cairo and Istanbul.

About ten thousand Karaites now live in Israel. Exact numbers are unavailable because Karaite law forbids their being counted in a census. Their status under Israeli law is ambiguous; they are considered Jews but have their own rabbis, chief rabbinate, national council, kosher slaughterers, *mohels,* and religious courts. They are not legally permitted to marry other Jews.

Thousands of Karaites are also left in Eastern Europe, nearly all of them in the Soviet Union. Most of those in pre-war Poland had lived in parts of Lithuania and Galicia which were annexed by Russia after the war. Their religion has virtually disappeared. Most are no more than "passport Karaites"—that is, Karaites by official classification alone.

* * * *

Israeli Karaites leave no doubt about what they think of themselves. A sign in front of their central synagogue in Ramla, a small city southeast of Tel Aviv, proclaims in Hebrew: "Center of the *Karaite Jews* in Israel." That phrase is also found on their books, walls, stationery, and lips. For them, "Karaite" is an adjective, not a noun. It is invariably accompanied by the word "Jew."

A visitor looking for that synagogue is likely to pass it by. It is housed in a plain-looking stucco building in an industrial zone at the city's edge, overshadowed by a larger construction site next door. Only a chest-high wall, half a dozen trees, and a courtyard with benches and a concrete fountain separate it from the trucks rumbling back and forth in front. It is not what one expects from the spiritual hub of a thousand-year-old faith.

The interior is equally unprepossessing. A corridor leads to a small front office, a kitchen with barely enough room for a coffee pot, an anteroom lined with shoehorns, and finally the synagogue itself. Rabbi Joseph Algamil, a young Karaite who is their most knowledgeable historian, warned his visitor not to enter it. "The synagogue is a holy place," he explained. "Unclean people may not enter. You are ritually unclean if you have been in a cemetery, had sexual intercourse, or touched a menstruating woman or anyone else who is unclean, since yesterday evening. Rather than cross-examine you to find out if you have done any of those things, we would prefer that you just didn't enter."

The differences between Karaites and other Jews are less obvious than in the case of most communities in this book. Israeli Karaites have no special costume, skin color, language, background, accent, or architecture. Their fundamental beliefs are little different from other Jewish ones. They differ only in their actual practices, how they interpret those beliefs.

Some of those practices are evident at a glance in the synagogue. Instead of pews, its floor is covered with Oriental carpets for Karaites to prostrate themselves on during prayer. The fountain in the courtyard is for Karaites to wash their hands in before entering. The anteroom is filled with shoehorns because Karaites wear no shoes inside. The reason, they say, is found in the story of the burning bush when God told Moses: "Put off thy shoes from off thy feet, for the place whereon thou standest is holy ground."[1]

Other differences are less conspicuous, but Rabbi Algamil was pleased to describe a few. Karaites do not separate meat from dairy products, he explained. The elaborate Jewish laws for separating meat and milk are based on a single sentence which appears three times in the Torah: "Thou shalt not seethe a kid in its mother's milk."

Orthodox Jews take that sentence metaphorically: using two sets of dishes, pots, pans, even tablecloths to ensure that meat and milk products do not touch each other. Karaites take it literally. They do not seethe kids in their mother's milk. Period.

Karaites observe the Sabbath strictly, performing no activity unrelated to prayer or basic human needs. Sex is forbidden on Friday night, and hot food on Saturday. Until recently they would not keep lamps or fires burning on the Sabbath even if they had been kindled on Friday afternoon. Other Jews made fun of them, calling them "sitters in darkness." Some strict Karaites still do not use electric lights on the Sabbath; the community is divided between "friends of light" and "friends of darkness."

Karaites do not use *tefillin*, mezuzahs, or a *mikveh*; none of these are mentioned in the Bible. They do not blow a *shofar* (ram's horn) on Rosh Hashanah. They do not celebrate Hanukkah. Their marriage laws are stricter, but divorce laws more lenient, than those of Orthodox Jews. Their calendar differs slightly from the Orthodox one, as do their methods of circumcision and ritual slaughter. Women may not enter their synagogues. And they reject the Orthodox definition of a Jew: for them, a Jew is the child of a Jewish father.

All these differences stem from a single source: the Karaite rejection of the Talmud. Although they believe in the same Bible as other Jews, they interpret it differently. Orthodox Jews rely on formal interpretations set forth in the Talmud and other rabbinical writings; these can be so subtle that they sometimes bear little relation to the Bible's original words. Karaites, on the other hand, accept no post-biblical writings other than their own. They prefer (at least in theory) the literal sense of the Bible. For this they were separated from the rest of the Jewish people more than a thousand years ago.

None of this seems particularly shocking today. The day is long past when you had to practice Orthodox Judaism—or even believe in God—to be a good Jew. Reform Judaism follows a similar line of reasoning; early Reformers were often labelled "modern Karaites." But Karaism survives from more rigid times, the remnant of a heresy which today would be mere dissent.

It began in what is now Iraq and Iran in the eighth and ninth centuries, as a popular rebellion against established Jewish authority—political, economic, and religious. It resembled, and was perhaps influenced by, the recent schism between Sunni and Shi'ite

Moslems in the same part of the world. The first dissenter to compile a systematic program was an ascetic Iraqi named Anan ben David in the 760's. He attracted few followers in his lifetime, probably because his interpretations made Jewish law even more burdensome than it already was. But, because his ideas laid the groundwork for Karaite theology, he is considered the father of Karaism.

Among those ideas was a distrust of all authority, including his own. "Search thoroughly in the Torah and do not rely on my opinion," he told his disciples.[2] They proceeded to do exactly that. Before long, in the words of one tenth-century Karaite writer, it was "impossible to find any two of them agreeing in everything."[3] These sectarian groups were reconciled only by turning Anan's distrust into a guiding principle: the free and independent study of the Scriptures. According to Karaite doctrine, no single interpretation is inherently "correct."

The Orthodox counterattack was led by a young philosopher known as Sa'adiah Gaon in the early tenth century. Sa'adiah hardened the boundary between Orthodox Jews and Karaites, declaring the latter to be heretics who should be ostracized by all good Jews. Those who remained in the Orthodox camp became known as Rabbanites, a word still used in this context for Orthodox Jews—who remain faithful to the Talmud and rabbinical authority—to distinguish them from Karaites.

The subsequent history of Karaism is a wide-ranging geographic odyssey. Karaites launched a missionary crusade to win new adherents in Syria, Palestine, Egypt, and as far away as Spain. First one and then another branch rose to prominence: Jerusalem, Cairo, Constantinople, the Crimea, and Lithuania. But Karaites never came close to dominating Jewish thought; Sa'adiah's ban had placed them beyond the pale for most believing Jews.

Curiously, few Karaites remained in Iraq or Iran after the tenth century. Only in the town of Hit, on the banks of the Euphrates in Iraq, did a tiny community survive into modern times. Thirteen Karaite families still lived in Hit in 1948 when their synagogue was destroyed and their Torah scroll confiscated during anti-Zionist riots. All sixty-seven Iraqi Karaites moved to Israel, where they settled in Beersheba.

Palestine, particularly Jerusalem and Ramla, was the next great Karaite center. Jerusalem's settlement was founded in the early ninth century by pilgrims from Iraq and Iran who came to the Holy City to lead a life of asceticism and piety, hoping to speed the coming of the Messiah. By the end of that century they formed a major part of Jerusalem's Jewish community, as they would continue to do for the next two hundred years, feuding with Rabbanites the entire time. But Karaite life ended abruptly in Jerusalem on July 15, 1099. Crusaders led by Godfrey of Bouillon entered Jerusalem on that day, herded all its Jews—Karaite and Rabbanite alike—into a synagogue, and set it on fire. Unlike the Rabbanites, the Karaites never returned in numbers.

About twenty Karaite families live in Jerusalem today. Their synagogue, supposedly nine hundred years old, which had been maintained for centuries by tiny Karaite communities dependent on charity from abroad, was destroyed in the 1948 battle for Jerusalem. Found full of rubble when Israel captured the Arab section of the city in 1967, it was cleared and restored as part of the reconstruction of the Jewish Quarter. A Karaite teacher was hired as caretaker and given a home upstairs. The restored synagogue was dedicated in 1978. But the hostility between Karaites and Rabbanites in Jerusalem had hardly abated in those nine hundred years. The ceremony was marked by jeering and debates, and ended in a fistfight.

In Egypt, Karaites lived uninterruptedly for more than a thousand years. They occupied the same street in Cairo's Jewish Quarter from the founding of that city in the eleventh century into the twentieth. Egyptian Karaites were traditionally goldsmiths, passing down their skills from generation to generation; Cairo's gold bazaar was just a short walk from the Karaite Quarter. Until Maimonides forbade it in the twelfth century, they freely intermarried with Rabbanites. But Maimonides also instructed that Karaites "should be treated with respect, honor, kindness, and humility as long as they [do not] slander the authorities of the Talmud."[4]

In the twentieth century young Karaites joined the general reawakening of Egyptian Jewry. Many went to universities and became doctors, lawyers, even composers. They began moving out of the old Karaite Quarter to newer parts of Cairo. A lavish domed synagogue was built in 1927 near the French Hospital in the neighborhood of Abbassie. More than three thousand Karaites lived in Cairo in 1947. Along with other Egyptian Jews, they began leaving after the anti-Jewish riots which followed the partition of Palestine.

The mobs made no distinction between Karaite and Rabbanite.

Among those who stayed after 1948 was a young Karaite doctor named Musa Marzouk, who helped organize the defense of the Jewish Quarter. He continued to work in Cairo's Jewish Hospital, and continued his Zionist activities on the side. Those activities were not limited to fund-raising and emigration. Marzouk was arrested in 1954 as a member of an Israeli spy ring. He and one other Egyptian Jew were executed the following January; they are remembered in Israel as "the martyrs of Cairo." Their remains were brought to Israel and reinterred in 1977.

The final exodus of Karaites followed the Sinai Campaign of 1956. In revenge for Egypt's humiliation, its Jews were fined, arrested, forbidden to practice their professions, and often deported. Synagogues, schools, and hospitals were closed. Only a few hundred Jews are left today, among them about forty Karaites. None of them still lives in the old Karaite Quarter. Both synagogues in that quarter are closed; all of Cairo's Karaites now pray in the new synagogue in Abbassie. Its archives contain about twenty priceless manuscripts, some illuminated, including an eleven-hundred-year-old Codex of the Prophets. The fate of those manuscripts has become one topic in Israel's internal debate over the Egypt-Israel peace talks.

The next great Karaite center, chronologically, was Constantinople. Under both Byzantine and Turkish rule, Karaite literature flourished in that city (and, briefly, in nearby Adrianople): Bible commentaries, liturgies, codifications of Karaite law, and works on secular subjects such as mathematics and astronomy. The community declined after the sixteenth century but never disappeared. It was reinforced in the 1920s by Karaite refugees from the Crimea, who were fleeing the Russian Civil War. The community is now split along ethnic lines; the native Turkish Karaites are pro-Jewish and pro-Zionist, while the newer refugees from the Crimea are often anti-Zionist and even anti-Semitic. An estimated two hundred Karaite families live in Istanbul today.

In none of those places—Iran, Iraq, Palestine, Egypt, or the Byzantine and Ottoman empires—did Karaites ever think of themselves as anything but Jews. In Turkish Constantinople there was even a modest attempt at reconciliation with Rabbanites. But the modern history of Karaites covers largely what is now Russian soil: the Crimea, Lithuania, and Galicia, although none of those lands belonged to Russia when Karaites first settled on them. In those places, Karaite history took a very different turn.

．　．　．　．

Catherine the Great annexed the Crimea to the Russian Empire in 1783, and Lithuania ten years later. Until the last few years before her death in 1796, Catherine was generally tolerant toward her empire's Jews. But in 1792 and 1794 she issued a pair of repressive decrees, the latter of which confined Jews to a "Pale of Settlement" and required Jewish merchants to pay a double tax. The following year, however, she made an exception to those rules. More than two thousand Karaites were among the Jews in the recently annexed territories, most of them in the Crimea. They were different from the Jews to whom Russians were accustomed, physically resembling Crimean Tatars and speaking a Tatar dialect. In 1795, Catherine exempted these Karaites from the double tax and permitted them to own land. This was to be the opening wedge between Karaites and other Russian Jews.

It soon grew into a chasm. Crimean Karaites were exempted from the draft in 1827, as were Lithuanian Karaites the following year. In succeeding decades they were granted permission to do business anywhere in Russia, given land, and declared to be an independent church with dioceses in Lithuania and the Crimea— equivalent to the status of Russian Moslems. In 1863 Karaites were awarded full civil rights. From then on they enjoyed a legal parity with Christians. Russian Jews, on the other hand, were still restricted to the Pale of Settlement, heavily taxed, and barred from government jobs as well as some other professions.

Karaite leaders encouraged the distinction. In appeals to Russian authorities they emphasized their differences from Rab- banites, often slandering them in the process. They were hard- working, honest, loyal citizens of Russia, they proclaimed—unlike "Jews." They even modified their vocabulary to eliminate traces of Jewishness: dropping their official designation of "Karaite Jews" in the 1830s in favor of "Russian Karaites of the Old Testament Faith," and later to just "Karaites." They completely eliminated the words "Jewish" and "Judaism," preferring "Mosaic" and "Mosaic Law." As recently as 1961, a Polish Karaite wrote an entire book about his sect without once using the words "Jew," "Jewish," or "Israel."[5]

To justify this attitude, they rewrote their history. Karaites denied being Jews who had rejected the Talmud; rather, they claimed that their ancestors had already lived in the Crimea before the Talmud was written. They had indeed been living there when Jesus was crucified, they added, and so had taken no part in the crucifixion—the ostensible justification for Russian anti-Semitism. This claim, of course, is not true, nor even original with Karaites. Medieval Jewish communities often proclaimed their innocence of the crucifixion by pointing to a pre-Christian origin. But in Russia it was given credence by the theories and fieldwork of a brilliant—if dubious—Karaite scholar named Abraham Firkovitch (1786–1874).

Firkovitch was an extraordinary figure by any standard: explorer, archeologist, educator, and forger. His place in history remains controversial to this day; the mention of his name in a roomful of Jewish scholars is still likely to produce an argument. Born in the Polish city of Lutsk, Firkovitch traveled widely in Russia and the Middle East before settling in the Crimea as a teacher. There, he was chosen by the newly founded Odessa Historical Society to gather information on Karaite history. He began in 1839 by excavating their cemetery in Chufut Kale (Jewish Fortress), which boasted one of the Crimea's oldest and largest Karaite communities. He claimed to discover Karaite tombstones dating to the first two centuries A.D. Over the next few years he traveled widely in the Crimea and the Caucasus, armed with the authority to confiscate old manuscripts and not bashful about using it. He later made expeditions to Syria, Palestine, and Egypt. The result: one of the world's greatest collections of Jewish, Karaite, and Samaritan manuscripts, tombstone rubbings, and inscriptions, which he sold to the Imperial Library (now the Lenin Public Library) of St. Petersburg (now Leningrad), where it remains to this day.

Unfortunately, Firkovitch was less than scrupulous in his standards of scholarly accuracy. His transcriptions were suspected almost as soon as they were published. Shortly after his death several of his forgeries were exposed, creating a worldwide scandal which embarrassed several eminent historians who had constructed theories around them.

Firkovitch tampered with dates and places with one purpose:

to demonstrate the antiquity of Karaite settlement in the Crimea. He was attempting to prove that Crimean Karaites were descended from a Turkic tribe called the Khazars. Those semi-nomadic warriors carved an empire out of southern Russia in the early Middle Ages, but are better remembered today for one bold political maneuver. At the height of their power in the eighth century, squeezed between Moslem armies to the south and Christian armies to the west, Khazar leaders declared their neutrality by converting to Judaism. They soon vanished from the world arena, but live on in the memories of amateur historians and pseudo-scientific theorists of race.

Karaites were neither the first nor the last Jews to claim descent from the Khazars. It has often been claimed for all the Jews from Eastern Europe, most recently by Arthur Koestler in his 1976 bestseller, *The Thirteenth Tribe.*[6] Koestler's theory, in brief, is that the Khazars migrated west and founded the *shtetls* of Eastern Europe which nurtured Ashkenazi Jewry. Firkovitch's theory was somewhat different. He claimed that the Khazars had converted not to Rabbanite but to Karaite Judaism, influenced by Karaites who already lived in the Crimea. They were never pushed west, he said, but stayed in the Crimea, and modern Karaites preserve their language and culture.

His theory is tempting, but has the unfortunate disadvantage—as does Koestler's—of not agreeing with the known facts. The Karaite language is completely different from that of the Khazars. It was not even spoken in the Crimea at the time when the Khazars flourished. Besides, it is now certain that the Khazars were Rabbanites. In addition to previous circumstantial evidence, a startling document from the Cairo *genizah* (a storage place for old religious books which may not be thrown out) was recently discovered: a Rabbanite manuscript from tenth-century Kiev, written in Hebrew but bearing an official endorsement in the Khazar language (in runic script). It puts to rest any lingering suspicion that the Khazars might have been Karaites.[7]

The true origin of Russian Karaites remains obscure, although scholars have pieced together a credible version from linguistic and other evidence. The Karaite language is an archaic dialect of the Tatar language spoken in the Crimea. Formerly written with the Hebrew alphabet, it also contains elements from Hebrew, Arabic, and Greek. (This peculiar patois is not yet extinct; in the 1979 Soviet census, 535 people listed it as their native language, and 112 as their second one.) The Greek elements in this language testify to the Karaites' probable origin in the Byzantine Empire, just across the Black Sea from the Crimea. After arriving, their numbers were probably augmented by converts from the various Turkic tribes which overran the Crimea at that time. These tribes (not related to the Khazars) had no monotheistic religion and converted in large numbers to Islam, Christianity, and both Karaite and Rabbanite Judaism.

From the Crimea, some Karaites emigrated to Lithuania in the thirteenth and fourteenth centuries. Their main settlement, and probably their oldest (they received a charter to live there in 1388), was the old Lithuanian capital, Troki. From there they spread to more than thirty other towns and villages in Lithuania and nearby Galicia and Volhynia, including Halicz, Lutsk, Nove Myasto, Kukizov, and Vilna, the modern Lithuanian capital just a few miles from Troki. None of those towns ever numbered more than a few hundred Karaites, and rarely that many.

After these regions were annexed by Russia, Karaites pros-pered, especially in the Crimea. Many, taking advantage of their privileged status, grew wealthy. They owned tobacco plantations, orchards, and salt mines. The Karaite population grew to nearly thirteen thousand by the turn of this century. But in the Civil War of 1920–21, Crimean Karaites joined the anti-Bolshevik "White Army." Hundreds had to flee to Turkey, Italy, France, or the United States when their cause proved a losing one. Those who stayed under Soviet rule underwent the same repression as did other opponents of the regime. They were discouraged from practicing their religion, and encouraged to disperse throughout Russia. Many moved to Kiev and other parts of the Ukraine.

Lithuanian and Galician Karaites found themselves under Polish rule between the two world wars. Their writers, now led by a young Polish Karaite named Ananiasz Zajączkowski, continued to debate Karaite history with Jewish scholars. Until his death in the 1960s, Zajączkowski clung to a modified version of Firkovitch's theory; he no longer claimed that the Karaites were actual descen-dants of Khazars, but regarded them as the "heirs to Khazar culture."[8]

Karaites won full autonomy in Poland in 1936. It was to last just three years. At the start of World War II, Germany and the Soviet Union carved up Poland, and its Karaites came under Soviet rule. Karaite religious life was repressed in Lithuania and Galicia as it already had been in the Crimea. Conditions were said to actually improve in 1941 when Germany invaded Russia—Hitler's government was less hostile to this Jewish sect than Stalin's.

•   •   •   •

Lithuania and the Crimea both lay in the path of Nazi troops in the surprise invasion of Russia that June. On the army's heels came the notorious *einsatzgruppen* (special-duty groups), with instructions to exterminate "undesirables" in the occupied territories. These were the commando formations which murdered one-third of the six million Jews who died in the Holocaust. They employed more primitive means than the gas chambers used in the death camps. When an *einsatzgruppe* entered a city it called the Jews together, lined them up next to a ditch, and simply shot them. It was an *einsatzgruppe* at work in Kiev for two horrible days that September, when thirty-three thousand Jews were shot in the infamous ravine known as Babi Yar.

The commanders of the *einsatzgruppen* had not been told whether to classify Karaites as undesirables—a broad grouping which was defined as including "Jews, Gypsies, insane people, Asiatic inferiors, Communist functionaries, and asocials."[9] When *Einsatzgruppe D* encountered Karaites in the southern Ukraine and Crimea, its commander, Otto Ohlendorf, wired back to SS headquarters in Berlin for instructions. The response, according to Ohlendorf's testimony at a Nuremburg war-crimes tribunal, was to spare them: "Karaites had the Jewish religion but could not be killed because they did not belong to the Jewish race."[10]

This decision was apparently made at a high level, because it was consistently applied in Lithuania, Volhynia, and Galicia as well as the Crimea and southern Ukraine. The only possible exception may have been Kiev itself. In his novel *Babi Yar*, Anatoli Kuznetsov writes that as a young boy he was told that Karaites had been marched through the streets on the first day of the massacre wearing long, loose robes and chanting, "Let us meet death bravely."[11] But the story is not authenticated, and is doubted by those familiar with the events of that era.

Ohlendorf also sent a second inquiry in regard to another group he encountered in the Crimea: the Krimchaks, native Crimean Rabbanites. The Krimchaks resembled Crimean Karaites in language, culture, and appearance—in everything, in fact, except the sect of Judaism they adhered to. They are thought to be descended from the same mixture of foreign Jews and Turkic converts as are the Karaites. Nevertheless, in Czarist Russia they had been lumped together with other Jews and not with Karaites. The Nazi attitude was the same. Ohlendorf was instructed to shoot them, and did. The difference, he was told, was that "some Jewish blood had entered the strain."[12]

Shot in the western Crimea alone in one month of 1941 were 2,504 Krimchaks. In the terse words of an official *einsatzgruppe* report, originally written about the city of Simferopol but applying equally well to the Crimea as a whole: "The Krimchak question was solved."[13] Individual Krimchaks survived the war, but as a people they no longer exist.

These decisions, seemingly so casual, actually stemmed from a debate which had lasted for years. The Axis powers began showing interest in the Karaites even before the start of the war. It was fascist Italy which first paid attention to them. A team of Italian anthropologists went on an expedition to Lithuania in 1934 and examined one hundred thirty Karaites, concluding that they "are not fundamentally of Turkic-Tatar stock, . . . but have adopted a Turkic language and probably a measure of Turkic-Tatar blood."[14] Nevertheless, Karaites were exempted from anti-Jewish legislation in Italy.

Immunity in Germany was slower to come. The eighteen German Karaites were Crimean refugees, mostly former officers of the White Army. To determine their status, a German Orientalist was dispatched to Leningrad to examine the Firkovitch collection. He returned with the opinion that the Karaites were an independent religious group which did not practice Judaism. But this did not satisfy German authorities, who were interested in the Karaites' racial rather than religious background. Twice in the autumn of 1938, as conditions for Jews deteriorated, the Karaites applied for independent status. They finally won a half-hearted endorsement from the Ministry of the Interior, known as the Decree of January 9, 1939, although it was actually issued the previous December. It declared: "The sect of the Karaites should not be considered a Jewish religious community, [although] it cannot be established that Karaites in their entirety are of blood-related stock. The racial categorization of an individual can [only] be determined by his personal ancestry and racial-biological characteristics."[15] Although this did not grant the Karaites absolute immunity, it was often cited to that effect in the more intensive debates to come. It led to the de facto exemption of Karaites from the Final Solution.

After the fall of France, the "Karaite problem" expanded to include approximately two hundred Karaites in the Paris area and another forty to fifty in southern France. Paris police did not at first require Karaites to register as Jews. But in the south, the collaborationist Vichy regime ruled otherwise: they "must be considered Jews in regard to the law."[16] After some debate the Vichy attitude prevailed throughout France. Karaites were instructed to register in November 1941.

French Karaites responded with a propaganda offensive. They cited the Decree of January 9, 1939, and obtained the support of high Catholic and Russian Orthodox clergymen, as well as from prominent anti-Semites. The director of the Nazi-sponsored Institute for the Study of Jewish and Ethnoracial Questions, Georges Montandon, declared that Karaites were probably descended from the Khazars and lacked the "Jewish mentality."[17] One French Karaite leader boasted of the "violent antagonism" between Jews and Karaites, which had "created a certain anti-Semitism among the Karaites."[18]

The Karaites won their battle. The *Statut des Juifs* was rewritten to exclude them from anti-Jewish measures. French Karaites suffered no further harassment. Moreover, these discussions apparently influenced the German authorities which later ruled on their status in Eastern Europe. No one knows who made the decision to spare them from the *einsatzgruppen,* or why. (The order is thought to have been issued by either SS chief Heinrich Himmler or his right-hand man, Reinhardt Heydrich.)[19] But the subsequent debate by German civil authorities, discussing how to deal with Karaites in occupied territory, is thoroughly documented.

In race-obsessed wartime Germany the debate reached fashionable proportions. Feature articles about Karaites appeared in German newspapers and magazines; one war correspondent described them as "determined enemies of the Jews."[20] Nazi officials visited Troki to interview Karaite leaders, and sent an expedition to the Ukraine. The Germans even thought they discovered a hitherto-unknown colony of four hundred Karaites near Bialystok; they turned out to be descendants of Moslem immigrants, who had been living in Poland for six hundred years.

The height of incongruity was reached when German officials consulted Jewish scholars, including some of those who had freely debated the question before the war. Six historians in three different cities were asked for their opinions. None were aware of the other requests, but all realized that an ill-conceived reply could endanger thousands of lives. Two historians in the Warsaw ghetto, Meir Balaban and Isaac Schipper, prepared reports declaring that Karaites were not of Jewish origin, even though they had taken an opposite position before the war. Neither, incidentally, survived the Holocaust himself.

Zelig Kalmanovitch, director of the YIVO Institute for Jewish Research in occupied Vilna, was ordered to collect and translate material on Karaites. The Nazis also arranged a debate between Kalmanovitch and a Karaite religious leader. Kalmanovitch, an impeccable scholar, allowed himself to be "defeated" by the comparatively unlearned Karaite, of whom he noted in his diary: "He has a better understanding of horses and weapons than of religion."[21] Kalmanovitch, too, died in the death camps.

Three historians in Lvov also had to prepare a report on the origin of the Karaites: Philip Friedman, Leib Landau, and Jacob Schall. Friedman, who survived the war, later wrote: "Both Landau and I saw clearly that a completely objective and scholarly treatment of the subject, indicating the Jewish origins of the Karaites, might mean a death sentence for them. . . . The memorandum was drafted to indicate that the problem of the origins of the Karaites was the subject of heated controversy, and great emphasis was given to the views of the Karaite scholars who adhered to the theory of Turkish and Mongolian origins."[22]

A final decision was reached in spring 1943, when the German Ministry for Occupied Eastern Territories declared that the Karaites are "a people of Turkic-Tatar origin closely related to the Crimean Tatars. . . . The Karaites should not be treated as Jews, but should be treated in the same fashion as the Turkic-Tatar peoples."[23]

As a result, the Karaites were allowed to live under the same conditions as the rest of the non-Jewish population: subjected to some hardships, but nothing remotely like those of other Jews. Their communal lands were confiscated, and the government salaries which had been paid to their religious leaders were discontinued. Most continued to work at their pre-war occupations. Some actively collaborated with the Germans.

The wartime behavior of the Karaites became a sensitive topic after the war, especially in Israel. When the new Jewish state announced that it would welcome Karaite immigrants, one Holocaust survivor protested in a letter to the *Jerusalem Post:* "I had the misfortune to spend four agonizing years in the vicinity of Troki (Polish Lithuania), where one of the most numerous Karaite communities in Poland lived, and could not escape observing their unworthy behavior towards the hounded Jews. Not only did the Karaites gladly accept the non-Jewish status bestowed on them by the Nazis; they were loyal servants of the Nazis and faithfully collaborated with them. They abhorred any association with the persecuted Jews. I know of Poles who rescued Jewish children, but I do not know even a single case of a Karaite who was prepared to shelter a Jewish child." [24]

Five to six hundred Karaites are said to have served in various branches of the occupying German army. Others worked for the Nazis as interpreters. In Lutsk, Karaites were said to have beaten Jewish women and children, and even have assisted in the liquidation of the ghetto during four horrible days in 1942, when seventeen thousand Jews were shot on a hillside near the town.

On the other hand, some Karaites are known to have assisted Jews. Vilna Jews often forged Karaite identification papers, and were sometimes shielded by local Karaites. In one case, a Jewish couple was captured and sent to Warsaw for questioning by Ananiasz Zajączkowski, who acted as liaison between the Karaites and the Germans. Zajączkowski agreed not to unmask the couple if they disappeared; the couple survived and now lives in New York. On the whole, says one recent student of the question, the Karaite attitude toward the Holocaust could be described most aptly as "apathetic." [25]

After the war a number of Karaites fled from the Soviet Union to Poland, Western Europe, and Israel. Several dozen families settled in Ashkelon and Ashdod in the 1950s, but soon moved on to North America. A single family of Russian Karaites lives in Jerusalem.

In post-war Poland, Zajączkowski presided over that country's several hundred Karaites until his death. The Polish government subsidized their religious needs, but attempts to reestablish synagogue services were unsuccessful.

An estimated five hundred Karaites now live in the United States, and a few hundred more in Canada and Western Europe. Those of East European origin, however, are outnumbered by Egyptian Karaites who emigrated in the 1950s. The largest western communities are in Chicago, San Francisco, Baltimore, and Paris. They have no synagogues, but gather in private homes on Karaite holidays.

Soviet Karaites are now scattered throughout that country. Many live in Moscow, Leningrad, Kiev, Vilna, and other major cities. A large proportion are educated professionals; the most distinguished one is a historian of contemporary Latin America, a Corresponding Member of the Soviet Academy of Sciences. Soviet citizens identifying themselves as Karaites in the 1979 census numbered 3,341. That number was substantially lower than the 4,571 in 1970 and the 5,727 in 1959, indicating a declining sense of community. (Soviet citizens may identify themselves as they choose in a census, not necessarily by the nationality which appears on their internal passports.) Census data also portrays the Karaites as one of the most urbanized and most "Russified" of Soviet ethnic groups. Only Jews and one other group have a higher percentage of members living in cities; only Jews have a higher percentage declaring Russian to be their native tongue.[26]

No Karaite synagogue remains active in the Soviet Union. The central synagogue in Troki was turned into a Karaite Historico-Ethnographic Museum after the war, and its aging religious leader was hired as the museum guide. The official Soviet line parrots that of both Czars and Nazis: that Karaites have nothing in common with Jews. The Great Soviet Encyclopedia still describes Karaites as "descendants of Turkic tribes in the Khazar Kaganate. . . . The Karaites have preserved a rich folklore, which reflects their historical ties with the Khazars."[27]

Ironically, a few young Karaites have been influenced by the Soviet Jewish revival of the 1960s and '70s, and are beginning to erase their long feud with Jews. Professor Mikhail Zand, an ex-dissident now living in Israel, tells of being contacted by two young

Karaites in Moscow. They wanted to take part in the Jewish dissident movement of which Zand was a well-known member. They told him they were thinking of applying for visas to Israel, hinting that they spoke for many other Karaites besides themselves.

Zand, an Orientalist by profession, interested himself in Soviet Karaites before emigrating to Israel. He found them even more ignorant of their religion than were other Russian Jews, without even the illusion of leadership which Rabbanites enjoy. Only a few educated Karaites were familiar with their history, referring to themselves as members of the Jewish people who had become estranged over the centuries. They told Zand that they understood the "fraud" which their ancestors had perpetrated.

But there is still no dialogue between Jews and Karaites in the Soviet Union, at least not in an organized fashion. Zand tells of meeting a mixed group of young Jews—Rabbanites and Karaites—while on vacation in the Crimea. Neither knew anything about their religion; all were trying to learn together. One young Karaite said he had learned he was Jewish from an English-language book called *Facts About Israel*, left behind by a tourist. The book said that in Israel, Karaites are considered Jews.

The accuracy of such a statement is questionable.

*   *   *   *

One summer afternoon in 1968, a young Karaite named Maurice Marzouk rose in a Tel Aviv courtroom to testify on his own behalf. Marzouk, a cousin of the Egyptian Karaite martyr Musa Marzouk, was on trial for the attempted murder of three nurses in Assaf Ha-Rofeh Hospital in Ramla. He testified that, as a patient in the hospital, he had fallen in love with a nurse. When she discovered from the hospital register that he was already married, she refused to see him again. On the morning of the incident she had telephoned her decision to him. Marzouk testified that he then got drunk and didn't remember a thing until he woke up at the police station, where he was told he had shot and wounded three nurses.

What had touched off his rage, Marzouk explained, was that he wasn't really married. That is, he was married but didn't actually have a wife. His "wife" was legally married to another man.

Marzouk was a victim—the most visible victim—of the Karaites' peculiar status in Israel. Legally, they do not exist. Only one form of Judaism is recognized in the Jewish state: Rabbanism. Yet, no one wishes to see Karaites labelled "non-Jews." So the Karaites possess neither the privileges granted to Jews nor those granted to non-Jews in Israel.

Israeli laws concerning personal status, including marriage and divorce, are based on the Ottoman system which formerly governed Palestine. That system was adopted more or less intact by the British Mandate (1920–48), and again by the state of Israel. It provides for each religious community to regulate the marriage and divorce of its members according to its own religious laws. Under the British Mandate, people who did not belong to a recognized community could marry according to civil law. But the Israeli government eliminated civil marriage in 1953, as part of a compromise with Orthodox politicians. Jurisdiction over all Jews was awarded to Orthodox rabbis in exchange for their support on a bill to draft women, which the rabbis had opposed.

This modification did not affect non-Jewish minorities. Moslems, Christians, Druzes (a semi-Moslem sect), and even Samaritans (who are not considered Jews in religious law) continued to regulate their personal status according to their own laws. It did affect Karaites. As a *Jewish* minority they were not granted autonomy.

This placed Karaites under the jurisdiction of their age-old adversaries, the Rabbanites. But the Rabbanites did not want anything to do with Karaites, whom they consider heretics and legally "bastards." The Hebrew word *mamzer*, usually translated as "bastard," actually has a slightly different meaning in Jewish law. It does not include all children of unmarried couples, only those resulting from incestuous relationships, or from the union of a married *woman* with a man other than her lawful husband—but not the other way around. This one-sided definition of adultery includes all women who remarry after an improper divorce. Rabbanites consider all Karaite divorces invalid, so all Karaites are potential *mamzerim* in their eyes. For this reason, Orthodox rabbis do not sanction "mixed" marriages between Rabbanites and Karaites.

Likewise, Karaites refuse to acknowledge the authority of Rabbanites. So, when they arrived in Israel, they continued to marry and divorce each other according to their own laws. These marriages and divorces had no legal validity, but town clerks routinely registered them anyway. It served everyone's purposes not to disturb this informal arrangement . . . until Maurice Marzouk challenged his own divorce.

Maurice and Sarah Marzouk had been married in October 1963. Marzouk, however, was a less observant Karaite than his wife. Although Karaite law forbids sexual activity on the Sabbath or during a woman's menstrual period, he insisted on making love at those times. Sarah applied for a divorce. Since Marzouk did not deny his actions, the divorce was granted by a religious court of three Karaite rabbis in Ramla in September 1965. The rabbis took the additional measure of excommunicating him.

Marzouk challenged the divorce in a civil court. He claimed that since Karaite rabbis are not legally recognized by Israeli law, they had no authority to grant it. The Supreme Court agreed with him. Following its instructions, the Ministry of the Interior sent letters in March 1966 to Sarah and to the clerks of Ramla and nearby cities, instructing them not to change her registration from "married" to "divorced."

It was too late. A clerk in Ashkelon had already issued Sarah a new identity card. She had married another Karaite man in February. She was not charged with bigamy because she had remarried in good faith, before her divorce was overturned.

But Marzouk's identity card remained unchanged. Since his divorce had been ruled invalid, he was still legally married. He had won a Pyrrhic victory: saving his marriage but losing his wife.

The clerk who checked him into Assaf Ha-Rofeh Hospital two years later was not concerned with Marzouk's legal history. He simply looked at the identity card and registered him as married. From there, one thing led to another. But the judge of Marzouk's trial for attempted murder remained unaffected by his plight. He sentenced Marzouk to twelve years in prison.

The "Karaite problem" has perplexed the Israeli government since the sect arrived in that country. Except for two Karaite families which lived in Jerusalem before independence, the first wave of about fifteen hundred immigrants arrived in 1949–50. After a brief stay in transit camps, the Iraqi immigrants settled in Beersheba and the Egyptian ones in Ramla and two *moshavim* (semi-communal farms): Rannen in the Negev desert, and Matzliah outside Ramla. Later immigrants, mostly from Egypt in 1956–57, settled in all those places plus Ashdod and Ofakim (a new town near Rannen). From there they dispersed throughout the country; there are now Karaites living in nearly every Israeli city. Their largest community is in Ramla, where about three thousand Karaites make their home. That city has two Karaite synagogues, including the large central synagogue with a community center under construction next door.

In 1950, the Israeli government decided to accept Karaites as Jews under the Law of Return. The decision was universally applauded (except by those Polish Jews who retained ill feelings from the war). The *Jerusalem Post* editorialized: "A Jew, it has been said, is a person who regards himself as one. Whether or not they accept the particular articles of faith and forms of ritual associated in people's minds with Judaism, the Karaites are Jews at least as much as are the many who have joined in the building of the Jewish National Home [but] nevertheless disregard or repudiate religion."[28]

Once in Israel, however, their status was less certain. Neither Karaites nor Rabbanites wished them under the jurisdiction of the Orthodox rabbinate. Nor did anyone wish to declare them a non-Jewish minority. The government settled on the uneasy compromise which stands to this day: their tacit, but not legal, recognition as a Jewish minority. It agreed to supply Karaite rabbis with marriage and divorce certificates, and to fund the Association of Karaite Jews in Israel. This association runs their social and religious institutions: synagogues, schools, cemeteries, religious courts, kosher slaughtering, book publishing, and the community center under construction in Ramla.

The association was initially funded through the Moslem section of the Orthodox-controlled Ministry of Religious Affairs. This deeply offended the Karaites. Under pressure from President Ben-Zvi, the ministry agreed in 1961 to set up a separate department for Karaites, Samaritans, and the "dispersed of Israel." Karaites still objected to the designation. They refused to participate until the name was changed to the Department of Karaite and Samaritan Affairs. The subsidy is so meager, anyway, that Karaite rabbis must work on the side as farmers and construction workers. The ministry provides Karaites with only one-seventh of the per capita support which it provides to Samaritans.

The marriage problem proved even more intractable than

their legal status. Israeli rabbis refused to allow the marriage of Karaites to anyone but other *mamzerim*. When they laid down that decision in 1956, a storm of public protest erupted. Prime Minister Ben-Gurion, taking the floor at the Knesset, demanded that such marriages be permitted: "A large part of the Jewish people would not accept a state of affairs where Karaites and non-Karaites who wished to marry were forbidden to do so by a law of the state." Ben-Gurion threatened to revoke the rabbis' monopoly on Jewish marriages unless they changed their decision. "After all," he continued, "many Jews in Israel could not be called either Karaite or Rabbanite, and yet no one questioned the fact that they form part of the Jewish people, nor their right to marry."[29]

Ben-Gurion's threats were hollow. Five years later, he had to admit on the Knesset floor that he had been unable to change the rabbis' minds.

Only a few exceptions have been allowed. The brother of Musa Marzouk, the Karaite "martyr of Cairo," was allowed to marry a Rabbanite girl after Orthodox rabbis checked the last three generations of his family tree and "assumed" that he was free of taint. They carefully added that this procedure was not to be considered a precedent. One Karaite rabbi was prompted to remark that you needed to lose a brother on the gallows before you could marry whomever you pleased.[30]

Another exception was made for the shotgun wedding of a twenty-two-year-old Karaite man to a fifteen-year-old Rabbanite girl who was five months pregnant. Orthodox rabbis expediently allowed the Karaite to "convert" to Judaism—a strange procedure for someone who was already Jewish.

More commonly, Karaites do not identify themselves as such when they wish to marry Rabbanite girls. (Israeli identity cards do not specify "Karaite" or "Rabbanite.") A few sympathetic rabbis can also be found to look the other way. Once such marriages are performed, Orthodox law considers them valid.

The "Karaite problem" cropped up again in 1961. Israeli citizens were asked to state their nationality in that year's census. The census form listed five categories: Jew, Moslem, Christian, Druze, and a fifth category marked "Other (Karaite, Samaritan, Bahai, etc.)." Karaites were outraged at being listed as non-Jews, and threatened to boycott the census. Prime Minister Levi Eshkol apologized. It was too late, however, to reprint the census forms. He told Karaites to answer the question however they pleased.

Karaite religious law forbids their being counted in a census, anyway. Karaite leaders once proposed an ingenious method of circumventing this problem. Each Karaite, they suggested, could donate a sheep. That way the sheep could be counted instead of the Karaites themselves. Census officials rejected this solution as "awkward."[31]

Karaite leaders have repeatedly tried to resolve their ambiguous status. They applied for separate recognition of their religious council in 1960, but were talked out of it by President Ben-Zvi. He and other secular Jews wished to avoid a legal distinction between Karaites and Rabbanites. Similar appeals were made in 1962 and 1965. But the government refused to act until the Marzouk case turned Karaites into a *cause célèbre*. Then it set up a committee.

The blue-ribbon Commission for the Examination of the Personal Status of the Karaites was formed in 1966. It was chaired by Supreme Court Justice Moses Silberg, who had sat on the Marzouk case. The Silberg Commission, as it became known, issued its recommendations after more than a year's deliberations. It called for granting the Karaites legal authority over their own personal status, and for recognition of their religious courts. After several years' delay and several more public appeals by Karaite leaders, a bill to that effect was introduced in the Knesset. It did not pass. Nothing, in fact, has ever changed. The Ministry of Religious Affairs continues to supply Karaite rabbis with marriage and divorce certificates, and town clerks continue to accept them even though they are legally worthless. Israeli Karaites continue to feel that they are second-class citizens. They hold occasional press conferences to plead their cause. Many have emigrated to France, Canada, and the United States.

A second Karaite divorce case reached the Supreme Court in 1976. This time the justices condemned government inaction. "The Karaite community is caught up in a vicious circle," the court complained. "A heavy responsibility for a whole community lies upon those who are not doing their best to bring this matter to its final stage with the utmost expedition."[32]

The synagogue of Venta Prieta. The community center (*el club*) is at left.

Passover seder in *el club*, 1980.

Dan Ross

An elderly woman in Venta Prieta cupping her hands as she blesses the candles, prior to the 1980 Passover seder. She is assisted by Margarita Marron de Gonzalez (holding book), wife of the congregation's president.

Baltasar Laureano Ramirez (right) preaching in the Venta Prieta synagogue, 1939, assisted by a Turkish Jew from Mexico City. The tablecloth is inscribed with the words, "Iglesia de Dios," the name of a Protestant church with which Venta Prieta's Jews were once affiliated.

Baltasar Laureano Ramirez, 1980.

Dan Ross

A rare photograph of a secret Passover seder, taken near Belmonte in 1967 by a young Israeli who was one of the few outside Jews ever allowed to witness this Marrano rite.

The village of Belmonte ("beautiful mountain") seen from one kilometer away. The castle (right) dates to the fourteenth century.

Shlomo Carmeli

Dan Ross

Encyclopedia Judaica Photo Archive, Jerusalem.

Rabbi Jacob Shababo (second from right) with three of his students at the Rosh Pinah Yeshiva in Oporto.

Captain Artur Carlos de Barros Basto

Amílcar Paulo, the foremost student of the Portuguese Marranos and himself from a Marrano family, and his wife, demonstrating a Marrano "Sabbath lamp."

Dan Ross

Estudio Zero, Oporto.

The Kadoorie Synagogue in Oporto, as it appeared in May, 1979, painted with a swastika and the slogan, "Death to the Jews."

A small clothing factory in Belmonte, owned by two Marrano brothers. The slogan on the right refers to a right-wing Portuguese political party; the one on the left says, "Jew, the fascists will always persecute you."

Dan Ross

Moisés Abraão (Moses Abraham) Gaspar with his family in the village of Rebordelo, Portugal. He is holding a book of Marrano prayers which dates to the early 1800s. The gatepost was carved with a star of David by his father, at the height of the Marrano "renaissance" in 1931.

Dan Ross

Amílcar Paulo

A Marrano girl in the province of Trás-os-Montes, wearing a secret prayer shawl.

An elderly Marrano couple in the province of Beira Baixa.

Amílcar Paulo

Some of the twenty-four Majorcans who were brought to Israel in 1966, seen unloading their baggage in the Tel Aviv suburb of Nes Ziona.

Nissan "Nico" Aguiló, the only Chueta who has converted to Judaism, seen in front of the Jerusalem yeshiva where he studied in 1979.

Dan Ross

Museo del Prado, Madrid

"Auto de fe en la Plaza Mayor de Madrid," a painting by Francisco Rizi (1608–1685).
Various activities of the auto-da-fe are depicted as though occurring simultaneously. The
prisoners are led in from the upper right, brought around the plaza, and finally presented
to King Carlos II (seated at top). One of the prisoners at this *auto* was a Majorcan
silversmith named Raphael Crespi Cortes, who subsequently returned to Palma where
he was burned at the stake on May 1, 1691.

From the collection of Mashiah Levy, Tel Aviv

A one-of-a-kind photograph of a Moslem school in Mashhad, Iran, patronized almost exclusively by secret Jews, c. 1917. After studying Koran in this school, most of the pupils went home to study Torah.

Sixty-three years later: Levian Nasrullayoff (circled, above) in his Jewish religious-goods shop in Jerusalem. He is now president of the Mashhadi community in Jerusalem.

"The Life of a Jadid al-Islam (New Moslem)"

The six photographs on these two plates depict the life of Azizollah Jamshidoff (1894–1975), later known as Azariah Levy. All photos are from the collection of Mashiah Levy, Tel Aviv.

1909: Azizollah (standing, center) with his family in Mashhad, photographed with their Persian carpets. His bearded father, Hajji Jamshid, had just returned from a pilgrimage to Mecca. On the return trip he stopped in Jerusalem to say Kaddish at the Western Wall.

1912: Azizollah's two marriage contracts: a public one in Persian (above) and a secret one in Hebrew. As was customary, witnesses signed the Persian contract in Hebrew script even though they were ostensibly Moslems.

1918: Azizollah's Iranian passport. His photograph is attached at top. In the entry for religion (center) is the word "Moslem," in Persian. On the reverse side is a Russian visa for a trip to Bukhara.

1924: In Jerusalem with his family after immigrating. Azizollah (standing, upper right) changed his name to Azariah Levy, his father to Menashe Levy, and his brother Rajah to Mishael Levy.

1929: A portrait taken in Bombay on a business trip.

1962: With Israeli President Isaac Ben-Zvi (wearing glasses, partially obscured by his wife) at a reception for the Mashhadis in the president's home in Jerusalem. Azariah Levy (third man from right) was at that time president of the Mashhadi community in Tel Aviv.

From the collection of Ephraim Levy, Jerusalem

The Hajji Ezekiel Synagogue in Jerusalem, c. 1910. In this photograph the Mashhadis are joined by other immigrants from Bukhara, Aleppo, and Herat.

When the Mashhadis immigrated to Jerusalem they built their homes around private courtyards, as they were accustomed to in Iran. This turn-of-the-century building in Jerusalem includes the Hajji Adoniyahu Synagogue (second floor, right), the oldest Mashhadi synagogue in Israel.

Dan Ross

A page from a book of illustrated Bible stories, used for secretly teaching Jewish children in Mashhad. The colorful illustration shows Joshua's spies returning from the "land of milk and honey." The text is in Persian, written in Hebrew script.

From the collection of Rahamim Levy, Tel Aviv

Frederick Moore

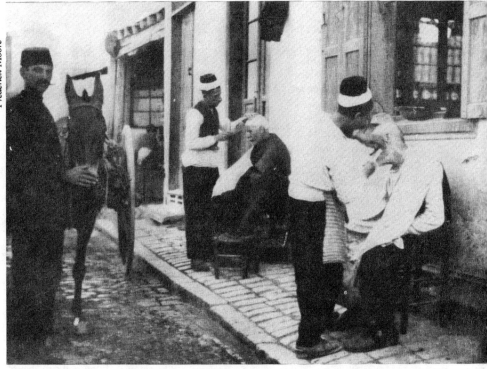

A rare photograph of the Dönmeh in Salonica. When it appeared in *National Geographic* in 1916 the caption read, "Street Barbers in the Turkish Quarter." They were presumably Dönmeh, who held a monopoly on that city's barbers.

The population exchange between Greece and Turkey, 1924. Macedonian Turks are seen here boarding a freighter in Salonica, bound for new homes in Asia Minor.

The Holocaust in Salonica. On July 11, 1942, six to seven thousand Jewish males between the ages of 18 and 45 were assembled in Salonica's Place de la Liberté for deportation to labor camps.

From the collection of David A. Recanati, Tel Aviv

Leni Sonnenfeld

An anonymous German engraving entitled, "Fasting and atonement of the Jews in Salonica." The text reads:
"Frost, heat, hunger, death, burial in earth, Thorn, whip, will here be the Jews' penance,
To enter the kingdom promised by Sabatai, Who, bold and daring, proclaims himself the Jews' Messiah."

Djavid Bey, a Dönmeh who was active in the Young Turks and became their first Finance Minister, founding the first native Ottoman bank. He was hanged in the 1920s as a possible threat to power.

Yad Itzhak Ben-Zvi, Jerusalem

Photo Archive Yael Braun, Jerusalem

Beginning of the Samaritan Passover, 1968.

Samaritans pray as the slaughtered lambs are hung upside down to drain, 1968.

Photo Archive Yael Braun, Jerusalem

A Samaritan couple smoking a hookah at the entrance to their tent on Mt. Gerizim during Passover week, 1942.

Central Zionist Archives, Jerusalem

Samaritan men recording songs and prayers in a taping session at the Hebrew University in Jerusalem.

From the collection of Binyamim Tsedaka, Holon

Yonel Sharvit

Samaritans on the summit of Mt. Gerizim during the pilgrimage of Sukkot, 1978. The high priest is carrying their most ancient Torah scroll.

Samaritans praying in their Holon synagogue during Sukkot, 1963, when they were not allowed to make the pilgrimage to Mt. Gerizim, then held by Jordan.

Government Press Office of Israel

Crimean Karaites, painted in 1862. The
seated man is Rabbi Abraham Firkovitch,
the controversial Karaite archeologist and
forger.

The interior of the Musa Dar'i Synagogue, the last remaining Karaite synagogue
in Cairo.

Micha Bar-Am, courtesy of Beth Hatefutsoth, Museum of the Jewish Diaspora, Tel Aviv

Dan Ross

The Central Synagogue of the Karaite Jews in Israel, in Ramla.

The synagogue interior, during Shavuot services, 1971. The photographer was not allowed to pass through the doors because he might have been ritually unclean.

Micha Bar-Am

Daniel Friedenberg

An armed Falasha
standing guard outside
his village, 1953.

A Falasha priest,
standing next to his
synagogue in the
village of Woozaba,
1953.

Daniel Friedenberg

Faitlovitch collection, Tel Aviv University

A Falasha boy with the European couple who adopted him, as part of Jacques Faitlovitch's program to educate Falashas in modern Judaism.

Four young Falashas at a press conference in Tel Aviv on January 2, 1979, called to protest Israeli government policy toward the Falashas. Left to right: Rahamim Eliezer, Zimne Berhane, Zechariah Yonah, and Avraham Yirday.

Isaac Freidin

Dov Goldflam

A conference of Falasha priests, 1976. Some priests who came from the remotest villages were so strictly religious that they brought their own food, refusing to eat food prepared by other Falashas.

A Falasha village market.

Dov Goldflam

Dov Goldflam

The school in Teda, a Falasha village. The inscription reads, in Hebrew and Amharic, "School of the Jews, Teda."

A Falasha funeral, 1976, The priests are carrying parasols, part of their ritual paraphernalia.

Yerachmiel Munitz

Above left: Kaifeng Jews as tourist attraction: American photographer Harrison Forman making what he described as the first motion picture of the Chinese Jews, 1938. Above, right: A close-up by Forman of the same Jewish man seen on the left.

Klau Library, HUC-JIR, Cincinnati

The two Kaifeng Jews who went to Shanghai in 1901: Li Ching-sheng (right) and his son Li Tsung-mai. Ching-sheng died there in 1903 and Tsung-mai stayed until shortly before his death in 1948, working for a Jewish-owned company and known by the name "Samuel Lee."

A Jewish family in Kaifeng, early twentieth century.

Two pages from the Kaifeng memorial book, perhaps the only Chinese-Hebrew manuscript in the world. Some Jews were listed by their Hebrew names and others, presumably those without Hebrew names, by Chinese ones. Among those listed on these pages is the most illustrious of all the Jewish mandarins, Chao Ying-ch'eng (1619–56 or 57), listed under his Hebrew name "Moses ben Abram."

Key to selected names (indicated on overlay):

1) R(abbi) Joseph ben Chao Yun-pai
2) Pinchas ben Shemaiah
3) Chao Shang-ho and Chao Shang-piao, ben Pinchas
4) Moses (the Chinese characters under his name stand for "doctor"), Chao Ying-k'uei, and Chao Shang-piao, ben Abram.

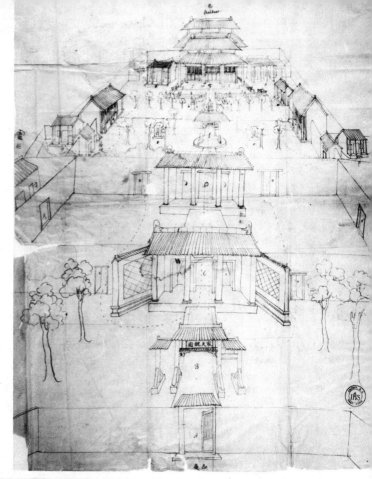

The courtyard of the
Kaifeng synagogue,
drawn by Jesuit
missionary Jean
Domenge in 1722.

*Istituto Storico
della Compagnia
de Gesu, Rome*

A model of the synagogue
building, based on Domenge's
drawing.

*Beth Hatefutsoth, Museum of the
Jewish Diaspora, Tel Aviv*

The synagogue site, 1910, half
a century after the synagogue
was torn down. Only one stone
inscription remained, at the
edge of a stagnant pond.

William C. White

The interior of the Kaifeng synagogue, also drawn by Domenge in 1722.

Istituto Storico della Compagnia de Gesu, Rome

A drawing by Domenge of a Kaifeng Jew reading the Torah from the "throne of Moses," assisted by two prompters.

Juif de Caifum lisant la Bible à la chaire de Moyse, avec deux souffleurs.

A Bene Israel hazan reading
the scroll of Esther at Purim
services in the same
synagogue.

Carmel Berkson

Carmel Berkson

Auctioning honors at
the Tifereth synagogue
in Bombay

Rosh Hashanah in Bombay: Bene Israel, dressed in their holiday finery, gathering at the Arabian Sea to perform Tashlich, the symbolic casting of sins into water.

An illustration from an 1874 Passover haggadah, printed in Poona, demonstrating how to make matzo. The title is printed in Hebrew and Marathi.

A Bombay Jew (of Baghdadi, not Bene Israel, origin) kneading matzo dough precisely as shown in the haggadah (upper right corner).

A Bene Israel woman in a sari, shopping in Dimona, Israel.

Dan Ross

A bus ticket "for Jews only" in Bombay, enabling the Bene Israel to take public transportation to and from their synagogues on Saturdays and Jewish holidays without using money.

American Jewish Committee, New York

A Bene Israel family, c. 1892.

Encyclopedia Judaica Photo Archive, Jerusalem

A Bene Israel family on a sit-down strike in Jerusalem, 1963, as part of their campaign to win equal rights in Israel.

Photo Archive Yael Braun, Jerusalem

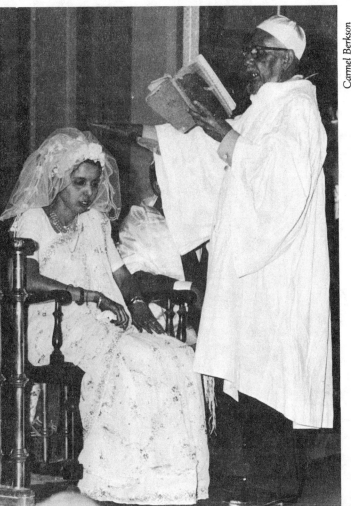

Carmel Berkson

A Bene Israel bride being blessed by the hazan after the ceremony. Note the bride's hands, painted with henna.

A close-up of hands painted with henna at a "*mendi*" ceremony before a Bene Israel wedding.

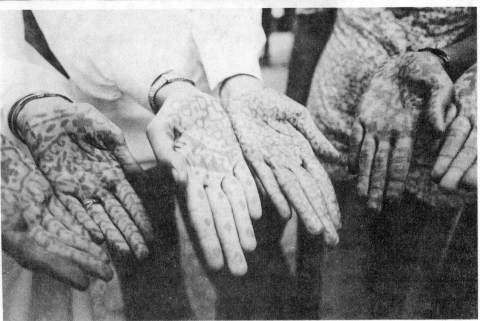

Joan Borsten

Carmel Berkson

Bene Israel women preparing a feast to celebrate the departure of community members for Israel.

The last family of Bene Israel oil-pressers, the traditional Bene Israel occupation, seen with their press in the village of Alibagh.

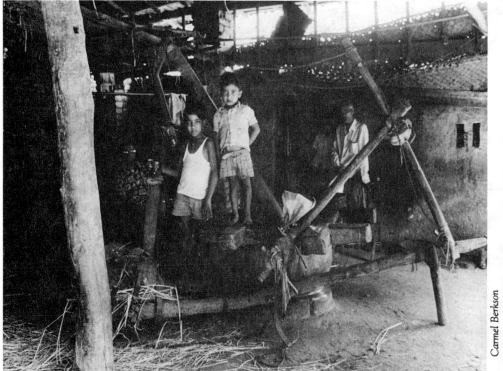

Carmel Berkson

CHAPTER EIGHT

Falashas:
"Is Zionism Only for White Jews?"

On the second day of 1979, four young Israelis ushered in the new year with a press conference in Tel Aviv, where they gave reporters a harrowing account of persecution against Jews abroad.[1] Such conferences are not uncommon in Israel. Demonstrations are regularly organized there with tacit government support, to protest the treatment of Jews in such countries as Syria, Argentina, and the Soviet Union. But this conference differed from the traditional ones. For one thing, the persecution was taking place on a scale of barbarity unheard of since World War II, including murder, physical atrocities, and child slavery. For another, they were occurring in a country which many people do not even realize Jews live in: Ethiopia. But what most distinguished this conference was its lack of government support—for a simple reason. These four young Falashas, as the black Jews of Ethiopia are usually called, were protesting what they charged was indifference on the part of the Israeli government.

As many as one-third of Ethiopia's twenty-eight thousand Jews were already dead or homeless, they told the press. The survivors were eager to come to Israel. But the same Israeli government which waged world-wide campaigns on behalf of white Jews in Syria, Argentina, and Russia came up with one excuse after another not to help black Jews in Ethiopia. Why? We don't know for sure, said the four Falashas in Tel Aviv; draw your own conclusions.

The gloves were off. That press conference marked the turning point in a long campaign to aid Falashas. After running into one bureaucratic dead end after another, Falashas were appealing over the government's head to the public. They claimed they had met only apathy—and sometimes hostility—from Israeli officials. A few days later one hundred Falashas demonstrated in front of the Knesset. Prime Minister Begin invited a delegation into his office but only asked them to be patient. Two hundred supporters demonstrated in front of the Israeli consulate in New York. Young Falashas went on publicity tours of the United States, and their supporters launched a letter-writing campaign to Israeli and Jewish Agency officials. Charges of racism were freely bandied about, not so much by Falashas as by some of their less politic supporters.

Perhaps the saddest irony was that Falashas had only recently won acceptance by world Jewry. Long considered a curiosity—or at best a quasi-Jewish fossil—they had usually been ignored or rejected by official Jewry. Not until after World War II did a few Jewish welfare organizations come to their aid. Not until the early 1970s did Israel's rabbinate recognize them as Jews. And not until 1975 did the Israeli government agree to admit Falashas under the Law of Return. Yet, few were actually brought to Israel.

That Falashas have had so much trouble winning acceptance is not surprising, though not justified, either. On the surface they seem to have little in common with other Jews. Not only are they black but their religion is a rudimentary sort of Judaism, resembling in some ways Samaritanism or Karaism. But unlike Samaritans or Karaites, Falashas are not the product of any schism, heresy, or doctrinal dispute. They were simply isolated so long that they evolved in a different direction.

Today, Falashas are embracing modern Judaism. They were electrified by the birth of Israel, turning to Zionism with a messianic fervor. Most Falashas who have managed to emigrate to Israel had to overcome tremendous obstacles to do so—including, at one time, the opposition of the Israeli government. They have successfully adapted to Israeli life. Most Israelis who have had contact with Falashas have been impressed by their sincerity, productivity, and commitment to being Jewish. But that acceptance, charge Falashas, is limited to the general public: the Israeli government has been hesitant in promoting their immigration.

Israel's approximately twelve hundred Falashas (as of this writing) are in despair. Letters from home continue to bring news of atrocities. They wonder why nothing is being done, and inevitably ask the questions they fear most. One recently voiced them in a letter to an American friend. "Is Zionism only for white Jews?" he asked. "Is the state of Israel only for white Jews?"[2]

.   .   .   .

"If there is any country in existence today where biblical life is the way of the people," an Ethiopian Jew recently wrote, "it is Ethiopia."[3] He was referring not just to Falashas but to all Ethiopians. Although on the map it is part of Africa, Ethiopia has always been the meeting ground of two civilizations: African and Semitic. Throughout its history it has been in close contact with the Arabian Peninsula, just across the Red Sea. The people of Ethiopia display a mixture of African and Semitic influences. Genetically the African strain is dominant, although Ethiopians are lighter-colored and possess more finely drawn features than most other Africans. Culturally the accent is on the Semitic. Ethiopians speak Semitic languages, write with a Semitic alphabet, and worship the Semitic God.

Ethiopia's national religion is a form of Monophysite Christianity (rejecting the man/God duality of Christ) which preserves many Jewish customs. Ethiopians claimed to be descended from Jews, and their emperors claimed Solomon and the Queen of Sheba as their ancestors. The Old Testament is as sacred to them as the New. They circumcise their children on the eighth day, observe the Sabbath on Saturday, do not eat pork or other forbidden foods, build their churches on the pattern of the Jerusalem Temple, and practice some Old Testament laws of purity. Visitor after visitor has been struck by the parallels between Judaism and Ethiopian Christianity. A Portuguese Jesuit, one of the first Europeans to visit Ethiopia in the seventeenth century, commented: "Their present religion is nothing but a kind of confused miscellany of Jewish and Mahometan superstitions, with which they have corrupted those remnants of Christianity which they still retain."[4] More than three hundred years later, in the 1960s, an Orthodox Jew living in Addis Ababa could still observe to a visitor: "When I first came here from Eastern Europe I was simply overwhelmed at how 'Jewish' everything was. Have you been to one of the traditional religious services? What does it remind you of if not a Sabbath morning in an Orthodox *shul*? I found among the various Ethiopian amulets things very close to my own phylacteries and mezuzah. I was exhilarated to discover the high holy days also falling in September, the Sabbath being celebrated on Saturday, and time reckoned from sunset."[5]

Falashas fit comfortably in this biblical world. They could be described as the most biblical of all Ethiopians. A rural people in the hills of northwest Ethiopia, their population is now estimated at twenty to twenty-five thousand—down somewhat from the twenty-eight thousand counted in a 1976 survey. All numbers are inexact because of the inaccessibility of their villages. Few are near a road; to reach them you must head overland through some of Africa's most spectacular mountain scenery. From Gondar, the largest city in the area, it is a full day's hike or two hours' jeep ride to Ambober, their largest village. In better times visitors were met outside their villages by an honor guard of armed Falashas. Several have written of their surprise at the sudden silhouette of armed Falasha men on a hilltop. "The strong, resolute expression of these men and the mountainous surroundings brought to mind the times when the Falashas fought for their independence against the Ethiopian kings," wrote Wolf Leslau, one of the foremost authorities on Falashas, after his first visit. "I confess that I was very much impressed by this sight."[6]

Since their conquest in the seventeenth century, Falashas have been scattered throughout the northwest without a homeland of their own. Forbidden to own land, they tenant-farm and work at handicrafts considered beneath the dignity of other Ethiopians. In their regions, they are the blacksmiths, weavers, and potters par excellence. Other Ethiopians used to believe (and some still do) that Falashas were sorcerers, because of their skill at those crafts. Popular legend held that Falashas turned themselves into hyenas after dark, and spent their nights digging up cemeteries. This superstition was so widespread that it was almost a national myth. As recently as Italy's 1935–41 occupation of Ethiopia, it was reinforced by leaflets dropped over the countryside by Italian planes.

Falashas are physically indistinguishable from other Ethiopians. Although the word falasha means "exile" or "stranger" (Falashas prefer to call themselves beta esra'el—"House of Israel"), not even Ethiopians claim that they differ in any way other than religion. Ethiopians say the easiest way to tell a Falasha is by the "smell of water" coming from him, because of his frequent washings for ritual purposes. Visually, the only way is by the women's shaved heads (as opposed to the long braided hair of Christian women), or by their different jewelry.

They now speak the same languages as other Ethiopians, too. Until the nineteenth century Falashas spoke their own dialect of Agau, a non-Semitic language still used in a few remote mountain areas. But today they speak Amharic, the national tongue, where that is commonly spoken, or other local languages. Their clothing and housing are also identical to those of other Ethiopians. They wear the ubiquitous toga-like *shamma*, the national dress of Ethiopia, and live in the same round thatched huts, called *tukuls*. Some now wear Western clothes.

Falasha villages are also typically Ethiopian: clusters of *tukuls* on a hilltop. They are always built near running water so Falashas can perform their ritual ablutions. The *tukuls* are built of sticks and branches in a circular wooden frame, sometimes plastered with mud, and topped with a roof of thick grass. They rarely contain any furniture other than animal skins, handwoven blankets, and sometimes a wooden bench. Fires burn in the center of the huts; smoke either escapes through the roof or not at all.

Outdoors, the villages are littered with the paraphernalia of their trades: looms, pots, pitchers, charcoal fires, and scraps of iron. Falasha blacksmiths work in teams. One man holds the iron in tongs, another hammers it, and others fan the flames with goatskin bellows. Women potters work without wheels or kilns, shaping their wares by hand, baking them on heated stones, and polishing them with glass-bead necklaces. Young girls spin thread from raw cotton to be woven into *shammas* by old men who sit on the ground with their legs in holes dug beneath the looms.

Falasha villages differ from others by a special structure found on its edge: a "hut of blood." Like Samaritans, Falashas do not touch women during menstruation or after childbirth. But unlike Samaritans, Falasha women spend their menstrual periods in separate huts. Circles of stones mark a perimeter around those *tukuls* beyond which men may not pass. Additional huts are built for women to live in during their forty or eighty days of impurity after childbirth; these are burned afterwards.

Ethiopian Christians follow Old Testament laws of purity, too, but not as strictly as Falashas. Any Ethiopian who (among other things) performs a circumcision, has sexual intercourse, enters a room where a child was born, or touches a corpse, grave, or even a dead animal becomes unclean. Unclean Christians may not enter a church or touch holy articles until sunset. But unclean Falashas must isolate themselves completely, until they can be purified by immersing their entire bodies in water.

Falashas also become unclean every time they touch a non-Jew. Because of this they always live apart, usually in their own villages. Where they must share a village with Christians they build a separate neighborhood. When selling goods in a public marketplace they carry a bowl of water to receive money in. This attitude has earned them the nickname "touch-me-nots" from other Ethiopians.

Even among themselves Falashas used to have a formal hierarchy of purity. Falasha monks would not eat with laymen. "Hill Falashas" would not eat with "town Falashas" (those who have moved to Gondar or elsewhere for better jobs) because they came into frequent contact with non-Jews. When the Italians built a road near one of their villages, Wolleqa, many Falashas fled to remoter locales rather than live so exposed. Only a few stayed in Wolleqa, where they now live by selling sculptured figurines to passing tourists.

The Falasha Bible is in an old Ethiopian language called Ge'ez, which is also used by Ethiopian Christians. They knew no Hebrew until they were introduced to it by foreign Jews. Falashas use the same Bible translation as Christians, including several books of the Apocrypha but not the New Testament. The only Falashas who understand Ge'ez are monks and priests, who translate for the others as they read the scriptures aloud.

They also have a small literature of their own. These manuscripts, also in Ge'ez, were stored for centuries in Falasha synagogues and monasteries. Most are now held by various European libraries. Only a few are original; the others were adapted from Christian versions with the most blatantly Christian passages deleted. Among their original works are sermons and homilies written by monks, compilations of Falasha commandments, and legends woven around the life and death of Moses. Their prayers are also of their own composition.

Their synagogues resemble ordinary *tukuls*, except that they may be larger or, in the last few years, marked with a Star of David on the roof. Inside they are divided in two parts: a common area for laymen and a "holy of holies" for priests and monks. Priests pray seven times a day but other Falashas rarely join them except for morning and evening prayers. Women, except a few unmarried girls and honored elders, may not enter at all. Nor may non-Jews or "unclean" Falashas. One foreign Jew reported that he was only allowed to enter after a wooden board was placed on the floor for him to stand on.

Outside each synagogue is a stone altar. Falashas formerly sacrificed an animal every Passover, like Samaritans, and on a few other occasions as well. Unlike Samaritans they did not sacrifice only lambs, but sometimes bulls or goats. The animals were slaughtered with a special knife, skinned, washed, boiled, and eaten by Falasha men. Sacrifices were abandoned in the late 1950s and early 1960s under the influence of foreign Jews.

Every Friday, Falashas put down their work at mid-day and begin to prepare for the Sabbath. They wash themselves and their clothing, grind grain, brew beer, and bake bread. Beginning at sunset, Falashas do no work, light no fires, draw no water, make no love, and do not leave their villages. In former times, according to Ethiopian chronicles, Falashas even rested on the Sabbath in wartime—fighting only when attacked.

Falashas celebrate all biblical holidays plus a few of their own. Each year, for example, they observe a "Festival of the Eighteenth" (named after the day of the month it is held on) to mark the deaths of Abraham, Isaac, and Jacob. On that day they read the lives of the patriarchs from the Bible. They also celebrate monthly holidays to commemorate *other* holidays: the tenth of each month is a holiday in honor of Yom Kippur, the twelfth in honor of Shavuot, and the fifteenth in honor of Passover and Sukkot. All Falashas fast on the twenty-ninth of each month; priests and old men fast every Thursday.

Like Karaites they slaughter animals according to biblical rules, but do not separate meat from milk. They do not eat raw meat, unlike other Ethiopians who consider it a treat. They rarely eat meat, anyway. Like other poor Ethiopian villagers, Falashas subsist almost entirely on a spongy, flat bread called *injera*, made from wheat or a native Ethiopian grain called *teff*. Meat, fresh fruits, and vegetables are reserved for special occasions. Falashas wash their hands and recite blessings before and after every meal.

Falashas are led by priests, called *kahens* (an Amharic word analogous to the Hebrew *kohen*), and "learned men" called *dabtaras*. Priests lead the prayers, read the Scriptures, perform marriages, hear confessions from dying Falashas, and generally counsel and lead the community. They receive offerings of food and beer, but also work alongside other Falashas. *Dabtaras* teach the children and assist the priests until they qualify for the priesthood themselves. Unlike that of Samaritans or ancient Jews, the Falasha priesthood is not hereditary. Priests are elected by the community. Their learning and character must be of a high order, and their families free of adultery or physical defects for the last seven generations. Larger communities also elect a high priest. Like Ethiopian Christian priests, Falasha priests carry parasols which they unfurl for ritual occasions. When the Falasha scholar and Ethiopian government minister Ta'amrat Emmanuel studied in New York in the 1930s, he was said to cut a dashing figure as he made his way around town with an umbrella under his arm, under blue skies as well as gray.[7]

Falashas have monks and, formerly, a few nuns as well. They live in self-denial on the edges of villages or in monasteries of their own. They frequently fast, and sometimes retreat to deserted spots to receive inspiration, later returning as preachers or "saints." Monks are the guardians of Falasha religion, resistant to change. They do not touch other Falashas, even priests, or speak to non-Jews or "town Falashas." In one village, Falashas tell the story of a monk who refused to speak to a Jewish officer in the British army (which liberated Ethiopia from the Italians in 1941), because he rode into that village on muleback on a Saturday.

Falashas are the only Jews in the world with a monastic tradition, which they apparently borrowed from their Christian neighbors. According to their traditions, Falasha monasticism was founded by a fifteenth-century saint named Abba Zabra, who is the hero of many of their legends. He is said to have converted the son of Ethiopia's king to Judaism and, when the king came after him, he was miraculously transported to a distant cave. Falashas credit Abba Zabra with instituting their laws of "touch-me-not," and with writing one of their few original books, the *Te'ezaza Sanbat* (Precepts of the Sabbath). The cave where Abba Zabra lived became the largest Falasha monastery. Last century, two hundred monks were said to be living there.

There are few—if any—monks left today. In the mid-1950s only a half-dozen were said to be left, none under eighty years old. While still revered, they were no longer blindly obeyed. Because they are so conservative, villages with monks had the most trouble adjusting to the changes of the last few decades.

. . . .

When the great Scottish explorer James Bruce returned to Britain in 1773, claiming to have traveled the length of the Blue Nile from Ethiopia to Egypt, he was met with outright scorn and ridicule. Few believed his outlandish tales of Ethiopian natives who cut steaks from the flanks of living cattle and ate them raw, or wore rings through their noses (instead of their ears). Dr. Samuel Johnson set the tone for all England when he declared that he did not believe Bruce had even been in Ethiopia. "He is not a distinct relater," Johnson also told his biographer, James Boswell, after dining with Bruce, "and I should say, he is neither abounding nor deficient in sense. I did not perceive any superiority of understanding."[8]

Offended, Bruce sulked in Scotland for seventeen years before publishing his *Travels to Discover the Source of the Nile,* which became an immediate sensation. Even then it was considered more fiction than fact. That verdict has since been reversed. Today it is considered a classic of exploration literature, and its author, in the words of the noted Ethiopist Edward Ullendorff, "one of the great universal *savants* and men of action of the eighteenth century."[9] His travelogue was so precise that later explorers were able to use it as a guidebook.

Thought to be among Bruce's most fantastic "inventions" was his description of one of "the stranger nations" he came across: a tribe of black Jews called the Falasha. "I did not spare my utmost pains in inquiring into the history of this curious people," Bruce wrote, "and lived in friendship with several, esteemed the most knowing and learned among them, if any of them deserved to be so called; and I am persuaded, as far as they knew, they told me the truth."[10]

We now know, of course, that Bruce's account of Falashas was remarkably accurate. He must have gone to great lengths to obtain his information. His book, which dwells at length on Falasha history, conforms closely to what we have learned in the intervening two hundred years. Bruce was the first to unearth their own explanation of their origin—"supported only by tradition," he carefully noted.[11] He reported that Falashas claimed to have come from Palestine in the retinue of Menelik, the son of Solomon and the Queen of Sheba. In this, Bruce pointed out, "they perfectly agree with the Abyssinians [Ethiopians] in the story of the Queen of Saba, who, they say, was a

Jewess, and her nation, Jews, before the time ofaf17Solomon."[12]

The story of Solomon and Sheba, somewhat embroidered, was and still is the national myth of Ethiopia. The Ethiopian version is more explicit than the biblical. Where the Bible only hints at a sexual liaison, Ethiopian chronicles describe a seduction in detail. The queen left Solomon immediately afterward, continues this legend, and nine months later gave birth to a son named Menelik. As a grown man Menelik visited his father in Jerusalem before returning to found a dynasty which ruled (intermittently) until the overthrow of Emperor Haile Selassie in 1974. The Ethiopians were converted to Christianity, legend and historians agree, by Syrian missionaries in the fourth century A.D.

Falasha traditions depart from that national one when the Israelites arrive in Ethiopia. Bruce's account continues: "Being very industrious, these people multiplied exceedingly, and were very powerful at the time of the conversion to Christianity, or, as they term it, the apostasy. . . . At that time they declared a prince of the tribe of Judah, and of the race of Solomon and Menelik, their sovereign. The name of this prince was Phineas, who refused to abandon the religion of his forefathers."[13]

Bruce was skeptical about this Falasha tale. His restrained appraisal was that "many difficulties occur in this account of the Falasha."[14] Few since Bruce have taken it any more seriously than he did, which is not to say that their alternatives have been more reasonable. The origin of the Falashas has inspired more nonsense than James Bruce ever dreamed of. Even today, when the speculation has turned from the imaginative to the scientific, it is difficult to find any two opinions which agree. The mystery of Falasha origins is not much closer to being solved today than it was in Bruce's time.

Ruling out some of the more fanciful theories is the easiest thing to do. It is not very likely that Falashas are descendants of Moses's followers who turned right out of Egypt instead of left, ending up in Ethiopia instead of Palestine. Nor is it likely that they are descendants of the lost tribe of Dan (as Israel's chief rabbis claim), or of Jewish soldiers posted in upper Egypt by the Persian emperors (as President Ben-Zvi believed), or of refugees from the destruction of one Jerusalem Temple or the other. In fact, it is not very likely that Falashas are descendants of Jews at all. Most historians now believe that the ancestors of Falashas were Ethiopians, who *adopted* their

Judaism long ago. What they are less sure of is when, and how.

Historical thought has come full circle since Bruce's day. The now-favored line of thinking is not so far from the Falasha legend uncovered by that explorer. As set forth by Edward Ullendorff, it is that Falashas are descended from ancient Ethiopians who stubbornly refused to abandon their religion for Christianity. Before the conversion, according to Ullendorff, the biblical style of Judaism which Falashas still practice was far more widespread in Ethiopia.

Ethiopian chronicles appear to agree. Before the conversion, they relate, "One part of the people was under the Mosaic Law, the other was worshipping the Serpent [i.e., paganism]."[15]

Where did this Judaism come from? Almost certainly from southern Arabia, what is now Yemen. Travel and even war across that neck of the Red Sea were frequent in ancient times. Ethiopian languages are closely related to those once spoken in southern Arabia. Before the spread of Islam, Judaism was one of the major religions in southern Arabia. There was even an Arabian Jewish kingdom called Himyar which was toppled by Ethiopian armies in 525 A.D. Exactly how Judaism crossed the Red Sea is still a subject for speculation. It may have been brought by traders, perhaps by missionaries, or perhaps by prisoners of war.

Not all historians agree. The French Semitist Maxime Rodinson points out that there is no solid evidence behind this theory. He presents credible arguments for Judaism being home-grown on Ethiopian soil, out of imitation of the Old Testament—as occurred in Venta Prieta (see Chapter I). There is no reason to believe this happened earlier than the Middle Ages, he says. "We are faced with a historical problem which will not be resolved without patient effort and stamina," Rodinson concludes. "Nothing up to now demonstrates an important immigration of Jews at any time, nor a massive Judaization of Ethiopia before the Christianization."[16]

All we really know for sure, until the arrival of Europeans, is what we are told by Ethiopian chronicles. These do not mention Falashas until the fourteenth century, and even then only when describing wars waged against them by Ethiopian kings. They pick up Falasha history while they are still independent, and trace their gradual subjugation through a series of wars, treaties, broken alliances, and forced baptisms. Falasha independence came to its final end three hundred years later, in 1632. A last-ditch rebellion was suppressed by a massacre of Falasha men, women, and children. They were dispersed from their homeland, forbidden to own land, encouraged to convert to Christianity, and generally reduced to penury. Without their own land they turned more and more to handicrafts for a livelihood; they have been on the bottom rung of Ethiopia's social ladder ever since. Ethiopian chronicles do not mention them again. But by this time, the first Europeans were on the scene.

Even before James Bruce the outside world was not entirely ignorant of Falashas. A few Jewish and Arab travelers mentioned them in passing, mostly from hearsay. An occasional Falasha slave turned up in the Arab world. The religious wars of Ethiopia were well known in Egypt by the 1500s. The Portuguese and Spanish began to frequent Ethiopia at that time, too. A few brief missionary and explorer accounts preceded Bruce's, revealing little more than that Falashas existed. The state of European knowledge prior to Bruce was summed up by the German Orientalist Job Ludolf in 1681: "The Jews formerly held several fair and large Provinces, stoutly Defending themselves by means of the Rocks; at that time they also liv'd according to their own Customs, under a Prince of their own. Now they are dispers'd, getting their livings by Weaving, and exercising the trade of Carpenters. Most of them still keep up their own Synagogues, have their own Hebrew Bibles [sic], and speak in a corrupt Talmudic dialect [sic]."[17]

Falashas also had their first contact with a foreign Jew at that time. In one of the most curious and least known episodes of that era, an otherwise unknown Viennese Jew surfaced in the capital of Ethiopia in the early 1600s. His name was either Solomon or Abraham, depending on whose account you believe, and he was dressed as a merchant. He is known to have held a religious disputation with Catholic missionaries, but the results are as uncertain as his name. According to Portuguese accounts (which call him Solomon), the Jew was out-debated and he was expelled from Ethiopia. But a Falasha tradition (which calls him Abraham) claims that he won, and that his victory saved them from massacre.[18]

None of those reports attracted much attention in Europe. It was Bruce's detailed narrative, published in 1790, which first piqued Western curiosity. A series of scholars and Protestant missionaries contacted Falashas in the 1800s, the former to find out more about them and the latter to win their souls. The missionaries were by far the more successful of the two. Forbidden by the king from seeking converts among Ethiopian Christians, they spent all their energy on Falashas, with considerable results. Their widely advertised success disturbed European Jews. A prominent German rabbi, Azriel Hildesheimer, published a full-page appeal in the *Jewish Chronicle* in 1864, calling for a mission to rescue Falashas before they were all converted. "It is our duty to deliver them from the pernicious toils in which they are ensnared by men who have no regard for the bonds of family and religion," he declared.[19]

Three years later, the *Alliance Israélite Universelle* dispatched a French linguist named Joseph Halévy to report on the situation. Halévy was a forty-year-old teacher and Orientalist, born in Adrianople, whose success in this mission would launch a spectacular career in Oriental philology, lasting another fifty years. After a dangerous and irregular journey he finally reached a Falasha village. They refused to believe he was Jewish. "What!" he wrote that they told him. "You a Falasha! A white Falasha! You are laughing at us. Are there any white Falashas?"[20]

He won them over by telling them he came from Jerusalem, which he had visited along the way. "I assured them that all the Falashas of Jerusalem, and in other parts of the world, were white," Halévy wrote, "and that they could not be distinguished from the other inhabitants of their respective countries. The name of Jerusalem, which I had accidentally mentioned, changed as if by magic the attitude of the most incredulous. A burning curiosity seemed all at once to have seized the whole company. 'Oh, do you come from Jerusalem, the blessed city? Have you beheld with your own eyes Mount Zion, and the House of the Lord of Israel, the holy Temple?' . . . I must confess I was deeply moved on seeing those black faces light up at the memory of our glorious history."[21]

Halévy's mission could not have been more well-timed. Only five years earlier a feud between missionaries and Falashas had ended in a disastrous millennial movement. Three Protestant missionaries had debated five Falashas in the presence of the king, attempting to convert them by reinterpreting the Falashas' own scriptures in a Christian light. They argued over the unity versus trinity of God, over the practice of sacrifice, and over the unwillingness of Falashas to convert. The king's verdict is not known; again, it depends on whose version you believe. But by all accounts, Falashas embarked on a mass pilgrimage to Jerusalem following the debate. Entire villages and parts of others packed their belongings and began walking in that general direction. They knew only that Jerusalem was somewhere beyond the Red Sea, but believed that their exodus would be attended by miracles as had that of their "ancestors" out of Egypt. Their leader, a Falasha monk, assured them that the Red Sea would part for them as it had for Moses. But no miracles appeared, and they were forced to stop before even sighting water. Most perished during three years of hardship in northeast Ethiopia. Only a few managed to return.

Halévy, in his travels, saw many empty homes abandoned by the pilgrims. He toured Falasha villages, observed their customs, interviewed priests and monks, and brought back the first Falasha manuscripts to Europe. He also brought back two young Falashas in person, who insisted on accompanying him to Europe. On his return he declared unequivocally that Falashas were Jews.

His assertion was received with skepticism. Halévy's mission won no immediate support for Falashas. The *Alliance* launched no programs to aid them, as it had for other impoverished Jews. It remained for a student of Halévy's, Jacques Faitlovitch, to become their champion. Not so dispassionate as his teacher, Faitlovitch was as interested in helping Falashas as in studying them. He lived with them for eighteen months in 1904–05, and returned to Europe to plead their cause. He, too, brought back two young Falashas, the first of several whom he placed in European schools.

Faitlovitch initially won no more support than Halévy had. Still skeptical, the *Alliance* sent another envoy in 1907–08: a prominent Turkish rabbi named Haim Nahoum. Rabbi Nahoum was considerably less enthusiastic. "It does not seem to me desirable that anything should be done," he told one journalist on his return. "In view of their small numbers and wide distribution, the creation of schools seems to me impossible."[22] The *Alliance* agreed.

Undaunted by rejection, Faitlovitch formed "Pro-Falasha" committees to raise funds in Italy and Germany. On a third visit in 1913–14, he founded a mobile school to tour Falasha villages. He continued fund-raising in the United States after World War I, and in 1923 founded a Falasha boarding school in Addis Ababa. The school was headed by a young Falasha named Ta'amrat Emmanuel, whom Faitlovitch had sent to Europe and America for education, and who later became a minister in Haile Selassie's government before dying in Israel in 1963. Faitlovitch's efforts were interrupted by the Italian invasion of 1935 and not resumed until the post-war years, now from Tel Aviv. He lived just long enough to see his labors taken over by organized Jewry. His funeral in 1955 was attended by twelve Falasha children, who had just arrived in Israel as part of the first contingent brought there for an education.

The 1950s saw the first real effort by Jewish organizations to aid Falashas. In 1953 the Jewish Agency opened a teacher's school in Asmara, near the Ethiopian coast. It began with half a dozen priests who returned to their villages after a two-month introduction to modern Judaism, and with a dozen children who stayed for a broader education. The following year fifteen young Falashas (averaging ten years old) were brought to Israel for a three-year program in basic farming skills, Orthodox Judaism, and hygiene. They lived alongside young Israelis in an Orthodox boarding school, *Kfar Batya*. A total of twenty-eight came by 1958, and eighteen of them returned to Ethiopia at the end of their studies. Together with the graduates of the Asmara school, they formed an educated Falasha nucleus to begin the task of bringing their people into the modern world. More than twenty schools were opened in Falasha villages. Most offered only a two-year course, but the best students graduated to a boarding school in Ambober for another four years. A few went on to high school in Gondar.

A new generation of Falashas grew up whose vistas were not limited to traditional lore. They learned about the outside world in school, listened to Israeli radio at night, and occasionally met Jewish tourists. Their new role models were their teachers, rather than the priests and monks schooled in the old ways. They learned that their religion was not the "real" Judaism, and began to change it. Falashas celebrated Hanukkah for the first time; they had never before known about that post-biblical festival. They built their first *sukkah* for Sukkoth. They lit candles in their synagogues on Friday nights, and wore prayer shawls during services. They switched to the Jewish calendar from their own; calendars were printed in Ethiopian languages in Israel and mailed to them.

More than religion is now changing. Ethiopia in the 1970s was a country in the grip of social, political, and economic upheaval. A terrible famine, killing hundreds of thousands, led to the overthrow of Haile Selassie in 1974. He was followed by a succession of Marxist-oriented military regimes. The weakened central government was challenged by revolution in the northeast (Eritrea), invasion in the southeast (from Somalia), and counterrevolutionaries in the northwest, where Falashas live.

Falashas had always been loyal to Haile Selassie. Shortly before his downfall he allowed them to participate in a land reclamation program along the Sudanese border. Thousands of acres were assigned to Falasha farmers, but the program was a fiasco. Life in the lowlands was much different from what Falashas were used to: prairies instead of mountains, hot dry weather instead of their rainy climate, and cash crops instead of subsistence farming. Wild West conditions prevailed. Roads were rare, squatters seized vacant land, and weapons were a necessity of life.[23]

The first Falasha settlement in 1969 was actually on the wrong side of the border, in Sudan. They were forced to retreat after a pitched battle with Sudanese troops. Malaria was widespread. Only men went to the new villages, and few volunteered for a second tour of duty. Support from foreign Jews enabled a few Falashas to turn a modest profit, but the venture petered out after four years.

Conditions grew worse after the 1974 revolution. When the new government announced a land reform, all Ethiopians were supposed to receive twenty-five acres. Falashas were hopeful they could own their land for the first time in centuries. But the central government was too weak to impose the reforms in the north, and the landlord class led a counterrevolution. Some Falashas were actually expelled from land they had tenant-farmed for generations.

The revolution soon degenerated into chaos, peaking in the catastrophic years of 1977–78. A wave of terror gripped the country. Even the slave trade flared anew, one of the last places on earth where it survives. Murder, rape, and physical mutilations became commonplace; children were often sold into slavery. Old tribal animosities were revived, and Falashas were caught in the crossfire. Those in the far north were trapped by the rebellion of Moslem Eritreans. Thousands of Falashas fled to refugee camps in Sudan and other countries. Others were not so fortunate. The most widely quoted casualty figures (which can be neither confirmed nor refuted) are that two thousand Falashas were killed and seven thousand driven off their land—one-third of the total Falasha population.

Most of the schools are still operating, but in a new

atmosphere of suspicion. They are no longer operated by the Jewish Agency but by ORT, a Jewish vocational-training organization. ORT accepts Falashas and non-Falashas on an equal basis—an admirable policy in peaceful times but which appears to have backfired in fractured Ethiopian society. The schools fell victim to ethnic animosity. Feuding between non-Falasha directors and Falasha teachers ended in the arrest of six teachers in December 1978, and the deaths of two of them. Those teachers had been the most active Zionists, and their activities came to a halt.

"Ethiopians are living in a tribal society," explains an Israeli who worked with Falasha teachers, "each tribe on its own, each tribe against the others. How much more so with the Falashas who used to be, and still are, 'strangers' and even enemies. Just remember one of the Falashas' laws—having to wash after touching non-Falashas! You cannot expect that they will accept instructions from non-Jewish teachers, and you cannot expect that non-Falashas will look upon Falashas as equals. When we first went there it even took us, the Israelis, a long time to be accepted by the Falashas. You cannot expect them to forget hundreds of years of history."[24]

■ ■ ■ ■

Even after his death, Jacques Faitlovitch continues to be a "good Samaritan" to the Falashas. He bequeathed his spacious home to the Tel Aviv municipality, which turned it into a public library and folklore center. Falashas use it as a meeting place and home-away-from-home in Tel Aviv. It was in the basement of that house that two Falasha students agreed to discuss their lives in Ethiopia and Israel.

"Life has changed for Falashas," said Zechariah Yonah, the secretary of the Association of Ethiopian Jews in Israel. "Most of the young ones no longer practice as they did. There are no more monks, except maybe in a few distant villages. In another ten to fifteen years there will be no more priests, either. Because of the state of Israel and the activities of the Jewish Agency, we stopped bothering to learn the old customs. Everyone thought the schools were preparation for immigration, and we would go to Israel soon. No one thought it would take thirty years."

"And thirty years looks like only the beginning," interjected his close friend Rahamim Eliezer. "Who can say when the rest of the Falashas will join us here?"

Anyone who thinks of Falashas as primitive African tribesmen would have been quickly disillusioned by meeting Zechariah or Rahamim—or, for that matter, any of the other Falashas in Israel. Both these young men were handsome, well-spoken, with a quiet dignity. Zechariah sported a small goatee and Rahamim a mustache. In appearance they resembled nothing so much as middle-class black Americans, perhaps graduate students or young professors. Otherwise they were much the average Israelis, except in their polite and respectful manner. Their Hebrew was fluent and their English nearly so. Each wore a small button on his lapel which said in English, "Save Falasha Jewry."

"Not only did they destroy our old religion," Zechariah continued, "but the children, too. They prepared the children to want to go to higher education. But the only option was to go to government schools where they were forced to convert. The best of the children have left us: either converted or simply no longer Jewish. They will never return to their villages. They are no more Falashas."

"Once a Falasha leaves his village he can no longer practice his religion," explained Rahamim. "He must pretend he is a Christian, or he can't get a job or get along in school. But he still remembers he is a Jew. Every Falasha wants to practice what is in the Torah—they *feel* that. I had to pretend I was a Christian, too, but I only did it because people made me.

"When I came to Israel I finally felt free to be a Jew," Rahamim continued. "It was a shock to see Jews here driving and playing the radio on the Sabbath. And then *they* asked *me* to convert to Judaism! In Ethiopia I felt everything as a Jew, and practiced as in the Bible. But here they said I'm not a Jew and had to convert. So what's the use of everything I did there? Now I don't do what I did there or what they do here. But I believe. You can believe and not practice, even as a Jew."

Zechariah agreed. "I went to synagogue every Sabbath in Ethiopia, but here I stopped. They told us we had to be converted. The rabbis said it was very different from the conversion of a non-Jew, but for me who is no rabbi there's no difference. I can't deny all my history and accept a new one."

The ceremony about which Zechariah and Rahamim were

complaining is one which all Falashas must undergo before Israeli rabbis will accept them as Jews. It is not a full conversion, just an immersion in the *mikveh*—the same one required of Venta Prietans (see Chapter I). In 1971 and 1972, when Zechariah and Rahamim immigrated, the rabbis were calling this a "token conversion." Since 1973, when the rabbis ruled that Falashas were already Jewish, they have been calling it a "renewal of the covenant." The ceremony is the same. Most Falashas do not care what it is called, and get it over with as soon as they arrive. Some, like Zechariah and Rahamim, consider it an insult. A few have refused.

Until the 1970s there were few Falashas in Israel. The first was one of Faitlovitch's students, who brought his family to what was then Palestine. Next came the Falasha wives of a few Yemenite traders, who had lived in Ethiopia before moving to Israel shortly after its independence. Then there were the ten young Falashas who did not return to Ethiopia after studying in *Kfar Batya:* three boys who moved to a kibbutz and four girls who became nurses in various parts of the country. These began to be supplemented in the late 1960s by young Falashas who began sneaking into the country, mostly by working on Red Sea fishing boats and deserting in Eilat. The first one came in 1965, followed by five in 1966, eight in 1967, eight more in 1968, and four in 1969.

As few as they were, these Falashas raised the first disturbing questions about their Jewishness. In 1966 the rabbinate refused to allow twenty-seven-year-old Benjamin Gitye, one of the *Kfar Batya* students who stayed, to marry a Jewish girl. Gitye's father had been one of Faitlovitch's students and converted to Judaism at that time, but his mother had not. Therefore, said the rabbis, Gitye would have to undergo the "token" conversion. "I have the impression," explained one rabbi, "that the scholars are convinced that the Falashas are a people not of Jewish origin who were once converted to Judaism."[25]

But Gitye refused, telling reporters: "I'm a Jew just like any other Jew."[26] Instead, he sued the rabbinate. Two years later the Supreme Court finally decided against him. It did not rule on whether Gitye was Jewish, but that the rabbinate has the legal authority to determine who is a Jew for purposes of marriage and divorce. Gitye was forced to undergo the conversion before he could marry.

The pace of immigration picked up in the early 1970s.

Zechariah came as a student in 1971 and never left. Others continued to come on fishing boats or as tourists. "Every Falasha would come to Israel if he could," contends Zechariah. "The Falashas have never in history believed they would stay in Ethiopia forever. This belief has always strengthened them in times of trouble. The desire to go to Israel is like a religion with them. But there was always one problem or another."

The problem used to be that the Israeli government did not consider Falashas to be Jews. It refused to issue them immigration papers, and hindered those Falashas who wished to come on tourist visas. Falasha tourists had to show a round-trip ticket (costing $560) and $100 cash before receiving an Israeli visa. (The annual income of the average Falasha at the time was less than $100.) Only occasionally were these conditions ignored—if, for example, an Israeli citizen agreed to "sponsor" a Falasha. That is how Rahamim arrived in 1972, sponsored by an Israeli journalist who had met him in Ethiopia and written about him.[27]

The Israeli government was candid about its policy. "Israel indeed does not regard the Law of Return as being applicable to Falashas," responded one diplomat to a journalist's query in early 1973. "If any Falashas visit Israel as bona fide tourists, they are accorded the same courtesy as non-Falasha Ethiopians. However, we must note that surreptitious attempts by Falashas to immigrate illegally harm such people. . . . Israel is not enthusiastic about the prospect of Falasha immigration."[28]

This policy was unacceptable to a small but dedicated circle of Jews in Israel and abroad. They were drawn from all walks of life: Hazi Ovadiah, a staff sergeant in the Israeli army, had been born in Ethiopia to Yemenite parents; Meyer Levin was a well-known American novelist; David Kessler was the editor of London's *Jewish Chronicle*; Arieh Tartakower was the Israeli representative of the World Jewish Congress; Graenum Berger was a New York communal worker and educator. Between them, a worldwide campaign was launched to bring Falashas to Israel.

Their first breakthrough came in 1973, when Sephardi Chief Rabbi Ovadiah Yosef ruled that Falashas were Jews. "It is our duty to redeem them from assimilation and hasten their immigration to Israel," he wrote.[29] His reason? Falashas, according to Rabbi Yosef, are the lost tribe of Dan.

This explanation of the origin of the Falashas has existed as long as other Jews have known about them. It began when rabbis first encountered them and searched Jewish literature for a clue to who they were. There was only one: the writings of a mysterious traveler named Eldad Ha-Dani who appeared in Egypt in the ninth century, telling fantastic tales of Jewish kingdoms and professing to know the whereabouts of the ten lost tribes. His stories were the source of the Christian legend of Prester John, which later inspired Vasco da Gama and other explorers. Eldad himself claimed to belong to the tribe of Dan, which had a rich and mighty kingdom in the "land of Ethiopia." But Ethiopia, at that time, was a generic term which could refer to anything from India to southern Africa. To this day no one has figured out where Eldad really came from.

Egyptian Jews were the first to learn about Falashas in the sixteenth century, and immediately connected them with Eldad's strange story. This explanation was given the force of law by Cairo's chief rabbi, David ibn Abi Zimra, a famous scholar known to posterity by the acronym, "the RaDBaZ." An unusual case involving a young man in Cairo who sought permission to marry a Jewish girl was the occasion for the RaDBaZ's conclusion. The boy's father was an Egyptian Jew and his mother a Falasha slave, captured in Ethiopia. Her husband was presumed killed in the same battle in which she had been captured.

The RaDBaZ was a thinker noted for his logic and lucidity. He distinguished two separate questions which had to be answered. First, was the young man a Jew? And if so, was he a "bastard" (*mamzer*)? The first question was neatly disposed of. "It is well known," said the RaDBaZ, "that there is always war going on between the various kings of Abyssinia, since there are three kingdoms in it. Some of them are Moslems, some Christians, and some Israelites of the tribe of Dan. It seems that [the Israelites] belong to the sect who are called Karaites, for they only know a few of the commandments. They do not know the [Talmud] at all; and they do not kindle lights on the Sabbath."[30] On those grounds the RaDBaZ ruled that Falashas have the same status as Karaites, who were still allowed to marry other Jews if they renounced their separate ways.

The second question was resolved less favorably. The RaDBaZ declared that the young man was a *mamzer*, since he could not prove that his mother's husband had actually been killed. He could only marry a girl who was also a bastard.

Nearly every rabbi since the RaDBaZ has followed his

explanation of Falasha origins. Unable to account for Falashas any other way, they accepted them as the lost tribe of Dan. Today, as fantastic as it sounds, this is the de facto policy of Israel. Rabbi Yosef's 1973 ruling cited the RaDBaZ and other rabbis, concluding: "There is no doubt that the above sages, who established that they are of the tribe of Dan, investigated and inquired and reached their conclusions on the basis of the most reliable witnesses and evidence. . . . I, too, have decided that in my humble opinion the Falashas are Jews."[31] But because Falashas were so isolated, added Rabbi Yosef, they would still require the symbolic immersion in a *mikveh*. He described this as "an act of renewing their covenant with the Jewish people."[32]

Armed with Rabbi Yosef's ruling, Falashas appealed to the government for immigration privileges under the Law of Return. An interministerial committee was appointed. It announced its decision in 1975: Falashas would henceforth be considered Jews. The news was greeted with unrestrained glee, even by those who scoffed at the logic behind it: that Falashas are the lost tribe of Dan. In front-page stories Israeli and Jewish newspapers announced that an airlift, along the lines of the Operation Magic Carpet that had transported Jews from Yemen, was imminent. An anonymous "expert" was quoted as estimating that thirty-five percent of Falashas wanted to come to Israel.[33]

No such airlift materialized. In fact, not a single Falasha was brought to Israel for more than two years afterward. A census of Israeli Falashas in early 1977 counted only 165 in that country. The only operation even resembling an airlift began later that year, following secret negotiations with Ethiopia. Two planeloads of Falashas arrived: sixty-two in August and fifty-nine in December. But expectations that this could become a regular airlift were soon dashed. In February 1978, Foreign Minister Moshe Dayan revealed that Israel was secretly arming Ethiopia against Moslem rebels in Eritrea. Dayan's "slip of the tongue" baffled observers, but whatever the reason, the results were immediate. Secret contacts between Israel and Ethiopia came to a halt. So did Falasha immigration.

Another hiatus followed, until the Falashas went public with their frustrations in January 1979. After the press conference and demonstrations, two Falashas were brought out of Ethiopia. The publicity campaign stepped up in the spring, when Zechariah Yonah went on a speaking tour of the United States. Thirty-two Falasha refugees were brought from neighboring countries that summer. Yonah Bogale, Zechariah's father and the former director of Falasha schools, escaped to Israel in October. After a lifetime of advocating aid for Falashas *in* Ethiopia, he joined the campaign for their emigration. Another demonstration was held at the Knesset in November, and Rahamim Eliezer went on an American speaking tour in early 1980. Finally, emigration resumed on a significant scale. Some six hundred fifty Falashas were brought from refugee camps in 1980, and two hundred fifty more in the first eight months of 1981.

Falashas have not had as difficult a time adjusting to Israel as many people feared. "It was strange in the beginning," admitted Zechariah Yonah, "because we didn't know about such things as gas stoves or supermarkets. But after a few months there were no problems."

It is difficult to generalize about Israeli Falashas. Eager to assimilate, they have dispersed around the country. There are no Falashae ghettoes. Some live in kibbutzim, others in cities. One has been ordained an Orthodox rabbi; others no longer even attend synagogue. A few are students, although most take factory jobs in order to send money home to their families. Young immigrants serve in the army; two were killed during the Six Day War. A few have married non-Falashas. Their new in-laws were sometimes hostile, they say, but never for long. Everyone who meets Falashas in Israel seems to like them, at least partly because of what one writer calls "the considerable personal charm of their dignified, yet humble, bearing."[34]

Falashas say they experience no racial prejudice in Israel other than the ubiquitous nickname *kushi* (Negro). Even that is not meant as an insult. When, in the 1950s, the Falasha wife of a Yemenite immigrant asked Israeli police to stop a neighbor from calling her that, the police commissioner ruled that *kushi* is merely descriptive, not disrespectful.[35] Most Falashas are inured to it. "True," one told a journalist, "my young daughter in kindergarten will have to adjust to the term *kushi*, but a red-haired child is called a *jinji*, so what's the difference?"[36]

Most Israelis are happy to accept Falashas as Jews—whether or not they are the lost tribe of Dan. Opinion polls show overwhelming support for their immigration. "If the Falashas observe as Jews, believe they are Jews, and suffer as Jews, then in my mind they are Jews," said former President Zalman Shazar.[37] Skeptics doubt that even the rabbis really believe Falashas are the lost tribe of Dan, but adopted that expedient to justify the near-universal desire to accept Falashas as Jews. Why? The reason has little to do with Jewish law. As one rabbi testified in the Benjamin Gitye case: "The Falashas fought vigorously, proudly, and bravely in order to preserve their religion, and died to sanctify it."[38]

"Everyone knows we are Jews," says Rahamim Eliezer, "but the rabbis need an excuse to make it legal. What do we care what their reasons are, as long as they come to the right conclusion? But it's ridiculous that we have to pass a conversion just because we were isolated. We think it is because we are black. Say the truth! Is there anyone who can say all the Jews of Europe are perfect?"

Among those who agree with Rahamim is Israeli Supreme Court Justice Alfred Witkon, who took part in the Gitye decision. "This strictness . . . is not to my liking," he demurred. "Many [immigrants] from Western and Central Europe and from America had reached the very brink of assimilation. There were many cases of mixed marriages among them. . . . We are not accustomed to split hairs with these people and their descendants or to require witnesses and evidence as to their origin and relationships. I do not know why [Falashas] have not benefitted from the same degree of flexibility."[39]

CHAPTER NINE

The Assimilation of the Chinese Jews

The first European allowed to live inside China in modern times was a Jesuit missionary named Matteo Ricci, who entered that country in 1583 and lived in Peking from 1601 until his death in 1610. Ricci was a formidable figure in both personal appearance and mental endowment; the Church could not have made a more striking first impression on China. He stood over six feet tall and possessed, according to a Chinese contemporary, "a curly beard, blue eyes, and a voice like a great bell."[1] The Chinese were also impressed by his broad learning, which ranged from theology to clock-making, and his facility for mastering Chinese language and customs. When Ricci died his epitaph was composed by the governor of Peking: "To one who loved righteousness and wrote books."[2]

Ricci believed that for Christianity to succeed in China it needed to gain a foothold in the educated classes and filter downward to the common people. To that end he studied Chinese literature and adopted Chinese dress; a later Jesuit described him as "so like the Chinese in everything that he might be one of them."[3] He tried to reconcile Christianity with Confucian philosophy, which he considered essentially secular. In Chinese rituals such as ancestor worship or the public ceremonies honoring Confucius, he found nothing objectionable other than a few details which could be easily deleted.

To help him adapt Christianity to Chinese mores, Ricci searched for traces of Christians who had preceded him to China. Missionaries were known to have entered China sporadically throughout history. The Vatican had even sent an ambassador to the Mongol rulers in Peking, not long before Marco Polo. Polo himself had met both Christians and Jews in "Cathay," which Ricci personally helped prove was the same country as China. But three centuries after Polo, Ricci could find no trace of either Christians or Jews—until a surprise visitor showed up on his doorstep in the last week of June 1605. It has been called "one of the most romantic meetings in the history of religion."[4]

167

Ricci's visitor was an elderly Chinese mandarin (scholar-official) from the city of Kaifeng on the Yellow River, capital of Hunan province. He introduced himself as Ai (his full name is now known to have been Ai T'ien) and said he was in Peking to pick up an official appointment as school supervisor. According to Ricci, "his face was quite different from that of a Chinese in respect to his nose, his eyes, and all his features."[5]

Ai told Ricci that he belonged to a small religious sect which believed in only one God. Other Chinese, unable to distinguish his people from the far more numerous Moslems, called them "the Moslems who pluck the sinews from their meat" after their unusual method of butchering animals. But his people were not Moslems, Ai said, and in fact disliked the largr sect. They were an altogether different religion with many adherents abroad.

Unfortunately, they had not been in touch with those fellow believers for generations. This was what brought Ai to visit Ricci while in Peking. He told the Jesuit that he had read about him in a Chinese book which described Europeans as believers in one God, but not Moslems. "On entering our home," Ricci later wrote in his diary, "he seemed quite excited over the fact, as he expressed it, that he professed the same faith that we did."[6]

Ai was not the only one that day to make this mistake. The two men began comparing religions. Ai told Ricci that his sect's founder had twelve sons, and Ricci jumped to the conclusion that he meant the twelve apostles. Ricci led his visitor into the chapel, where pictures of four apostles were hanging. Ai asked if these were four of the twelve sons, and Ricci replied that they were.

Then, Ai saw a special altar, brought out that week for the festival of John the Baptist, with reliefs of Saint John on one side and the Madonna and Child on the other. He knelt before it in the Chinese style of venerating ancestors. But, simultaneously, he apologized for doing so. His apology is memorable. "Although I do not worship images," he told Ricci, "I want to offer reverence to my earliest ancestors."[7]

It did not take long for Ricci and Ai to straighten out their misunderstanding. When Ai complained that it was difficult for his people to keep their laws in China, because of circumcision and the ban on eating pork, Ricci realized he was speaking with a Jew. The "twelve sons" had been Jacob's. The "earliest ancestors" had been

Rebecca and her two sons, Jacob and Esau. Ai did not know the word "Jew" but called his people "Israel," pronouncing it, since like other Chinese he had difficulty making the sound "r," approximately "Yi-ssu-lo-yeh."

By Ricci's day Jews had already lived in China for hundreds of years. They formed a thriving community of nearly one thousand in their own quarter of Kaifeng. Unlike Jews in the West they had never been persecuted or confined to specific occupations. Some were merchants, others artisans, soldiers, shopkeepers, even farmers. Still others, like Ai, had entered China's literary elite: the mandarin class. Nor had all devoted themselves to Chinese studies; Jewish education also flourished. Many could read some Hebrew, and all were familiar with at least the Bible stories. Ai himself, who apologized to Ricci for his ignorance of Judaism, could no more than recognize the alphabet when Ricci showed him a Bible in Hebrew. But he recited stories of Abraham, Moses, Esther, and the twelve tribes. His brothers, Ai added, had preferred Hebrew studies to Chinese and were active members of the synagogue. Furthermore, it turned out that Jews—not Christians—had preceded Ricci in adapting their religion to Chinese customs. Ai's apology, while bowing to the altar, capsulized their religious blend: Chinese ancestor worship with the Jewish ban on graven images.

Isolated in far-off China, this tiny community forged a remarkable synthesis of two civilizations which otherwise remained unknown to each other: the Jewish and the Chinese. They produced what might be called a Judeo-Chinese culture, which flourished at about the same time as the European Renaissance. Chinese Jews studied Confucian philosophy, took part in Confucian ceremonies, and offered kosher sacrifices to their ancestors. Jewish thinking in China was devoted to reconciling these two systems of thought. The synthesis was inscribed on stone monuments in the courtyard of their pagoda-like synagogue. It was their staunch belief, one inscription records, that "the Confucian religion and this religion agree on all essential points, differing only on secondary ones."[8]

Ai T'ien's visit also resolved Ricci's quest for Christians in China. At first, Ai told the Jesuit that he knew of no Christians there. But in attempting to explain Christianity, Ricci had to invent a word for "cross," since there was no word in Chinese to express that concept. He fortunately hit on the Chinese word meaning "ten," which is written with a symbol resembling a cross. Hearing that word, Ai recalled another small sect in Kaifeng and one other town whose ancestors also came from abroad. They were known as "the Moslems of the ten" because they made the sign of the cross over their food and drink. Ai assured Ricci that he had no idea what the gesture meant, and that neither, any longer, did the people who made it.

The Jesuit was never able to visit Kaifeng himself, but three years later he sent a Chinese proselyte in his place. This lay brother was not received by Kaifeng's cross-worshippers, who did not want to admit they were descended from foreigners. But he was warmly welcomed by its Jews, eager to improve their knowledge of their religion. He delivered a letter from Ricci to Kaifeng's chief rabbi. Ever the missionary, Ricci informed the Jews that their Messiah had already arrived.

Kaifeng's Jews were better disposed to Ricci than to his Messiah. Hearing of his great learning, they offered to make him their chief rabbi if he would move to Kaifeng and give up eating pork. But as for the Messiah, replied the rabbis, he was not yet due for another ten thousand years.

Ricci wrote back to Europe that China's Jews would soon die out. Though premature, he was essentially on target. They prospered for another century or so but began losing their grip on Judaism. The last rabbi died in the first decade of the nineteenth century; the synagogue was torn down between 1851–66. By then the Jews could no longer read Hebrew or remember any but a few oddly misshapen rituals. A few of them converted to Islam or other religions, but most simply blended into their Chinese surroundings. One is known to have become a Buddhist priest. Another entered a Catholic seminary, but later dropped out.

In the late nineteenth and early twentieth centuries, the Chinese Jews became a well-known curiosity, though there was no longer anything very "Jewish" about them. Little remained beyond a memory of having once belonged to some unknown foreign people. To this day there are a few hundred residents of Kaifeng who can say, "I am descended from Jews." But that is exactly what they are. It has been a long time since anyone in Kaifeng has been able to say, "I am a Jew."

•   •   •   •

That Jews lived in China comes as no surprise; there are few places in the world untouched by the Diaspora. Still, the mention of Chinese Jews always seems to raise an eyebrow. "Were they Chinese or were they Jews?" is the question other Jews often ask, thinking of the foreign Jews who recently lived in China: Jews from England, Iraq, and India who began settling in Shanghai and other Chinese ports in the 1850s. After Hitler came to power, the Far East became a major stopping point for Jewish refugees from Germany and Russia. But those settlers were always considered foreigners, and even kept their European citizenships. Nearly all left China after the Communist revolution of 1949.

Not so with the Jews of Kaifeng. They became Chinese in spirit, temperament, and eventually even race. That did not—at first—prevent them from being Jewish, too. But the delicate balance could not be maintained; their Judeo-Chinese synthesis is now a thing of the past. Everything we know about it has been extracted from diverse scraps of information: the stone inscriptions in the synagogue courtyard, their Torah scrolls and other manuscripts, an occasional reference in Chinese records, the encounters with Ricci and later missionaries, and reports from travelers who visited Kaifeng from the mid-nineteenth century on. Only in the last few years, like a half-finished jigsaw puzzle, have scholars begun to piece together a coherent picture of their lives.

The earliest positive date for Jews in Kaifeng is the year 1163, the date given by one inscription for the founding of their synagogue. But it is reasonably safe to assume they had already lived there for several decades. They probably arrived before 1126—the year of the fall of the Northern Sung dynasty—when Kaifeng was still the imperial capital of China and perhaps the grandest city in the world. Its main thoroughfare was an Imperial Way leading to the palace, fully three hundred yards wide with a central lane marked off for the emperor alone. On either side were covered arcades crammed with stalls, pedestrians, and horses. Canals were lined with flowering plum, peach, pear, and apricot trees. The streets were filled with dancers, actors, jugglers, acrobats, storytellers, peddlers, prostitutes, and masses of unemployed beggars and loafers. China was in the throes of a mercantile revolution and merchants poured in from all over the world, selling corals, crystals, pearls, rhinoceros horns, and other exotic goods.

Kaifeng's Jews were undoubtedly among the foreign merchants

who came at that time. Their oldest inscription says: "Bringing tribute of Western cloth [cotton?], they entered the court of Sung and the emperor said, 'You have come to our China. Revere and preserve the customs of your ancestors and hand them down in Kaifeng.'"[9]

That these merchants traveled all the way to China is not so extraordinary as it might seem. Long before China became well-known to Europeans, well-used trade routes connected the Far East with the Near. The ports of South China were familiar territory to seamen and merchants from Moslem lands, whose return cargoes of silks, spices, and porcelains were sure to fetch high prices in the bazaars of Baghdad and Cairo. Similarly, overland caravan routes connected China with the Moslem world across the steppes of Central Asia.

Where did Kaifeng's Jews come from? It is impossible to say. Historians have suggested such wide-ranging origins as Persia, Afghanistan, India, Iraq, and Yemen. One of their inscriptions says they came from "India," but that was written three hundred years after the fact. Besides, the Chinese had little knowledge of foreign geography: "India" was a generic term used for all lands to the south and west. Another clue is that Kaifeng's Jews spoke and wrote the Persian language, and continued to speak it for hundreds of years after they arrived. But Persian was a lingua franca for Jewish merchants throughout the East; they would have spoken it no matter where they came from. Their liturgy, too, reflects general practice among Oriental Jews without pinpointing their origin to any particular country.

It is impossible, even, to say whether they arrived by land or sea. Jews were well-represented among merchants on both routes, traveling to China by both methods long before we hear of them in Kaifeng. Travelers reported seeing them as early as 879, when Jews were said to be among the one hundred twenty thousand foreigners massacred in Canton by a xenophobic Chinese rebel. The sea route was more active at the time Jews probably arrived in Kaifeng, but the land route may have been open, too.

Little is known of their early years in China. They generally seem to have been left alone to worship God in their own fashion—which was still the same as that of other Jews. Their treatment was closely linked with that of Moslems in China, of whom they were usually considered a sub-sect. But the degree of toleration varied from dynasty to dynasty.

Under the Sung dynasty (960–1126), when Northern Kaifeng's Jews probably arrived, foreigners in China were generally allowed to govern themselves. They lived in their own neighborhoods according to their own laws, settling their own disputes except when a serious crime was committed against a Chinese. They stayed apart from the native Chinese, rarely intermarrying or assimilating.

This policy was continued by the foreign Chin dynasty (1126–1279), which overran the northern half of China, including Kaifeng. The first synagogue in Kaifeng was built in the early years of the Chin. According to an inscription, a Rabbi Levi and a prominent Jew named Abdullah were in charge of the construction.

It actually became advantageous to be a foreigner under the Yüan (Mongol) dynasty (1279–1368). The Mongols distrusted their Chinese subjects and favored foreigners under their rule. Money-lending, tax-farming, most foreign trade, and the highest government positions were all reserved for non-Chinese. Foreigners from all over the world streamed into the Mongol capital. Marco Polo was one, and while in Peking he saw Jews and Christians debating their religions in Kublai Khan's presence. Another was an Arab named Ibn Batuta, who reported that one of Hangchow's entrances was named the "Gate of the Jews"—presumably after the people who lived in that quarter of the city.

Along with other religions in the Mongol Empire, Jews enjoyed a degree of self-government and their leaders were exempt from taxes. Mongol law specifically named them, calling Jews by the names *chu-hu* or *chu-wu*. These words baffled modern Sinologists until they recognized them as transliterations of *djuhud*, the Persian word for "Jew." In addition to Kaifeng, Hangchow, and Peking, Jews are thought to have lived in Canton, Nanking, Ningpo, Yangchow, and several other cities. Kaifeng's synagogue was rebuilt during Kublai's reign.

The pendulum swung in the opposite direction when the Mongols were overthrown by the native Ming dynasty (1368–1644), which launched a wave of anti-foreign repression. Foreigners were required to marry native Chinese and forbidden to assume Chinese names. Christianity, which had been spread under the Mongols by Armenians, Nestorians, and even a few Roman Catholics, disappeared except for the cross-worshippers found by Ricci. Moslems survived through sheer numbers but in less prosperous circumstances. Outside of Kaifeng, China's Jews did not. Jews were still considered foreigners in China, even though their great-great-great-grandparents may by then have been born there. They had never even taken Chinese names. Only in Kaifeng, thanks to the bravery of one prominent Jew—whose heroism reached the ear of the emperor himself—did they find a way to become Chinese without ceasing to be Jewish. This story was long misunderstood by historians. It was only recently pieced together through the detective work of a Chinese-American historian, Chaoying Fang.

The incident was originally known from one of the synagogue inscriptions. In the year 1421, the inscription says, a Jewish physician named An Ch'eng "made a report to the throne and was judged meritorious for it."[10] The Jews were rewarded with a gift of incense and permission to rebuild their synagogue. An was personally rewarded with a promotion and a Chinese name: Chao Ch'eng, or "Chao the Honest."

This brief anecdote barely hinted at the human drama involved. Its importance could only be speculated until 1965, when Professor Fang found the same story told from the other side in China's imperial archives. This version was quite different. For one thing, An was not a physician but a soldier. His original name was not An Ch'eng but An San. And the archives revealed what his report had contained: an accusation of treason against Kaifeng's Prince Su. An's charge had been upheld. Prince Su was brought before the emperor. According to the archives he "knocked his head on the ground and said repeatedly, 'My crime warrants the death sentence.'"[11] Prince Su was pardoned but ordered to humiliate himself by rewarding his accuser. He presented the Jews with a gift of incense, and permitted them to rebuild their synagogue.

These differences may appear trivial to the non-specialist, but Professor Fang goes on to explain their significance. Why had An's name been changed on the inscription? Because An San is an obvious transliteration of a foreign name, probably "Hassan." The Jews apparently wanted to downplay his—and their—foreign origin on their inscription. And why did the inscription not mention that Hassan was a soldier, or the contents of his report to the throne? The answer may appear strange to Westerners: because it was regarded as shameful. The relationship of a Chinese soldier to his prince is that of a slave to his master, and accusing one's master, no matter how justly, is an ignoble act of betrayal. But Hassan's higher loyalty—and by implication that of the entire Jewish community—was recognized by the emperor. The Chinese name was his reward.

Hassan paved the way for Kaifeng's Jews to become full members of Chinese society. The rest of the community soon took Chinese names, which had previously been forbidden. (They continued using Hebrew names in their communal records.) They also began entering government service.

China's civil service was far more egalitarian than any in the West at the time. It recruited officials on the basis of examinations leading to three successive degrees, roughly corresponding to the Western bachelor's, master's, and doctorate. The exams tested a student's knowledge of and ability to interpret Confucian scriptures. They were open to all Chinese citizens. The system was tailor-made for Jews, as similar systems would later be in the United States and other Western democracies. (In many ways, Kaifeng's Jews were precursors of today's "emancipated" Western Jews.) Education and interpreting scriptures were longstanding Jewish values. Within a generation of Hassan's breakthrough, Jews in Kaifeng began passing the exams and becoming mandarins.

The next three hundred years (c. 1421–1723) were their Golden Age. Ai T'ien and other Jewish mandarins attained a wide variety of positions: among them district magistrate, supervisor of schools, assistant editor of the Kaifeng gazetteer, senior secretary of the Board of Punishments, annalist of the household for the emperor's second son, and court president of imperial entertainments. When the synagogue was destroyed by a flood in 1461, the community already included several mandarins (including one with a "master's" degree) who rebuilt it "on a very spacious scale so that, glittering with gold and variegated colors, its splendor was complete," according to one inscription.[12] At one point Kaifeng's Jews included twenty Confucian degree-holders, fourteen military officers, and four official physicians—an extraordinary achievement for a community whose population is estimated at less than one thousand.

The most successful Jew was a mandarin named Chao Ying-ch'eng (1619–56 or 57), whose Hebrew name was Moses ben Abram. Chao was the first and perhaps only Jew to receive a "doctorate." He held several high positions, notably assistant governor of the southern province Fukien. He gained fame there when he defeated a bandit and "cut to pieces his associates," in the graphic words of a Chinese annalist.[13] After restoring peace he built schools, and "for the first time the sound of reading was heard among the people."[14] But after only three years in office Chao was called home for three years to mourn the death of a parent, as was customary in China. While there he helped rebuild the synagogue after another flood. He personally paid for a new Holy Ark and Rear Hall, and helped edit the waterlogged Torah scrolls. Afterward, he wrote a short book in Chinese called *The Vicissitudes of the Holy Scriptures*, which unfortunately has not survived. He died prematurely at the age of thirty-eight or thirty-nine.

But at the same time that they were rising in Chinese society, Kaifeng's Jews were beginning to drift away from Judaism. They lost all contact with foreign Jews. They adopted Chinese customs for marriages, funerals, and "capping" (a rite of passage analogous to the Bar Mitzvah). The examination system left little time for other interests—least of all, as Ai T'ien told Ricci, foreign scriptures in a foreign tongue. And Chinese officials were required to take positions away from home, to prevent corruption and nepotism. This made it difficult for successful Jews like Ai to keep the commandments. Ricci wrote that Ai "gave to understand that by following the affairs of the Chinese literati, he had been expelled from the synagogue by the Grand Rabbi, its head, and had become half excommunicated. He would readily abandon this creed if he could obtain the doctor's degree, as was done by the Saracens, who, once they received their doctor's degree, were no longer afraid of their mullah and gave up their faith."[15]

Ricci's account should not be taken literally. Either he misunderstood his visitor or exaggerated Ai's account, because Ai could not have been "expelled from the synagogue." Back in Kaifeng, Ai was the author of a short, quite Orthodox inscription in the synagogue courtyard. "The Heavenly Writings are fifty-three in number; with our mouth we recite them and in our heart we hold them fast," Ai wrote; "the Sacred Script has twenty-seven letters: these we teach in our families and display on our doors."[16] He was referring to the fifty-three weekly readings of the Torah (according to the Sephardi division; Ashkenazi Jews divide it into fifty-four portions), and to the twenty-seven letters of the Hebrew alphabet (including the five final letters).

In fact, Jewish mandarins were among the most active

participants in the synagogue. They donated heavily whenever the synagogue needed rebuilding. Many, like Ai, wrote inscriptions for its walls. This fit their Confucian ideology, which encouraged *all* religions for their social values. Chinese mandarins were expected to participate in all family and clan activities, according to whichever religion they happened to belong to. But it is also clear that there was tension, at least, between "traditional" and "assimilated" Jews in Kaifeng: the rabbis and the mandarins. In this, too, Kaifeng's Jews were precursors of today's Jewish communities.

Ai T'ien's story has a sequel. A few years later three young Jews visited Ricci in Peking. One was a nephew of Ai. It took little convincing for them to begin kneeling and praying to Ricci's statue of Christ. Ricci wrote: "These three were very sad seeing that their sect was thus to be extinguished, because nobody knew its scriptures, and that they would have to become either gentiles or Saracens, like the Christians who in olden times lived in this city. They said that their old Grand Rabbi, who had some knowledge, had already died and that one of his young sons had succeeded him through inheritance. But he knew nothing of the law and it seemed very bad in an extremely well-built temple which they had, that there was no image; neither was there any image in their chapels nor in their houses. If they had placed an image of the Savior in their temple and homes, it would have greatly blessed all the people. And especially Ai [the nephew] complained of the restrictions which the Grand Rabbi had placed on them, such as not eating any meat of animals which had not been killed by his own hand, saying that here in Peking, if they had wished to abide by this regulation, they would have died of hunger; and also the circumcision of babies eight days after their birth, which seemed very cruel to their gentile wives and relatives. They concluded that they would follow our law, provided we abolished these ceremonies, because it would not be very difficult to eat pork."[17] The three young Jews returned to Kaifeng with books on Christianity written by Ricci in Chinese. But we hear no further of any conversions at the time. Though beginning to ail, Judaism in Kaifeng was not yet ready to succumb.

In the early 1700s Jesuit missionaries often visited Kaifeng. A few grew friendly with the Jews, and met to discuss religion or compare scriptural texts. Their inquiries were limited only by the Jews' patience. "Consultations in China cannot last long," one

missionary noted, "especially in summer with people who outside
society wear only a simple pair of drawers even during the prayers in
their Temple, and who are certainly not interested in delicate
research concerning books and knowledge."[18]

These missionaries catalogued symptoms of the Jewish decline. Kaifeng's Jews used their Scriptures for Chinese-style fortune-
telling (drawing lots), they reported. A few tried to sell Torah scrolls,
but their leaders prevented it. Only forty to fifty men came to the
synagogue for holidays, and barely a *minyan* for the Sabbath. Rich
Jews avoided attending synagogue by donating new copies of the
weekly readings. Their pronunciation of Hebrew, added one missionary who spoke that language, was so unusual that "if I had not seen
the Hebrew before my eyes I would not have believed it was
Hebrew."[19] Another explained: "They pronounce [Hebrew] in a
Chinese manner, somewhat as our lay [Chinese] readers of the mass
pronounce Latin. As I appeared surprised by this and as I intimated to
them that their pronunciation was poor, they told me that it was a
very long time since they had any [visitor] from the west, and that
they had lost their Grammar, or as they say in Chinese, the book for
studying scripture."[20]

Another remarkable piece of evidence confirms this picture. It
is a bilingual "memorial book of the dead"—perhaps the only
Chinese-Hebrew manuscript in the world. In it Kaifeng's Jews
registered the names of their deceased. It was compiled in the mid-
seventeenth century, apparently from memorial books of the individual clans (there were seven Jewish clans in Kaifeng). Nearly a
thousand names are listed, some from as far back as the early 1400s.
Abandoned altogether around 1670, the manuscript was sold to
Europeans in 1851. It is now in the collection of the Hebrew Union
College-Jewish Institute of Religion in Cincinnati.

The memorial book provides vivid testimony of Jewish
assimilation in Kaifeng. Some Jews are listed in Hebrew and others,
presumably those who did not use Hebrew names, in Chinese. The
entries have been analyzed by Donald Daniel Leslie, a noted
Sinologist who has devoted his career to studying Kaifeng's Jews. His
analysis reveals a steady decline in the use of Hebrew. Many Jews who
had Hebrew names had sons who used only Chinese ones, but hardly
any Chinese-named fathers had Hebrew-named sons. The movement
was in a single direction: away from their traditions.[21]

• • • •

At the height of Jewish prosperity, in 1642, the Yellow river swept through Kaifeng in one of its worst floods ever. The synagogue was swept away and with it most of the Torah scrolls. Many Jews were among the hundreds of thousands who died in the catastrophe. Only a few hundred Jewish families survived.

Kaifeng was peculiarly vulnerable to such tragedies, because of its location in a broad plain actually below the level of the Yellow River. Its only protection was natural dikes and thick city walls, so frequently breached that the river has been nicknamed "China's Sorrow." A few hundred years later, in the mid-nineteenth century, it would actually turn at right angles not far from Kaifeng and dig a completely new channel to the sea, emerging hundreds of miles from its former outlet. But unlike Kaifeng's other floods, the 1642 disaster was man-made. It came during a popular uprising against the Ming emperors, when rebels in the Hunan countryside laid siege to Kaifeng. Jews were prominent in the city's defense; one commanded a mixed company of Jewish and Moslem soldiers.

The city could hold out only six months. What happened next is open to dispute. Some say the frustrated rebels cut the dikes and diverted the river into the city; others say that the governor sacrificed Kaifeng in a vain attempt to put them down. In any event, the city was inundated and fell to the rebels, who went on to overthrow the Ming dynasty two years later.

For weeks Kaifeng lay submerged. As the waters receded, weeds and grass sprouted in city streets and animals grazed in new-found pastures. The surviving Jews gathered on the opposite bank and rented a house for a temporary synagogue. One Jew, a captain-adjutant in the army who was involved in rebuilding the city, assigned his troops to protect the synagogue. Ten Torah scrolls were fished from its ruins. None were readable by themselves, but the chief rabbis—assisted by Chao Ying-ch'eng—collated the fragments and pieced together an entire Torah. New scrolls were copied from it.

Ten years later the Jews began rebuilding. Although the city was still "a jungle of weeds and brambles,"[22] the old synagogue's foundations could be located and the new synagogue built on them. It was completed in 1663. Kaifeng's highest officials honored it by composing inscriptions for its walls. One inscription boasted: "The plan of the synagogue was on the same sumptuous lines as that of the former time, but its decoration and color were still more beautiful." [23] This is the synagogue which survived until the mid-1800s. It is the one which was visited by the Jesuits, and which—through them—we know most about.

Kaifeng's synagogue was located near Earth Street, not far from the corner of Fire-God Shrine Street. It was reached down the narrow lane of the Li clan, one of the most prominent families of Chinese Jews. Another small lane on the other side of the synagogue was called "The Lane of the Religion Which Plucks the Sinews." In the twentieth century, after Kaifeng's Jews stopped following rules of kosher slaughter, it was changed to the more respectable "Lane of the Religion Which Teaches the Scriptures."

The synagogue stood at one end of a rectangular, two-acre walled compound, which was laid out in the same pattern as those of other Chinese temples except that it faced west, toward Jerusalem. A sign at the front gate announced that this was a "Temple of Purity and Truth," a name also used for Chinese mosques. Entering from the east there was a succession of ornamental archways and formal doors, leading to a courtyard and finally the Great Hall. The path was lined with marble lions, incense braziers, and carved vases. Trees gave the courtyard a garden-like air. The walls were lined with buildings: guest and assembly rooms, cottages for caretakers and guards, an office for the chief rabbi, a mikveh, and a recess for slaughtering animals.

Also in the courtyard were semi-enclosed wooden pavilions housing the stone inscriptions. These inscriptions commemorated major events in the community's life, as was customary in Chinese temples. Carved in the fifteenth to seventeenth centuries, the stones survived long enough for Western visitors to copy and eventually buy two of them. Shorter inscriptions were written on archways or hung from door frames throughout the courtyard.

The synagogue itself was built pagoda-style with a three-tiered roof. It had a balustraded porch where booths were built each autumn for Sukkoth. Inside, a long table held the "Five Ceremonial Objects" of all Chinese temples: two candlesticks, two flower vases, and an incense bowl. Behind it was a cushioned, embroidered lectern called the "Throne of Moses" on which the Torah was placed for the weekly readings. Behind that was the Holy Ark: square on the outside and round on the inside. The Ark contained a dozen curtained niches for twelve of their Torah scrolls—one for each of the twelve tribes—and a central position for the thirteenth, the ancient "Scroll of Moses" from which the others were copied after the flood.

Above the Ark hung a Chinese inscription offering fealty to the emperor—required in all Chinese temples. But above that, lest anyone forget who reigned supreme, hung a familiar Hebrew one, which included the *Shema:* "Hear O Israel, the Lord our God, the Lord is one. Blessed be the name of the glory of his kingdom forever and ever."

On either side of the Great Hall stood two smaller halls. Though common features of other Chinese temples, they were unique for a synagogue: halls of the ancestors. Kaifeng's Jews burned incense, offered food, and kowtowed to their ancestors in these halls. One, apparently, was for Abraham and the "early forefathers"; the other for Moses and the later ones. Each ancestor had his own bowl where incense was burned and food offerings were set out. But there were none of the portraits so prominent in other Chinese ancestral halls.

The ancestor cult was universal in China; it has been called that country's only national religion. Every family had an ancestral hall filled with wooden spirit-tablets representing dead ancestors. They gathered there on holidays and special occasions to pray, kowtow, burn incense, and sacrifice food and paper money. Kaifeng's Jews, in their halls, honored the forefathers of their entire nation: A-tan (Adam), A-wu-lo-han (Abraham), Mieh-she (Moses), A-ho-lien (Aaron), Yueh-shu-wo (Joshua), and Ai-tzu-la (Ezra), and others. They honored them at the spring and autumn festivals exactly as other Chinese did theirs—except for a few important deletions. They did not use pork in their sacrifices, did not post portraits, and rarely erected spirit-tablets. Over and over again in their inscriptions, Kaifeng's Jews emphasized that ancestor worship was compatible with monotheism. They were only *honoring* their ancestors, they insisted— not *worshipping* them. "Truly," says one inscription, "in the matter of honoring Heaven, if a man did not venerate his ancestors he could not then properly offer sacrifices to the forefathers."[24]

In this respect, Kaifeng's Jews agreed with Confucian philosophers. Although China's uneducated masses took the ancestral cult literally, as an appeal to those in the next world to aid their descendants in this one, the Chinese literati considered ancestor worship a secular ceremony. Its purpose was to channel the natural emotions, and bind together the family. It was in this philosophical spirit that the Jews, too, approached ancestor worship. It was not hard for them to find parallels in Jewish mourning rites.

These Jews were still devout. From their inscriptions we learn a great deal about their religious life. They prayed three times every day ("because there is not a day when Heaven is not among men").[25] They washed their bodies before entering the synagogue ("to dull the ardor of sensual desire").[26] They understood Hebrew. ("The twenty-seven letters are used to transmit the mysteries of the Mind, the Way, and Learning.")[27] They studied the Torah. ("To possess the Scriptures . . . was like to possessing the source of a stream.")[28] They kept kosher. ("In meat and drink [we] are careful to observe the distinction between what is permitted and what is not.")[29] They observed the Sabbath. ("The seventh day is specially for the cultivation of the virtues of purity and enlightenment.")[30] They celebrated Jewish festivals. ("At the four seasons of the year there is abstention for seven days.")[31] They fasted on Yom Kippur. ("On that day the scholar interrupts his reading and study, the farmer suspends his work of plowing or reaping, the tradesman ceases to do business in the market, and the traveler stops on his way.")[32]

Additional information can be gleaned from their Torah scrolls and prayer books, bought by Westerners in the nineteenth century and now in various European and American libraries. The Torah scrolls were written in black ink on parchment of sheepskin or goatskin sewn together with silk thread. They contain frequent copying errors, including the transposition of *lamed* (L) and *resh* (R), which were pronounced alike in China. Each week's Torah portion was also written separately on sheets of paper pasted together so they could be rolled without tearing, for the congregation to follow along. Kaifeng's Jews possessed prayers for all daily and Sabbath services, kiddush, grace before and after meals, kaddish for the dead, and for the holidays of Rosh Hashanah, Purim, Shavuot, Sukkoth, Hanukkah, Yom Kippur, the Ninth of Ab, the New Moon, and Passover, including a complete *Haggadah*.

We discover even more from the Jesuits who visited Kaifeng. They tell us the Jews observed the Sabbath strictly: preparing food on Friday to be eaten on Saturday when they would not light fires or cook. They still "gabbled a little Persian."[33] They called their religious leaders mullahs, as did Chinese Moslems, both pronouncing it "man-la." The chief rabbi was called the *chang-chiao* (ruler of the religion). Only he was allowed to enter the Holy Ark. They also possessed many more books of the Bible, and possibly part of the Mishnah (the first part of the Talmud), than have survived. Inside the synagogue they wore no ceremonial clothes other than blue skullcaps, which distinguished them from Moslems who wore white ones. (Kaifeng's Jews were sometimes known as "blue-capped Moslems".) Whoever read the Torah wore a white veil, and was assisted by two mullahs who corrected his errors. They took off their shoes before entering. One missionary had the good fortune to visit on Simchat Torah and watch the chief rabbi lead a procession around the synagogue with their Torah scrolls, wearing a sash of red silk which passed over his right shoulder and under his left arm.

Fortunately, our understanding is not limited to their external customs. The inscriptions afford a glimpse of their inner lives, too. Written by mandarins schooled in Chinese studies more than Jewish, they were apparently intended to explain Judaism to other Chinese. They make curious reading today. Consider these esoteric musings, found in one inscription to explain how Abraham invented monotheism:

"Abraham meditated upon Heaven:

"'Above, it is ethereal and pure; below it is most honorable beyond compare. The Way of Heaven does not speak, yet "the four seasons pursue their course, and all creatures are produced." It is evident that things come to life in the spring-time, grow during the summer, are harvested in the autumn, and stored up in the winter. Some fly, others swim, some walk, and others grow. Some are luxurious, others despoiled, some are blooming, others falling. Living things are produced from the sequence of life; transformations are due to the process of change; shapes are the outcome of the particular form, and colors are developed from their color source.'

"The patriarch, suddenly awakening as out of sleep, then understood these profound mysteries. He began truly to seek the Correct Religion. . . ."[34]

You could search far and wide in the Bible without finding these thoughts of Abraham's. In fact, they bear no resemblance to anything which the Bible attributes to him—or, for that matter, anything else in the Bible except perhaps Ecclesiastes, which was written more than a millennium after Abraham made his covenant with God. These ideas are from Chinese literature, which they even quote directly. The short quotation near the beginning ("the four seasons pursue their course, and all creatures are produced") is from a conversation between Confucius and a disciple, recorded in his *Analects*. The complete exchange goes like this:

"The Master [Confucius] said, 'I would prefer not speaking.'

"Tzu-kung said, 'If you, Master, do not speak, what shall we, your disciples, have to record?'

"The Master said, 'Does Heaven speak? The four seasons pursue their course, and all things are continually being produced, but does Heaven say anything?'"[35]

The inscriptions are a strange hodgepodge of religious ideas: Confucian philosophy, Jewish apologetics, and garbled history. They look at Judaism through Chinese eyes, citing Confucian writings frequently but never Jewish ones. Even Jewish beliefs and rituals were justified from Chinese literature. It can be difficult at times to bear in mind that they are Jewish literature. The Sabbath, for example, was "explained" in one inscription with this cryptic hexagram from the *I Ching*: "In seven days comes his return. In his return may be seen the purpose of Heaven and Earth."[36]

Moses's behavior on Mount Sinai was defended with an instruction from the Chinese book, *Record of Rites*. "Do not raise high places, do not dig pits, but sweep the earth and sacrifice thereon—which manifests simplicity."[37]

The inscriptions attempted to demonstrate that Judaism does not violate Confucian principles. "Although the written characters of the Scriptures of this religion are different from the script of Confucian books, on examining their principles it is found that their ways of common practice are similar."[38]

Another inscription is more specific. "The principles of establishing the mind and restraining the conduct are nothing more than honoring the Way of Heaven, venerating ancestors, giving high regard to the relations between the Prince and his ministers, being filial to parents, living in harmony with wife and children, preserving the distinction between superiors and inferiors, and having neighborly relations with friends. In short, these principles do not go beyond the Five Relationships."[39] Confucianism's "Five Relationships" are the basic human relations which lay the foundation of social order: sovereign to subject, father to son, elder brother to younger, husband to wife, and friend to friend.

Judaism and Confucianism are not actually difficult to reconcile. Confucianism is primarily an ethical and political code, less interested in the metaphysical than are Western religions. Confucius himself, while believing in a Supreme Being, was more concerned with the practical aspects of life in the here-and-now. He was a lover of ritual for the role it played in maintaining the social order, and of worship for the effect it had on the worshipper, but did not pretend to understand that which man is by nature incapable of understanding.

Confucianism, essentially, is what the French philosopher Jean Jacques Rousseau first dubbed "civil religion." Although belief in God was taken for granted, the details of worship were left to the individual. In that respect Confucian China resembled modern America, where every politician must pay lip service to God, no matter what his religion. When President Eisenhower declared, "Our government makes no sense unless it is founded in a deeply felt religious faith—and I don't care what it is!" he was merely updating Confucius.[40]

Besides, there are real similarities between Jewish and Confucian values. Both systems are based on written scriptures, interpreted for day-to-day guidance. Both honor men of words more than men of action. Both emphasize the family as the starting-point of religious life. Both insist that ritual is important for its own sake. Jewish prayers for the dead have similarities with Chinese ancestor rites. And Jews have no trouble agreeing with Confucians that human nature is essentially good—a positive outlook toward life on earth distinguishing both from, say, Christianity, with its concept of original sin. One modern student of Confucianism, Lin Yutang, has written: "The body of Confucian thought resembles most the laws of Moses, and it is easier to compare Confucius in the *scope* of his teachings to Moses than to any other philosopher. The *li* of Confucius, like the laws of Moses, covers both religious laws and laws of civil life and considers the two as integrated parts of a whole."[41]

Judaism took its place as a loyal Chinese faith, within the framework of China's "civil religion." One inscription boasted: "Reflecting on the three [Chinese] religions, it is evident that each of them has temples in which is honored . . . their Lord. Thus the

Confucians have the Temple of the Great Perfection, where Confucius is honored. The Buddhists have the Temple of the Holy
Countenance where Sakyamuni [Buddha] is honored. The Taoists
have the Temple of the Jade Emperor, where they honor the Three
Purities. And so the 'Pure and True' [i.e., the Jews] have the Temple
of Yi-ssu-lo-yeh [Israel] where they honor August Heaven."[42]

This theme may sound familiar to American ears. Kaifeng's
Jews were full members of the world around them, as Chinese as
American Jews are American. Like Jewish immigrants to America
they started out as despised foreigners, mostly merchants, and worked
their way up through education. Also like American Jews they
adopted local customs for marriages, funerals, and Bar Mitzvahs.
American Jews, too, joined public ceremonies honoring the dead
(Memorial Day) and the country's founders (Washington's and
Lincoln's birthdays). In a sense, Jews entered the modern world in
Kaifeng long before they did anywhere else. Chinese tolerance gave
Jews political rights which they would not enjoy elsewhere until
modern times. They were "emancipated" in 1421 when the emperor
rewarded them for Hassan's loyalty. This preceded the emancipation
of European Jews by four centuries. The very ideas of political
equality, religious freedom, and an aristocracy based on merit were
still unthinkable outside China.

But Kaifeng's Jews were also the first to face the dilemma of
modern Jewry: how to participate in the outside world and still
remain Jewish. To be a Jew in the modern world is to be without a
clear-cut sense of who you are. Before the era of emancipation a Jew
could be sure of that one thing, if nothing else. A Polish Jew was not
a Pole; he was a Jew who happened to live in Poland. But in China,
as in modern America and western Europe, a Jew could be both
Jewish *and* Chinese.

•   •   •   •

In 1843 a young Englishman named James Finn published a
book called The Jews in China. The Western world had lost contact
with Kaifeng's Jews more than a century before when the Chinese
emperors turned against the Catholic Church; the last missionary in
Hunan province had been thrown out bodily in 1724. Finn had never

been anywhere near China himself, but based his book on documents he found in the British Museum while researching Jewish history for the London Society for Promoting Christianity Among the Jews. As an attempt to gather everything known about Kaifeng's Jews in one volume, it was well-timed. The first Opium War had just reopened China's ports to the West. Hong Kong was ceded to the British, and an English-speaking community sprang up there. British consulates were opened in other ports as well. Finn's book was excerpted in a Hong Kong periodical and stirred up a great deal of interest.

No new information had come from Kaifeng since the expulsion of the missionaries. Everything written in the interim had been based on the Jesuit accounts, often with a healthy dose of imagination. Jews in Europe and America had written letters to Kaifeng in Hebrew, but with no response. No one knows if they were received; if so, it is not likely they could have been understood.

With typical English doggedness Finn set out to close that gap. He made the rounds of China-bound travelers, giving them copies of his book and urging them to contact the Jews. Among them was a diplomat on his way to a new post as British consul, who agreed to translate a letter to them into Chinese. Finn wrote the letter himself in English and Hebrew and mailed it to the consul, who forwarded it to Kaifeng. It was addressed to "The Honorable Sinew-Plucking Sect, Kaifeng."

Miraculously, Finn's letter was not only received but answered. A Chinese Jew named Chao Nien-tsu sent a reply to the consul in 1850.[43] His letter was a poignant cry for help from Jews who, for all they had known, might have been the only ones left in the world. "The receipt of your present letter," Chao wrote, "assures us that the holy religion contains still a germ of vitality, and that in the great English nation the history of its origin has not been lost."

Chao painted a gloomy picture of Jewish life in Kaifeng, on the verge of disappearing entirely. He described himself as one of the few Jews who still cared about their religion. "It is well that your letter reached the hands of the present writer," he wrote. "Had it been carried to others it might have remained unnoticed." But not even he understood the Scriptures, and only one old woman in her seventies remembered any of what their people once believed. "Morning and night," Chao wrote, "with tears in our eyes and with offerings of incense, do we implore that our religion may again flourish. We have everywhere sought about, but could find none who understood the letters of the Great Country."

At Finn's request Chao appended a list of festivals he remembered. They were barely recognizable as Jewish holidays. The "Feast of Dry Wheat," held on the "second moon, fourteenth day," was obviously Passover. In that festival, "cakes called *oil fragrant* are distributed to friends." And the festival on the "eighth moon, twenty-fourth day," when "the Scriptures are preached in the temple; the doors being closed, the scroll is opened out, and the Scriptures read—money colored red is distributed," was undoubtedly Simchat Torah. Others corresponded even more loosely to Rosh Hashanah, Yom Kippur, and the Ninth of Ab.

Chao reported that the synagogue was crumbling. "Our temple in this place has long been without ministers; the four walls of its principal hall are greatly dilapidated, and the compartments of the hall of the holy men are in ruins. The water-chamber [*mikveh*] and the treasury are in ruins likewise." To make things worse, some of the Jews were pulling it down. Chao named eight men who were mortgaging or selling parts of the building. "If any person be deputed hither," he said, "measures should be taken to put a stop to the scandalous proceedings of these people."

But Chao's letter arrived too late. Through a bizarre set of circumstances including the death of the consul, the disappearance of his wife, and the appointment of Finn as British consul to Jerusalem (where he became noted for, among other things, reestablishing contact with Samaritans), the letter did not reach Finn for twenty years—until 1870. By then the synagogue was already torn down. Its materials—even the earth beneath it—had been sold. The site became a stagnant pool, used as a public urinal. Only one of the stone inscriptions remained to mark the spot where a synagogue had stood for nearly seven hundred years, an achievement equalled by few Jewish communities anywhere.

What had gone wrong? Why, after living as Jews for more than half a millennium, did Kaifeng's Jews abandon their traditions?

A professor at Northwest Christian College in Oregon, Song Nai Rhee, has written a paper blaming their assimilation on "the overwhelming impact of the Confucian civil-service system," and "its potent power to absorb, disintegrate, and Sinify non-Chinese elements."[44] He points out that by participating in the civil service,

Kaifeng's Jews learned to behave and think as Confucian literati. They adulterated their religion with Confucianism, were often forced to leave Kaifeng, and were encouraged to intermarry.

But as true as this may be, it does not explain why they stopped being Jewish. On the contrary, it was precisely while the Jews were most successful in the civil service that Kaifeng's synagogue was in its heyday. Not until later did Judaism perish in Kaifeng. The problem was not that Kaifeng's Jews became Chinese, but that they lost the strength to remain Jewish at the same time.

Donald Leslie offers a different perspective. In his view it was the loss of contact with other Jews which caused their demise. They had lost touch with Jews in other Chinese cities by the early 1500s, and with foreign Jews probably earlier. Centuries of isolation left them without inner resources to draw on. Really, he says, it would be more appropriate to ask how they survived so long than why they eventually succumbed.

If anything, assimilation helped Kaifeng's Jews survive, rather than disappear. Internalizing Chinese values was the only way for Jews to succeed in Chinese society. Their success in the civil service sparked a Jewish mini-renaissance. And while adopting many Confucian customs they never violated basic Jewish principles. "Hardly anything crept in under Chinese influence actually contrary to a Judaism which is not over-rigid," notes Professor Leslie. "Rather a remolding occurred which reminds us of the phenomenon which is occurring amongst the Jewish communities of America today."[45]

The final stage of Kaifeng's Jewish community was as a tourist attraction. Visitors of every stripe and persuasion came to Kaifeng: American churchmen, European diplomats, Soviet military advisors, Japanese occupation forces. All reported the same impression: that only a memory of Jewish descent survived.

Information began reaching the outside world even before Chao Nien-tsu's letter was delivered to Finn. In addition to translating and forwarding Finn's letter, the British consul made some independent inquiries. He reported his first success in 1849: finding a Moslem sergeant from Kaifeng who was familiar with its Jews. He interviewed the sergeant with Finn's book on the table between them. The interview anticipated Chao Nien-tsu's bad news. The Jews no longer had a rabbi or understood their holy language, the sergeant reported. But they still kept up their synagogue and even the sanctity of the Holy Ark, which no one had entered in the forty to fifty years since the last rabbi died.

A year later the consul reported that the sergeant returned for a second visit. He said he had found an older friend from Kaifeng who remembered the days when the Jews still had a rabbi. This man recalled that the rabbis used to lead the Jews around the synagogue once a year, carrying something before him in his hands. This, of course, was Simchat Torah—the same festival witnessed by the Jesuit more than a century before, and described by Chao in his letter.

Still more information arrived that year. Inspired by Finn's book, Protestant missionaries in Shanghai and Hong Kong sent Chinese Christians to visit Kaifeng—just as Ricci had done before them. The two delegates left in November 1850 and spent five or six days in Kaifeng in December. They found the Jews "sunk in the lowest poverty and destitution—their religion scarcely more than a name."[46] They visited the synagogue, which was nearly in ruins. "We heard also," one delegate wrote, "that whenever any were known to belong to the Jewish religion, they were soon despised and became poor; none of the Chinese would make friends with them, and they were treated as outcasts by the common people."[47]

The Chinese delegates made a second trip in 1851. They spent two weeks in Kaifeng, long enough to estimate the Jewish population at three to four hundred. This time they returned with six Torah scrolls and assorted other manuscripts, including the memorial book. They also brought back two Jews in person. Both had been circumcised, a practice they still called by the Hebrew word mila. One died in Shanghai and was buried in that city's new Jewish cemetery. The two Chinese delegates were the last outsiders to see Kaifeng's synagogue. Civil disorder kept visitors away for the next fifteen years. By the time the first Westerners could visit Kaifeng in 1866, the synagogue was already torn down.

Several attempts were made to revive the community. The most promising was by the Society to Rescue the Chinese Jews, formed by Jews in Shanghai at the turn of the century. It brought down eight Jews from Kaifeng to study Hebrew in 1901–02. These Jews reported that nothing was left of their religion other than that they did not worship idols or eat pork. The society circumcised one sixteen-year-old boy and renamed him Israel. But after a few months he and most of the others returned to Kaifeng. The only two who stayed were an elderly flour-seller named Li Ching-sheng and his son Li Tsung-mai, who had been the first to arrive in 1901. Ching-sheng died in 1903 and was buried, like his predecessor half a century before, in Shanghai's Jewish cemetery. Tsung-mai stayed in Shanghai until shortly before his death in 1948, working for a company owned by a member of the society. He became known in Shanghai as "Samuel Lee."

Another attempt was made by Bishop William White, head of the Canadian Anglican Mission in Kaifeng. White bought the synagogue site and the two remaining inscriptional stones, promising to return them if the Jews ever resumed practicing their religion. In a series of meetings in 1919 he tried to reorganize the Jewish community, with no success. He called his last meeting in 1932 to introduce them to a visiting American Jew, David Brown. Brown noticed one old woman with curly hair but no other signs of Jewishness. He wrote: "They know they are Jews, but know nothing of Judaism. They realize they are Chinese, completely assimilated, yet there is pride in the knowledge that they spring from an ancient people who are different from the other Chinese in Kaifeng."[48]

During the Japanese occupation in World War II, two Japanese officials visited Kaifeng to report on the Jews. Though they were sympathetic and wrote objective reports, Kaifeng's Jews thought they were sent to persecute them. Some denied that they were Jewish. Since the war, only a few foreigners have visited. Two American journalists met them in 1946, as did a friend of Israel's future president, Isaac Ben-Zvi. Two European doctors working in Kaifeng were in contact with them until the 1949 revolution. A Czech Sinologist paid them a visit in 1957. So did a group of foreign students at the University of Peking that year, including two Jews. They were only allowed to meet them in front of their government guide. "Because of the presence of the cadre," wrote a Canadian Jew who was among them, "the discussion was formal and reserved. Nevertheless, when upon leaving the house I discreetly whispered to the old gentleman that two of us were Jewish, he beamed effusively and shook our hands."[49]

The most recent visitor was a UPI reporter in early 1980. She found a few dozen people who knew they were descended from Jews.

One confided that he shaved his head to disguise his curly hair. Otherwise there were no hints of discrimination. "Some people used to be afraid to say they were Jews," said one, "because minority groups were oppressed before the revolution. But not now."[50]

CHAPTER TEN

The Bene Israel of Bombay:
"We Survived"

The drowsy stillness of August afternoons in Jerusalem was shattered one Wednesday in 1964 by a sight which would have struck an unsuspecting observer as incongruous, to say the least. Two thousand East Indians were demonstrating in the streets, many wearing saris or Nehru suits. They were shouting slogans and carrying signs calling for an end to "religious fascist rule" in Israel, and warning of a "pharaoh in the cloak of the chief rabbi." Young marchers defied the caution of their more moderate elders by carrying an effigy of a rabbi with a rope around its neck. They were protesting the refusal of Israeli rabbis to allow them to marry other Jews.

The marchers wound their way through the city behind a contingent of about fifty non-Indian supporters. A sound truck exhorted them in three languages: Hebrew, English, and Marathi, a language spoken in the Bombay region. They paused for speeches in front of the Jewish Agency compound, where more than one hundred other Indians were waiting for them. The smaller group had been on a sit-down strike—practicing *satyagraha* (Gandhi-style passive resistance) for two weeks. Five of them were on a week-long hunger strike as well.

The march ended another hundred yards down King George Street, at the offices of Israel's chief rabbinate. A second effigy was brought out and burned, this one depicting a rabbi as a red-faced Hindu demon. "For two thousand years we lived as loyal Jews in India," a speaker declared, "only to come to Israel and suffer anti-Semitism at the hands of our brethren."[1]

It should come as little surprise by now, after reading of black Jews in Ethiopia and Confucian Jews in China, that Jews in India look and think like other Indians, too. But perhaps it should be even less surprising that Orthodox Jews would challenge their credentials. The protesters were indigenous Indian Jews, members of a community which has lived in the area around what is now Bombay for as long as anyone knows: the Bene Israel (children of Israel). Because of their Indian appearance and mysterious origin, their relationship with the larger Jewish world has been a two-century story of condescension and rejection. Only after that raucous afternoon in 1964 did they gain equal rights in the country where most now live: Israel.

The Jews of India are a varied lot, divided into distinct communities. The Bene Israel are only one of these, though by far the largest. When India's Jewish population was at its greatest (during the mid-1940s), Bene Israel made up two-thirds of its approximately thirty thousand Jews. The others fell into equally well-defined categories:

—The Jews of Cochin, on India's southwest coast. This, too, is an ancient community. Its existence has been traced to at least the eleventh century. But Cochin never lost contact with the rest of the Jewish world, as did the Bene Israel, so their identity was never challenged. More than ninety percent of Cochin's twenty-five hundred Jews have moved to Israel.

—Jews from Arab lands, called "Baghdadis" after the city many of them came from in the nineteenth century. Under the leadership of the Sassoon family, the "Rothschilds of the East," they grew wealthy and entered India's elite. There were sixty-five hundred Baghdadis in India in the mid-1940s (including war refugees from Burma), mostly in Bombay and Calcutta. Few remain. Wealthier Baghdadis tended to migrate to England, Canada, and other English-speaking countries rather than Israel.

—A few hundred Mashhadis (see Chapter IV). They went to Bombay (and an even smaller number to Calcutta) from Iran, Afghanistan, Russia (after 1917), and Pakistan (after 1947). They aligned themselves with the Baghdadis, and few people other than themselves took any notice of the distinction. All have since joined other Mashhadis in cities around the world.

—About thirteen hundred European Jews, most of whom fled to India (again, mostly Bombay) in the 1930s and 40s. Few ever considered India their home, and nearly all left immediately after the war.

From these communities the Bene Israel stand apart—not only because they are the only ones whose Jewishness has been doubted, but for the very reasons that it was. Judaism took a novel turn on India's northwest coast. Where most Jewish communities were molded by Christian or Moslem environments, the Bene Israel were molded by the Hindu. Added to that is the gap in their history, the hundreds of years when other Jews knew nothing about them. The Bene Israel, in turn, knew almost nothing of Judaism. They never forgot they were Jewish, but had to relearn completely what that means. It was those missing centuries which gave other Jews an excuse to challenge their identity.

. . . .

Like so many communities in this book, the origin of the Bene Israel is unknown. And like so many of those other communities, they claim descent from the ten lost tribes. But in India the legend receives an added fillip, and is interwoven with Hindu mythology. An Indian myth credits one light-skinned Brahman caste with descent from fourteen shipwrecked foreigners, found on a beach and brought back to life by an incarnation of the Hindu god Vishnu. The Bene Israel's tradition is parallel: they claim to have sprung from fourteen Israelites (seven men and seven women) who survived the wreck of their trading ship near the village of Navgaon, twenty miles south of what is now Bombay. The old Bene Israel cemetery in Navgaon is said to contain their graves. Historians offer a variety of alternative origins, generally believing they came from some Middle Eastern country in the first millennium A.D.; in actuality there is no more evidence for this theory than for the Bene Israel's own. Nothing is definitely known about the Bene Israel before the 1700s.

From Navgaon, continues Bene Israel tradition, descendants of the shipwrecked Israelites dispersed to more than one hundred villages along the narrow coastal strip of northwest India, known as the Konkan coast. They claim to have multiplied without marrying native Indians. The names of their original villages are preserved in their surnames. Each Bene Israel has a traditional family name ending with the suffix "–kar," as in "Kehimkar," where it means "from the village of Kehim." Such a surname is not always still used, especially in Israel, though it is always remembered.

In these villages they took up the trade of oil-pressing, and became known as the caste of *Shanwar Teli*, meaning "Saturday oil-pressers," because they would not work on the Sabbath. They were not, strictly speaking, a caste in the traditional Hindu sense. As Jews they were outside the spiritual hierarchy ordained by Hindu law. But they functioned as a caste in everyday life: a corporate body with a specific occupation and specific rank in society. Higher-caste Indians refused to eat with Bene Israel and would wash their cooking utensils if touched by them. Likewise, Bene Israel would not eat or even share water with those farther down on the scale than themselves.

As *Shanwar Teli*, they practiced a basic Judaism, stripped to its essentials. They circumcised their children on the eighth day, rested on Saturdays, abstained from forbidden foods, and observed a few more-or-less-Jewish festivals. They recited their only prayer, the *Shema*, on every religious occasion. Other than that they knew nothing of Judaism: they had no Jewish books, spoke no Hebrew other than the *Shema*, and had no contact with foreign Jews.

This did not change until they were discovered by a passing Jew named David Rahabi. Rahabi, according to their traditions, stumbled on them by accident and stayed to reintroduce them to Judaism. Since he was not absolutely sure they were Jews, he tested them by giving their women an assortment of seafood to cook. Only after they correctly separated the kosher fish—those with both fins and scales—from the forbidden did he agree to instruct them. Rahabi taught them the Hebrew alphabet, Jewish prayers and Scriptures, and several new holidays. Before his death he trained three young men as religious leaders, called *kajis*, who traveled from village to village sharing their new knowledge.

Just when this happened was long disputed. According to Bene Israel tradition, Rahabi came hundreds of years ago—perhaps five hundred, perhaps as many as nine hundred. Some Bene Israel claim he was David ben Maimon, a brother of Maimonides, who is known to have vanished in the Indian Ocean in the twelfth century. As evidence they point out that *Rahab* is one of several biblical names for Egypt, where Maimonides lived. Also, Maimonides may have known about the Bene Israel: he once wrote a letter to French rabbis which said, "The Jews of India know nothing of the Torah and none of the laws except the Sabbath and circumcision"—a description which could fit them. But this turns out to be wishful thinking. Rahabi is now known to have lived in the mid-1700s. His full name was David Ezekiel Rahabi, and he belonged to the Jewish community of Cochin, five hundred miles south of Bombay. The existence of the

Bene Israel was just then becoming known in Cochin, where the Rahabis were one of the leading families. According to family records, David Ezekiel Rahabi encountered the Bene Israel in the course of his travels as an agent of the Dutch East India Company.

Bene Israel began moving to the growing city of Bombay in the last third of the eighteenth century. British colonial policy favored minorities, and the "native Jew caste"—as they called the Bene Israel—won a reputation as hard-working and loyal. The first Bene Israel to prosper there were five brothers of the Divekar family, all of whom were army officers. The most successful, Samaji Hasaji (Samuel Ezekiel) Divekar, was a commandant in the native infantry. He was captured during the second Anglo-Mysore War (1780–84) but freed through a strange coincidence. Apparently, a member of the Rahabi family was in the camp of the sultan who captured him, and arranged for his release to Cochin. Grateful, and impressed by his glimpse of organized Judaism in Cochin, Divekar vowed to build a synagogue when he returned to Bombay. In 1796, he founded the first Bene Israel synagogue: *Shaar Harahamim* (Gate of Mercy). It still stands, rebuilt, on Samuel Street, which was named after Divekar. He died the following year in Cochin, while on a return trip to obtain a Torah scroll for the synagogue.

Bombay became the Bene Israel's new spiritual center. Previously, while dispersed in dozens of villages with just a few families in each, they had never needed a synagogue. Their religious life had always revolved around the home; every male knew how to lead their few ceremonies. But by the 1820s, some two thousand Bene Israel were concentrated in Bombay. There, they came under the influence of three groups of outsiders who brought them closer to Judaism: Cochin Jews, Baghdadis, and, ironically, Protestant missionaries.

India became one of the few places in the world where Jews had cordial relations with missionaries. Mostly from Great Britain and the United States, these missionaries were notoriously unsuccessful. In more than a century of avid proselytizing, perhaps one hundred and fifty Bene Israel switched religions. But the missionaries also taught them about their own religion: translating parts of the Old Testament into Marathi, publishing a Hebrew-Marathi grammar, and opening a school where Bene Israel children studied Marathi, English, and Hebrew. More than one-fourth of Bombay's school-age

Bene Israel were enrolled in mission schools by the 1830s, giving them one of the highest literacy rates of any non-Brahman caste.

The Jewish missionaries from Cochin were more successful. Five Cochin Jews moved north in 1826 to work among the Bene Israel, and another dozen followed in the 1830s. They worked as teachers, preachers, *mohels*, slaughterers, and *hazans*, opening schools, expounding the Scriptures, teaching religious law, and publishing books. Some stayed in Bombay; others circulated to the larger villages. Several stayed for more than a decade.

The last outside influence was by example alone, because the Baghdadis never seriously tried to assist their native brethren. Still, their mere presence set a standard of Orthodox Judaism for the Bene Israel to judge themselves by. Arabic-speaking Jews began coming to Bombay in the last years of the eighteenth century. They remained insignificant until David Sassoon brought his banking house from Baghdad in 1823, building it into an economic empire. The Sassoon companies became the most potent economic force in the East, with branches from Shanghai to London. In Bombay their mills offered employment to Jews who flocked there from throughout the Orient. Their charities became famous for funding hospitals, libraries, synagogues, schools, yeshivas, and reformatories. Later generations of Sassoons became assimilated English gentlemen, but David and his contemporaries in Bombay were traditional Orthodox Jews.

It was Baghdadis who first questioned the Jewishness of the Bene Israel. Pointing to their dark skins, they doubted the Bene Israel's Jewish origin. In fact, the name "Bene Israel" came into use to distinguish them from genuine "Jews," i.e., the Baghdadis. (Curiously, even the Bene Israel employed this terminology.) But Bene Israel claim the Baghdadi attitude had less to do with religion than with prestige and caste. In British India, natives were disdained. The lighter-skinned Baghdadis preferred to align themselves with Europeans.

The earliest immigrants from Arab countries showed no compunction toward sharing the Bene Israel synagogue and burial ground. As late as 1834, the leader of the Baghdadis was buried in the Bene Israel cemetery. But two years later, David Sassoon and other leading Baghdadis asked British authorities to build a wall down the center. "Two components and distinct tribes of Jews inhabit this country," declared their petition, "one having adopted the customs of the natives of India and the other faithful to their Arabian fathers. . . . For a long while [they have been] in a state of painful excitement against each other, occasioned by the place of sepulchre."[2] As the Baghdadis grew more numerous and prosperous, they isolated themselves completely. They opened their own synagogues, cemeteries, and schools from which Bene Israel were excluded. They refused to marry Bene Israel or even count them as part of a *minyan.* Indigent Bene Israel were not eligible for the monthly stipend received by other poor Jews from the Sassoon charities. Nor could they enter Baghdadi old-age homes. As late as 1934, Baghdadis tried to exclude Bene Israel from the "Sassoon Wing" of a Bombay hospital.

Despite their ostracism, Bene Israel prospered in the nineteenth century. They remained poor by Western and Baghdadi standards, but by their own they were rising rapidly. They became a "clerk caste" of skilled tradesmen, mechanics, building contractors, and office workers. Their English literacy qualified them for government service, especially as postal and railroad clerks. Although most lived near each other in a few mixed neighborhoods of Bombay, they did not isolate themselves in any one ghetto. Some joined the emigration of Indians around the rim of the Indian Ocean to Burma, Calcutta, Aden, Karachi, and East Africa, as well as the closer cities of Poona, Thana, and Ahmedabad. Joseph Halévy, on his way to study Falashas in 1867 (see Chapter VIII), spent Rosh Hashanah with Bene Israel on the Ethiopian coast.

A growing number of Bene Israel entered the professions: medicine, law, engineering, architecture, journalism, and academia. One served as mayor of Bombay in the 1930s. Others became prominent in India's film industry, in positions from scriptwriters to movie stars. Bene Israel women, freer than their Moslem and Hindu counterparts, often became nurses and teachers. One represented India in the 1959 Miss Universe contest. These successful Bene Israel left Bombay's communal neighborhoods for more comfortable suburbs or other cities, such as Karachi and Ahmedabad, their wealthiest communities. Some who never left their Konkan villages also prospered, becoming landowners. Few poor families still pressed oil for a living (today only one remains, in the village of Alibag). One Bene Israel academic, Moses Ezekiel, described the social situation he faced as a young boy in 1905 when his father retired to the countryside: "We were shocked to be described as Telis [oil-pressers], and my mother as Telin, the feminine of Teli. I knew for certain that not for three generations behind had we known any one in our family who had done the oil man's trade. Even in the John Elphinstone High School, most boys took delight in calling us by that very irritating name 'Teli.' I found to my surprise that some boys in the school had *ghanis* or oil-presses in their houses and their main source of income was the oil-press. They were real Telis, but we always protested that we were not."[3]

Professor Ezekiel made no attempt to conceal his concern for status. The Bene Israel, in fact, keenly share this most Indian of obsessions—to the point of internalizing the caste system. Though they no longer like to talk about it, Bene Israel used to be divided into two separate castes which would not eat, drink, pray, or marry together. The higher caste was called *gora* (white), and the lower one *kala* (black). *Gora* Bene Israel were considered somehow "purer" than *kala*, who were said to be the offspring of intermarriage with non-Jews. But *gora* were not necessarily lighter-skinned than *kala*; it was simply a matter of knowing who belonged to which. Caste distinctions took on less importance after the turn of the century, but were never forgotten. Even in Israel all Bene Israel still know who is which. During the marriage crisis of the 1960s, some Bene Israel suggested at a public meeting that they should provide a list of *kala* families to the Israeli rabbinate, in order to remove the stigma from the rest. Bene Israel leaders declined. Today the distinction has no remaining force in everyday life, in either Israel or India.

(A black-white caste system also existed among the Jews of Cochin, though based on different criteria. Cochin's "black Jews" were Indian-looking, and thought to be descended from that colony's original settlers. Its "white Jews"—unlike the Bene Israel's—were actually lighter-skinned. They were comparatively recent immigrants, although they, too, have claimed to be the original settlers. Cochin also boasted a third Jewish caste: the *meshuararim* (freedmen), descendants of manumitted slaves or of concubines with their Jewish masters. Separation between the castes was much stricter in Cochin than among Bene Israel, but even there it has disappeared. The barriers were already crumbling when mass emigration to Israel finished them off. No color bar remains today—at least partly because virtually no black Jews remain in Cochin.)

Bene Israel resemble their Indian neighbors in other ways, too. Actually, it is misleading to make that distinction: Bene Israel *are* Indians who differ from their neighbors in religion alone. They share Indian customs, morals, lifestyles, and attitudes. Many live in Hindu-style "joint families," where married brothers continue to live in the same household even after their parents die. A few practiced polygamy even after it was banned in other Jewish communities. (Although polygamous marriages are illegal in Israel, Bene Israel men who immigrated with two families were given two adjacent apartments.) Most Bene Israel do not eat beef. (Many believe beef is not kosher, though better-informed Bene Israel say they don't like its taste or that they refrain out of respect for their Hindu neighbors.) And they practice many Indian customs, most conspicuously a prenuptial *mendi* (henna) ceremony, where the bride's hands are painted with henna in preparation for the wedding. *Mendi* is still practiced in Israel.

They also have a peculiarly Indian attitude toward Judaism. Most are pious Jews, but in a different sense than the traditionally Orthodox. Theirs is a religion of faith and piety, more than the detailed observance which looms so large in the Orthodox mind. It is a different view of what Judaism is, and of the role of religion in their lives.

Religious Bene Israel are selective about which Jewish laws they obey. Even the most observant, who attend synagogue daily, are willing to work on Saturdays. They separate milk from meat, but do not use different sets of dishes for the two. They use mezuzahs, but not *tefillin*. The Bible is their only scripture. While not actually denying the Talmud (as do Karaites), they pay no attention to it. One reason is that they have no Orthodox rabbis trained in Jewish law; their services are run by *hazans* who are schooled only in liturgy. A foreign rabbi who visited Bombay in the early 1950s wrote of his initial admiration for a Bene Israel *hazan*'s chanting of the Torah: "Every word, every accent, every intonation was perfect, and since the cantillation accentuates and groups the words according to their sense, it was impossible to believe that he was reading without full awareness of the meaning. Almost shamefacedly I asked him what he had read, and he, with no shamefacedness at all, frankly admitted that he did not understand a word."[4]

This attitude is as characteristic of Bene Israel who profess to be Orthodox as of those who adhere to the less-rigid Conservative movement. Curiously, there is no difference between the Judaism practiced in their Orthodox and Conservative synagogues. The religious disputes which divide those movements in other parts of the world are irrelevant in Bombay; the two groups are separated only by community politics. The only exception is the Jewish Religious Union, which has been India's only Reform temple since it was founded in 1925. But even there, membership depends less on theology than on education and class. The Jewish Religious Union is patronized exclusively by the Bene Israel elite: doctors, lawyers, and other well-educated members of the community. Services are conducted in English and rabbis are imported from England and America. Two promising youngsters were sent to the United States in the 1960s to study for the rabbinate at the Hebrew Union College, but neither returned to serve the community. One dropped out; the other married an American girl and returned only briefly before going back to America.

The most popular Bene Israel festival is one that is only minor for other Jews: *tashlikh*, the casting of sins into the sea on Rosh Hashanah. Outside India only the very Orthodox practice *tashlikh*, usually individually or in small groups. But Bene Israel gather by the thousands at several sites on the Bombay waterfront, dressed in their finest clothes, to symbolically empty their pockets into the sea. These "sea prayers," as they call them, are the high-water mark of their social season. Why? Sociologist Carl M. Gussin suggests that they resemble a Hindu ritual called *avabhrta snana*, a similar ceremony of washing sins away in water. *Tashlikh* was turned into a major celebration by the Bene Israel just as Hanukkah was by American Jews because it coincides with Christmas.

Another popular rite is peculiar to the Bene Israel: a thanks-offering to Elijah called *Eliahu Hannabi* (Elijah the prophet), or simply *malida* after a ground-rice-and-sugar dish served during the ceremony. It is performed on all sorts of occasions: Saturday evenings, at all rites of passage, or simply to give thanks. It varies according to the occasion: from a brief prayer to a complex series of blessings and foods, culminating in the passing around of a plate of *malida*. This rite is only part of the Bene Israel's cult of Elijah, who they claim miraculously visited India. Bene Israel still make pilgrimages to the village of Khandalla, where the tracks of his horse-drawn chariot are said to be preserved. They used to hold an annual fair in his honor on the fifteenth of Shevat, the Jewish New Year for the trees. It was held in Khandalla until 1796, when it was moved to Bombay's new *Shaar Harahamim* synagogue. The fair, but not the pilgrimage, was later discontinued under the influence of Cochin Jews. (In Israel the Bene Israel make pilgrimages to Elijah's Cave on Mount Carmel.) This, too, is a thoroughly Indian practice. Hindus and Indian Moslems also have patron saints to whom they look for protection; Elijah is simply the Bene Israel's. Educated Bene Israel may no longer believe literally in Elijah's influence, but still take part in the rite.

Bene Israel selectivity has also produced a unique curio of Judaica: a "Jewish bus ticket." Bene Israel take public transportation to and from their synagogues, ignoring the Orthodox prohibition against riding on the Sabbath or Jewish holidays. But in order not to use money—another Orthodox prohibition—they formerly purchased special tickets marked "for Jews only," available in synagogues during the week. This practice was discontinued in the 1950s after city councilmen complained that the ticket discriminated against non-Jews—a curious line of reasoning, given that the ticket cost more than an ordinary fare. Bene Israel simply switched to cash, and continued riding the bus on Saturdays.

Granted, Jews being selective about which commandments to obey is hardly out of the ordinary in this day and age. Most Bene Israel are far more observant than the mass of Jews in America or Israel. But American or Israeli Jews who work on Saturdays do not profess to be Orthodox. The Bene Israel think differently: that what makes a Jew "religious" is not the degree of his observance but the depth of his belief. "The essence of their faith," wrote Bene Israel leader Haeem Kehimkar in the late nineteenth century, "is 'Hear O Israel! The Lord our God is one Lord' [the *Shema*]. These words the Bene Israel retained in memory even during their dark ages, and repeated on every occasion of birth, marriage, death, vow-making, etc. In fact, these words were and are the watchwords of the Bene Israel, who repeat them with heart and soul thrice a day. The Bene Israel also ends his earthly existence with the repetition of these words."[5]

Even today the *Shema* serves that terminal function. One young Bene Israel woman from a sophisticated family—her father was chief justice of an Indian state supreme court—recently told a journalist that the *Shema* was the only Judaism she ever learned. "When I was seven years old," she recalled, "I was given strict instructions that if I were knocked down by a car I should say this before I died."[6]

The Bene Israel do not deny they have been influenced by their Indian environment. But, they point out, the influence was never contrary to Jewish principles. Rather, it is a difference of emphasis. "Our assimilation of Hindu and Moslem practices was restricted to social matters," writes their foremost contemporary author, Benjamin J. Israel, "and did not extend to religion proper. In these respects we hardly differ from Jews elsewhere living like us in conditions of close, free, and friendly association with their non-Jewish neighbors."[7]

By mid-twentieth century, two hundred years of contact with the outside world had transformed the Bene Israel from "an obscure Hindu caste with a vague folk-memory of Judaism,"[8] as one sociologist puts it, into full members of the modern Jewish world. So far, being both Indians and Jews had posed no conflict of interest. This was to change. By entering the Jewish mainstream, the Bene Israel also accepted those dilemmas of identity and allegiance which being a modern Jew entails. Latent at first, this identity crisis emerged with the parallel growth of Zionism and Indian nationalism.

The Bene Israel began debating the relative merits of Indian versus Jewish nationalism even before the turn of the century. Invited to send delegates to the First Zionist Congress in Basel in 1897, they declined. They replied that the return to Zion was subject to the "Divine Hand," adopting the anti-Zionist line then prevalent in Orthodox circles.

They soon reconsidered. Indian nationalism threatened their favored position under British rule. The Bene Israel Conference, founded in 1917 to unite the community, took a stand against Indian independence. Only a few educated Bene Israel disagreed, particularly outside Bombay, and founded a rival All-India Israelite League which came out in favor of the nationalist movement. One Bene Israel doctor in Ahmedabad, local secretary of the National Home Rule League, circulated a petition declaring: "We are Indian first, and Muslim or Jews or Parsees afterwards."[9] But the prevailing winds faced west, toward Palestine. The Bombay Zionist Association, founded in 1919, gradually came to represent the entire community.

Intellectuals who declared themselves "Indian first" found themselves alone. The rest of the country shattered into a myriad of tribes, castes, and religious groupings.

The Bene Israel's fate was sealed by independence in 1947. They were doomed to powerlessness in India's new politics of caste. Of Bombay's nearly three million residents (by the 1951 census), only sixteen thousand were Jewish. The civil service closed to them. Land reform deprived rural Bene Israel landlords of their livelihood. The Karachi community, finding itself in Moslem Pakistan, fled across the new border to a diminished India. Only educated professionals, who could succeed on individual merit, continued to think of themselves as more Indian than Jewish. The others looked toward Israel.

Even so, the Bene Israel were the slowest Indian Jewish community to emigrate. First went the wartime refugees from Burma and Europe, many of whom left even before independence. They were followed by the majority of Baghdadis. From Cochin, the poorer black Jews and meshuararim emigrated in the late 1940s and early 1950s. Most of the better-off white Jews followed over the course of the next two decades. Bene Israel emigration was even more cautious. Although they had made up two-thirds of all Jews in India, they were less than one-fifth of Israel's Indian population by its fourth birthday in 1952. Their exodus did not pick up steam until the marriage crisis was resolved in 1964. Subsequently, Bene Israel left India at the rate of more than one thousand a year until the mid-1970s.

Educated Bene Israel sometimes left for countries other than Israel, especially England. Three hundred families are estimated living in the London area. They have little contact with one another, and nothing resembling a Bene Israel community. Ironically, some had their first taste of anti-Semitism in England. "In India no one had ever heard of the Jews," one told an interviewer. "Here they talk against them." [10]

Jewish life still thrives in India, though on a vastly reduced scale. Fewer than five thousand Jews are now thought to remain, most of them Bene Israel. Empty synagogues stand with unused Torah scrolls where Jewish communities once prospered. An "all-synagogue convention" was called in 1970 to dispose of communal property. Nine synagogues still function in Bombay, though the two Baghdadi ones have to pay Bene Israel to help form a daily minyan. In Poona, too, two synagogues remain open: one Bene Israel and the other

Baghdadi. Bene Israel synagogues survive in Ahmedabad and Delhi, a Baghdadi synagogue in Calcutta, and the oldest of all Indian synagogues in Cochin: an exquisite edifice of blue tile and chandeliers which is now a national monument. Prime Minister Indira Gandhi attended its four hundredth anniversary celebration in 1966.

But what Judaism remains is fervent and alive. That special quality of Bene Israel religion, what one writer calls "their genuine simplicity, their deep and uncomplicated love for Judaism,"[11] still shines through. "There is a very active life here," reports a foreigner who recently settled in Bombay. "Synagogues are much more full than the ones I attended just last summer in New York. A terrific religious spirit is here, which for me is a revelation and reflects the fact that the Bene Israel are living in a country where religion is alive and real."[12]

Bombay's few hundred Baghdadis still live apart from the Bene Israel, but are no longer hostile. It is now class and habit which sets them off more than anything else. The Baghdadis are generally wealthier, more westernized, live in nicer neighborhoods, and have their own larger, plusher synagogues, though both communities have their share of charity cases. They join together for most community activities. A few Baghdadis have even married Bene Israel. But the closest contact is between old Baghdadis and old Bene Israel who are spending their final days together in a joint old-age home—as are, in a sense, the entire Baghdadi and Bene Israel communities.

• • • •

"Leaving for Israel is not like going to the park," the heroine of Meera Mahadevan's novel, *Shulamith*, cautions her son. "It is nearly eight years since we emigrated from Karachi and I still feel unsettled. Can you imagine what it would be like for me now to settle in a completely different country? Do you think I could fit into any kibbutz? Or for that matter how do you see yourself committed permanently to a commune? You know very well how annoyed you get if the food you eat is not cooked exactly as you like it."[13]

Shulamith is a fictional portrayal of the Bene Israel's predicament in India: an ancient past, but no future. Shulamith's husband, Michael, has gone ahead to Israel to carve out a niche for his family.

But Shulamith does not want to follow. The battle is waged over the future of their son, Uriel, who finally joins his father in Israel. But the novel concludes with an unexpected twist: Michael returns to Shulamith in India. "The moment I left this country," he tells her, "I realized how Indian I was. I may be Jewish but I cannot live like an American or Baghdadi Jew. I am Indian, and my culture is an Indian culture. India is my country." [14]

This story may be fiction, but it captures the essence of the Bene Israel's dilemma. They feel no more welcome in their adopted homeland than they do in their native one. Migration to Israel was traumatic for them. Everything there was strange: not only language but housing, jobs, sports, family life, drinking habits, even sexual habits. Israeli food was disagreeable; that bland cuisine did not sit well on palates formed by curry, chile, and coriander. The Bene Israel reacted by withdrawing into themselves—forming the ghettoes they had always avoided in India. "Our Bene Israel community has created a mini-India wherever they have settled," Michael says in *Shulamith.* "Whenever you visit these communities you see our women in saris. You smell the scent of Indian cooking. You hear Hindi and Marathi being spoken, and in the background the soft notes of Indian devotional music." [15]

Most Bene Israel live in the poor "development towns" at the fringe of Israeli life: Dimona, Lod, Yeruham, Kiryat Shemonah, Kiryat Gat, Ashdod, or Beersheba. Few were happy on kibbutzim or *moshavim*; most who tried that communal life eventually left for the towns. Only a few have risen in Israeli society. As in India, those moved out of the communal neighborhoods to more prosperous ones in Tel Aviv, Haifa, or Jerusalem. Among them is Samson J. Samson, a librarian in Jerusalem's National Library and general secretary of the Federation of Indian Jews. Samson is a quiet, well-spoken man in his forties, one of the few Bene Israel professionals who stays active in communal affairs. But even he, as he sat in his well-appointed Jerusalem apartment, could only shrug his shoulders at what is referred to in Israel as "the Indian problem." "We lived well in India," he says. "Not by American standards, but with a good standard of living. We had no idea of what it would be like in Israel. The East Europeans who rule this country lumped together all the non-Europeans into the slums. Even those of us who are professionals and could have gotten good jobs were sent there."

Israelis discovered they had an "Indian problem" almost as soon as the Bene Israel arrived. In November 1951, one hundred fifty Bene Israel went on a sit-down strike in front of the Jewish Agency building in Tel Aviv, asking to be sent home to India. They had been in Israel at most twenty months, but were unable to adjust to either kibbutz or urban life. On the kibbutzim they could not adjust to communal living: the lack of control over their children, the unfriendly kibbutzniks, and the bland cooking. After a few months they drifted into Beersheba, where they felt discriminated against: allotted the poorest housing, given menial jobs, and ridiculed by their neighbors. Two weeks before the sit-in they had petitioned Prime Minister Ben-Gurion to send them home. "We shall wait eight days for an affirmative reply from you," said their letter, which was signed by ninety adults and forty-eight children. "If none is forthcoming, we shall go to the Jewish Agency building and wait there for another two days. If this is not enough, one by one, all our members will go on a hunger strike."[16]

A hunger strike was not necessary. Their protest made headlines from New York to New Delhi, and prompted the Jewish Agency to strike a deal. It agreed to send the protesters back to India if they would first give Beersheba a second chance, this time with the personal attention of social workers.

Four months later, most were back in Tel Aviv. Only twenty-five had been able to adjust to Beersheba; the majority still wanted to go home. The Jewish Agency kept its word and put them in a nearby transit camp to await a flight to Bombay. About one hundred more Bene Israel tried to join the exodus (mostly unmarried men, about half of them soldiers), and also sat down in front of the Jewish Agency. This time the agency flatly refused, even after the second group went on a hunger strike. They returned to their homes after a few days.

Meanwhile, foreign journalists interviewed the India-bound Bene Israel in the transit camp. The world learned that they were leaving Israel "because they have discovered that they are more Indian than Jewish." One Bene Israel told a reporter: "In religion we are nearly the same as the other Jews here, but in every other way we are 100 percent Indians." Others complained that the men could only find work as laborers, and the women were not prepared for Israel's pioneer conditions. "Our ladies are gentle," one Bene Israel said. "No good in queues. They don't argue—they go home and cry." [17]

The Jewish Agency responded with a statement to the press. "The complaining group seems to be caste-conscious and tends to ascribe every normal difficulty to 'racial discrimination,'" it said. "It is unfortunate, but conditions in Israel now require all housewives, and men, to stand in queues. This applies to persons in all stations of life, including the wife of the Prime Minister of Israel." [18]

In April, one-hundred-fifteen Bene Israel were flown to Bombay, and in May, twelve more. But life in India was not as they remembered it. Within a week of their arrival, they began asking the Jewish Agency to bring them back to Israel. They threatened another hunger strike if it didn't. The Jewish Agency representative in Bombay reported that they were "so disillusioned by the conditions they found in India that they had almost overnight been transformed from critics of Israel into ardent propagandists for her." [19] That October, they sent a second petition to Prime Minister Ben-Gurion. "We are now repenting for our actions," this one said. "We humbly request Your Honor to take us back to Israel and we assure you that we shall give you entire satisfaction." [20] Nearly all were brought back in December 1954. Each signed a statement agreeing to pay the fare himself if he wanted to return to India again.

"The moment they went back they were sorry," recalls Samson Samson. "They had a lot of trouble in India. They were insulted, they couldn't find jobs, they couldn't eat. But the only reason there was a noise was because they were poor. Other immigrants went home quietly to Europe or America or wherever, but our people couldn't afford the fare."

The second crisis came a decade later: the marriage dispute. "It was a complete surprise," says Samson. "In India a 'bastard' is a serious insult; you break someone's jaw for it. When they called us bastards we thought—at first—that they meant we didn't know who our fathers were. And when they explained to us what a *mamzer* is in Jewish law [see Chapter VII], it was no better. They were casting aspersions on our fathers and our fathers' fathers, all the way back."

The marriage crisis grew out of their rivalry with Baghdadis. As early as 1843, Iraqi-born Jews had questioned the Bene Israel's Jewishness. Calcutta's fledgling Jewish community wrote a letter to Baghdad rabbis that year, asking how to deal with them. The reply is not known. Similar queries were sent to rabbis in Baghdad and Palestine in 1869, 1893, 1914, and 1944. The results were mixed. Some rabbis accepted the Bene Israel as Jews, others called them *goyim*, still others put them on a par with Karaites: *mamzerim* who were technically part of the Jewish people but not allowed to marry other Jews. Like Karaites, the Bene Israel had not obeyed the details of Jewish marriage and divorce laws over the centuries. But while Karaites had disobeyed them because of theological differences, the Bene Israel had simply known nothing about them.

At the time of the birth of Israel, the 1944 ruling was in force. It had been issued by Ashkenazi Chief Rabbi Isaac Herzog (the Israeli rabbinate is presided over jointly by two chief rabbis, one Ashkenazi and the other Sephardi), who took a flexible stand. The Bene Israel were definitely Jews, he said, and not necessarily "bastards." The latter determination had to be made on a case-by-case basis. Whenever a Bene Israel wanted to marry another Jew, his or her family history was to be checked for improper marriages or divorces in the last few generations.

During Rabbi Herzog's lifetime this ruling was interpreted leniently. Few individuals were affected, and no protests made. But Rabbi Herzog died in 1959 and was not immediately replaced, because of intra-rabbinical politics. For five years the chief rabbinate was in the sole hands of Sephardi Chief Rabbi Isaac Nissim, a native of Baghdad. Rabbi Nissim again raised the possibility that all Bene Israel were *mamzerim*.

In early 1961, four rabbis in four different cities—Jerusalem, Beersheba, Netanya, and Kiryat Shemonah—independently refused to marry Bene Israel to other Jews. The Bene Israel blame this on Rabbi Nissim, who, they believe, was influenced by Baghdadi prejudice. "The problem was that the Iraqi rabbis never wanted to believe we were Jews," says Samson. "They were influenced by the Iraqis in Bombay." Samson was one of the organizers of the Bene Israel Actions Committee in May of that year. The committee decided on a series of protests: suspending further immigration from India, appealing to public opinion, and ultimately threatening *satyagraha*. "God alone knows what has come over the rabbinate," said the committee's first president, Professor Haim Ezekiel. "Surely Israel is not going to introduce castes?"[21]

That October, the Supreme Rabbinical Council issued a long-

awaited report on Bene Israel status. It calmed them—temporarily—
by declaring: "There are no doubts concerning the Jewishness of the
Bene Israel."[22] But there was less to that declaration than met the
eye, because it did not address the possibility that Bene Israel might
be *mamzerim*. Accordingly, under heavy political pressure from ultra-
Orthodox rabbis, the rabbinate issued "implementary directives" the
following February. These prohibited Bene Israel from marrying other
Jews until their families had been investigated "as far back as
possible."

The Actions Committee resumed its protests. "We thought
they had accepted us," says Samson, "but then they took away
everything we had won. They should have settled it quietly instead of
holding us up to scorn. We have never forgiven the rabbis for that.
And our people who are so religious—maybe not in the Orthodox
sense, but they are believers—lost all respect for the rabbis."

The controversy lasted another two-and-a-half years. Letters
were written, telegrams sent, and articles printed in the local and
foreign press. A resolution was quickly introduced in the Knesset,
though not acted on. Bene Israel in India boycotted a rabbinical
delegation sent to investigate fifteen *kala* families. In the summer of
1963, one hundred young Bene Israel went on a sit-down strike (not
sanctioned by the Actions Committee) to be sent back to India, but
gave up after a month of camping in an empty lot. The crisis came to
a head the following summer, in 1964. A second sit-down strike—
this one supported by the Actions Committee—was held for the
purpose of winning full marriage rights. It culminated in the mass
demonstration on August 5, attended by more than one-fourth of all
Bene Israel in the country. A contingent of non-Indian supporters
was led by Professor (later Deputy Prime Minister) Yigael Yadin and
other prominent Israelis.

On August 17, the Knesset met in special session to resolve
the dispute. Rising above his usually uninspiring rhetoric, Prime
Minister Levi Eshkol delivered a fiery speech in favor of a government
resolution calling on the rabbinate to rewrite its directive. The
resolution declared that Bene Israel are "Jews in all respects, without
qualification, and with the same rights as all other Jews."[23] Eshkol
enjoyed a rare measure of support from the leader of the opposition at
the time, Menachem Begin, who, though devoting most of his
famous oratory to criticizing the burning of the rabbinical effigy,

agreed on their right to marry other Jews. Even most Orthodox politicians, embarrassed by the rabbinate, supported the government resolution. It passed by forty-three to two. The two "no" votes were from an ultra-Orthodox party. Thirty other members abstained because they thought the resolution too weak.

That night the rabbinate announced a face-saving compromise. "Religious law must be observed," a spokesman announced, "but we are seeking a formula to assuage the feelings of the Bene Israel."[24] A new directive was issued two weeks later, with the words "Bene Israel" deleted. Instead, the background investigation was to be required of any Jew for whom there was doubt as to "the ritual purity of his family status." This gave the Bene Israel official parity with other Israelis, though it also gave individual rabbis a loophole through which they could continue refusing to preside over their marriages. And, in fact, some rabbis still require the Bene Israel to be immersed in a ritual bath before marrying other Jews.

Why did the rabbinate change its policy? Because Israeli public opinion overwhelmingly disagreed with it. The Jewish man-in-the-street considered the Bene Israel to be Jews "as we the Jews understand it" (see Chapter I).

"A Jew is first of all someone who is conscious of being a Jew," commented Moshe Sharett, then executive chairman of the Jewish Agency, when the marriage crisis began. "Consciousness determines the sociological and political facts of life."[25]

Yes, even for Orthodox rabbis. Not even *they* follow the letter of the law if there are other overriding considerations. Or, to be more precise, they bend the law to fit those other considerations. In the case of the Bene Israel, as would be the case of the Falashas a few years later, the prime consideration was that nearly every Jew considered them Jewish. Jewish identity is an evolving phenomenon; it does not exist in a vacuum. It is best defined as Gershom Scholem defines Judaism itself: "that which faithful Jews in a given generation rule it to be."[26]

"Till recently," wrote Bombay author Benjamin Israel during the marriage crisis, "the Bene Israel harbored a pathetic compulsion to establish that they stemmed from the veritable stock of Jacob. Now that we know that, in fact, for the last two thousand years and more, there has been no such thing as a Jewish race; *that what makes a Jew is not his ancestry but his commitment to Judaism (in the wider sense of a way of life as well as religion)*; it is sufficient that our people have for centuries been identifiable as Jews in all essential respects and distinguishable from their Hindu and Moslem neighbors."[27]

Here, perhaps, is the ultimate assertion of Jewishness: "We survived." The Bene Israel's tenacious will to be Jewish, their identification with the historic struggle of the Jewish people to survive, cannot be denied. *That* is the criterion most Jews use. "After two thousand years of living in a land where there are so many gods and it is so easy to assimilate," says Samson Samson, "they should have been proud of us instead of giving us a slap in the face." Most Jews are. To be a Jew, above all, is still an act of faith—if no longer in God, then in another phenomenon whose existence cannot be objectively proven: the Jewish people.

Acknowledgments

So many people contributed in some manner to this book that to mention each of them by name is unfortunately not possible. I offer this communal note of gratitude in the hope that none will be offended by its insufficiency. I especially would like to express my appreciation to all who consented to be interviewed, both those who are mentioned by name in the text and those who could not be. To all who kindly provided me with photographs. To Tony Holmes for his superb prints. To all, particularly Diana Villa, who assisted me with the translation of research materials from the Hebrew, Spanish, French, Portuguese, Catalan, German, Italian, or Turkish originals. To librarians in general, of whose resourcefulness I am in awe. To librarians in particular at the New York Public Library, Jewish Theological Seminary, Ben-Zvi Institute for the Study of Oriental Jewish Communities, Jerusalem Post Archives, Jewish National and University Library, Oporto Municipal Library, and others. To the following scholars for reading and commenting on individual chapters in manuscript: Yosef Hayim Yerushalmi, Thomas Glick, Azariah Levy, Gershom Scholem, Theodor Gaster, Leon Nemoy, Wolf Leslau, Graenum Berger, Donald Daniel Leslie, and Raphael Patai, who was also kind enough to contribute a foreword. Their comments have almost without exception been taken into account in the completed book, which is not to lay the blame for its deficiencies on any lap but my own. I owe a particular debt to my literary agent, Barbara Lowenstein, without whose loyalty and dedication this book would never have reached print; to my family and friends, without whose support I could never have attempted it; and last, but certainly not least, to Lisa Brailoff, whose love and encouragement saw me through it. I thank you all.

Bibliography and Notes

GENERAL BIBLIOGRAPHY

Baron, Salo W. "Who Is a Jew?" *Midstream*, Spring 1960, pp. 5-16.

Ben-Zvi, Itzhak. *The Exiled and the Redeemed*. Philadelphia: Jewish Publication Society, 1957.

Blidstein, Gerald J. "Who Is Not a Jew—the Medieval Discussion." *Israel Law Review* 11 (1976): 369-90.

Goldberg, Avraham. "Mamzerim and Marriage." *Jerusalem Post Magazine*, 17 September 1971.

Gouldman, M.D. *Israel Nationality Law*. Jerusalem: Institute for Legislative Research and Comparative Law, 1970.

Herman, Simon. *Jewish Identity: A Social Psychological Perspective*. New York: Herzl Press, 1977.

Hertzberg, Arthur. "Jewish Identity." In *Encyclopedia Judaica*, vol. 10. New York: Macmillan Co., 1971.

Kohn, Moshe. "Two Ways of Being Jewish." *Jerusalem Post*, 31 July 1978.

Litvin, Baruch, comp. *Jewish Identity: Modern Responsa and Opinions on the Registration of Children of Mixed Marriages*. Edited by Sidney B. Hoenig. Jerusalem: Feldheim Publishers, 1970.

Mourant, A.E.; Kopec, Ada C.; and Domaniewska-Sobczak, Kazimiera. *The Genetics of the Jews*. London: Oxford University Press, 1978.

Patai, Raphael. *The Jewish Mind*. New York: Charles Scribner's Sons, 1977.

———. *Tents of Jacob*. Englewood Cliffs, N.J.: Prentice-Hall, 1971.

———, and Wing, Jennifer Patai. *The Myth of the Jewish Race*. New York: Charles Scribner's Sons, 1975.

Roshwald, Mordecai. "Marginal Jewish Sects in Israel." *International Journal of Middle East Studies* 4 (1973): 219-37, 328-54.

———. "Who Is a Jew in Israel?" *Jewish Journal of Sociology* 12 (1970): 233-66.

Rubinstein, Amnon. "Law and Religion in Israel." *Israel Law Review* 2 (1967): 380-414.

Zucker, Norman L. *The Coming Crisis in Israel: Private Faith and Public Policy.* Cambridge, Mass.: MIT Press, 1973.

Chapter One: Venta Prieta

BIBLIOGRAPHY

Gutmann, Enrique. *"Indios Israelitas: Los Judios Mexicanos de Venta Prieta."* *Hoy,* 21 October 1939, pp. 38-43.

Liebman, Seymour B. "A Dying Branch." *Jewish Spectator,* February 1962, pp. 22-23.

———. "The Mestizo Jews of Mexico." *American Jewish Archives* 35 (1967): 144-74.

Patai, Raphael. "The Indios Israelitas of Mexico." *Menorah Journal* 38 (1950): 54-67.

———. "Venta Prieta Revisited." *Midstream,* March 1965, pp. 79-92.

Plenn, Jaime. "A Pious Fairy Tale: There Are No Jewish Indians." *Jewish Digest,* February 1966, pp. 69-70 (condensed from *Mexico City News,* 29 July 1965).

Shapiro, Sraya. "Probing the Past of Mexico's 'Indian Jews.'" *Jerusalem Post,* 30 July 1968.

Vorspan, Albert. "Mexico Mitzvah Corps: This Is No Fairy Tale." *Jewish Digest,* June 1966, pp. 8-12.

NOTES

1. *Mexico on $5 & $10 a Day,* 1973-74 ed. (New York: Frommer/Pasmantier, 1973), p. 103.

2. Robert Silverberg, "Dybbuk on Mazel Tov IV," in *Wandering*

Stars: An Anthology of Jewish Fantasy and Science Fiction, ed. Jack Dann (New York: Harper and Row, 1974), p. 101.

3. Patai, *Jewish Mind*, p. 15.

4. Albert Memmi, *The Liberation of a Jew* (New York: Orion Press, 1966), pp. 27-28. This translation, which differs slightly, is from excerpts in *Commentary*, November 1966, p. 76.

5. Baron, p. 14.

6. "With Gershom Scholem: An Interview," in Scholem, *On Jews and Judaism in Crisis* (New York: Schocken Books, 1976), p. 3. The same story is told in somewhat different words in Scholem's autobiographical *From Berlin to Jerusalem* (New York: Schocken Books, 1980), pp. 42-43.

7. "Diary of the Nazi Ghetto in Vilna," *YIVO Annual of Jewish Social Science* 8 (1953): 9-81, s.v. "30 April 1943" (pp. 50-52). This translation, which differs slightly, is in Norman E. Frimer, "'Who Is a Jew' in the Vilna Ghetto?" *Tradition*, Fall 1977, pp. 55-62.

8. Qtd. J.H. Hertz, *Pentateuch and Haftorahs* (London: Soncino Press, 1960), p. 59.

9. See Kohn, "Two Ways of Being Jewish."

10. *The Jewish Encyclopedia*, s.v. "Moses Mendelssohn."

11. *The Jewish Encyclopedia*, s.v. "Conversion to Christianity."

12. Compiled in Litvin.

13. Qtd. Zucker, p. 179.

14. Qtd. Solomon S. Bernards, *Who Is a Jew: A Reader* (New York: Anti-Defamation League of B'nai Brith, 1966), pp. 18-20. See also Gouldman, pp. 23-26.

15. *Jerusalem Post*, 7 November 1978. See also *New York Times*, 10 September 1980, p. B12.

16. Gutmann, p. 41.

17. Marie Syrkin, "Jewish Indians in Mexico," *Jewish Frontier*, October 1940, pp. 13-15.

18. Patai, "Revisited," p. 81.

19. Patai, "Indios Israelitas," p. 63.

20. Ibid., p. 64.

21. Ibid., p. 67.

22. Patai, "Revisited," p. 81.

23. *Enciclopedia Judaica Castellana*, s.v. "Mexico."

24. Qtd. Patai, "Revisited," p. 89.

25. Ibid., p. 92.

26. Qtd. Plenn, p. 69.

27. Liebman, "Mestizo Jews," p. 147.

Chapter Two: Portugal

BIBLIOGRAPHY

Bethencourt, Cardozo de. "The Jews in Portugal from 1773-1902." *Jewish Quarterly Review*, o.s. 15 (1903): 251-74.

Javal, Lily (Léon-Lévy). *Sous le charme du Portugal: visages et paysages.* Paris: Librairie Plon, 1931.

Novinsky, Anita, and Paulo, Amílcar. "The Last Marranos." *Commentary*, May 1967, pp. 76-81.

Paulo, Amílcar. *Os Criptojudeus.* Oporto: Livraria Athena, 1969 or 70.

———. *"Judeus e Cristãos-Novos na Cidade do Porto."* O Primeiro de Janeiro (Oporto), 9-20 July 1979.

———. *"Judeus Secretos em Portugal."* O Primeiro de Janeiro (Oporto), 20-29 November 1978.

———, and Steinhardt, Inacio. "The Hidden Jews of Belmonte." *Jewish Chronicle Colour Magazine*, 17 March 1978, pp. 6-19.

Portuguese Marranos Committee, The. *Marranos in Portugal: A Survey, 1926-1938.* London: 1938.

Révah, Israel S. *"Les Marranes."* Revue des études juives, 3rd s. 1 (1959-60): 29-77.

Roth, Cecil. *A History of the Marranos.* 4th ed. New York: Schocken Books, 1974.

Salomon, Herman P. "The Captain, the *Abade,* and 20th Century 'Marranism' in Portugal." *Arquivos do Centro Cultural Português* 10 (1976): 631-42.

———. "The Portuguese Inquisition and Its Victims in the Light of Recent Polemics." *Journal of the American Portuguese Cultural Society,* Summer-Fall 1971, pp. 19-28.

Schwarz, Samuel. "The Crypto-Jews of Portugal." *Menorah Journal* 12 (1926): 138-49, 283-97.

Wolf, Lucien. *Report on the "Marranos" or Crypto-Jews of Portugal.* London: Anglo-Jewish Association, 1926.

Yerushalmi, Yosef Hayim. *From Spanish Court to Italian Ghetto: Isaac Cardoso; A Study in Seventeenth-Century Marranism and Jewish Apologetics.* New York: Columbia University Press, 1971.

NOTES

1. Schwarz, p. 138.
2. Wolf, p. 6; see also *The Jewish Encyclopedia*, s.v. "Spain."
3. For a discussion of nomenclature see Yerushalmi, pp. 16–21.
4. The following story is told in Schwarz, pp. 140-44.
5. *Os Cristãos-Novos em Portugal no século XX* (Lisbon, 1925). Schwarz's article is a translation of extensive excerpts from this book.
6. Qtd. Javal, p. 41.
7. Qtd. Daniel M. Friedenberg, "The Jewish Catacombs of Portugal," *Midstream*, Spring 1960, p. 106.
8. Cecil Roth, "The Apostle of the Marranos," *Jewish Guardian*, 16 June 1930, pp. 7.
9. Wolf, p. 17.
10. Ibid., p. 16.
11. Ibid., p. 17.
12. Ibid., p. 15.
13. Qtd. Portuguese Marranos Committee, p. 6.
14. Ibid., p. 22.
15. Ibid., p. 23.
16. Qtd. Javal, p. 30.
17. Qtd. Portuguese Marranos Committee, p. 12; see also p. 10.
18. *Ha-Lapid*, no. 51 (December 1932).
19. Eduardo Carvalho (Bragança), personal interview, 1979.
20. *Ha-Lapid*, no. 16 (December 1928-January 1929).
21. All quotations in this paragraph are from Paulo, *"Judeus e Cristãos-Novos,"* no. 10: *"Antijudaísmo em Portugal,"* 20 July 1979.
22. Mordechai Van Son, "Was a Synagogue Justified?" Letter to *Jewish Chronicle*, 14 January 1938.
23. "Catholics Who Celebrate Passover," *Time*, 11 April 1977, p. 66.
24. *Ha-Lapid*, nos. 10-12 (April-June 1928).
25. Qtd. Salomon, "Captain," p. 638.
26. Amílcar Paulo, *Os Marranos em Trás-os-Montes (Reminiscências Judio-Portuguesas)* (Oporto, 1956).
27. In Schwarz, p. 287.
28. Ibid., pp. 286-87.
29. Paulo and Steinhardt, p. 15; see also Novinsky and Paulo.
30. In Schwarz, pp. 292-93; see also Novinsky and Paulo, pp. 80-81. Raphael Patai adds that the concept of twelve roads through the Red Sea

(one for each tribe) is from a Talmudic Midrash, not from the Old Testament itself. This is further evidence for the direct descent of Marrano traditions from medieval Portuguese Jewry, rather than being a spontaneous imitation of the Old Testament, as "revisionist" historians suggest.

31. Amílcar Paulo, *Romanceiro Criptojudaico* (Bragança, 1969).

32. Benzion Netanyahu, *The Marranos of Spain* (New York: American Academy for Jewish Research, 1966), p. 3.

33. Gerson D. Cohen, review of Netanyahu, in *Jewish Social Studies* 29 (1967): 181.

34. Wolf, p. 14.

Chapter Three: Chuetas

BIBLIOGRAPHY

Braunstein, Baruch. *The Chuetas of Majorca.* 1936. Reprint. New York: Ktav Publishing House, 1972.

Forteza, Miquel. *Els descendents dels jueus conversos de Mallorca: Quatre mots de la veritat.* 2nd ed. Palma de Mallorca: Raixe, 1970.

Glick, Thomas F. Book review. *Jewish Social Studies* 33 (1971): 230-32.

———. Book review. *Jewish Social Studies* 36 (1974): 339-42.

———. Book review. *Jewish Social Studies* 40 (1978): 323-24.

Graves, Robert. "'A Dead Branch on the Tree of Israel': The Xuetas of Majorca." *Commentary* 23 (1957): 139-46.

Isaacs, A. Lionel. *The Jews of Majorca.* London: Methuen and Co., 1936.

Kohn, Moshe. "Marrano Immigrants Settled in Own Trades," *Jerusalem Post,* 7 June 1966.

Markham, James. "After 300 Years, Inquisition Still Taints Some Majorcans," *New York Times,* 25 April 1978, p. 3.

Moore, Kenneth. *Those of the Street: The Catholic-Jews of Mallorca.* South Bend, Ind.: University of Notre Dame Press, 1976.

Patai, Raphael. "The Chuetas of Majorca." *Midstream,* Spring 1962, pp. 59-68.

"When Marrano Descendants Met Their Israeli *Landsleit.*" *Jewish Digest,* June 1967, pp. 61-67.

NOTES

1. Santiago Rusiñol, *Isla de la Calma* (Barcelona: Pulide, 1905); tr. Moore, p. 37.

2. Qtd. Markham.

3. Frederick Sternberg, letter to *Jewish Chronicle*, 21 May 1880, p. 6.

4. Qtd. Braunstein, p. 88, n. 98.

5. The most thorough etymology of "Chueta" is found in *Diccionari Català-Valencià-Balear*, vol. 10, s.v. *"xuetó."*

6. George Sand, *Winter in Majorca*, tr. Robert Graves (London: Cassell and Co., 1956), p. 89.

7. Qtd. Markham.

8. In Forteza, ch. 17.

9. Moore, p. 39.

10. Llorenc Villalonga, *Mort de Dama* (Barcelona: El Club dels Novel-listes, 1967), p. 98.

11. Qtd. Graves, p. 145.

12. Qtd. Markham.

13. In Graves, p. 145.

14. Ibid.

15. *Jerusalem Post*, 22 May 1960.

16. *Jewish Chronicle*, 5 July 1963.

17. Repr. *Kol-Sepharad*, September 1963.

18. Qtd. Graves, p. 145.

19. *L'Arche*, July 1966, p. 25.

20. *Jerusalem Post*, 6 June 1966.

21. Moore, p. 197.

22. Glick, 1978, p. 323.

Chapter Four: Mashhad

BIBLIOGRAPHY

Fischel, Walter J. "The Marrano Community in Persia" (Hebrew). *Zion*, n.s. 1 (1935-36): 49-74.

———. "Mulla Ibrahim Nathan (1816-1868): Jewish Agent of the British During the First Anglo-Afghan War." *Hebrew Union College Annual* 29 (1958): 331-75.

———. "Secret Jews of Persia." *Commentary* 7 (1949): 28-33.

———. "With the Marranos in Persia." *Jewish Forum* 15 (1932): 77-81.

Kashani, Reuben. *Anusei Mashhad* [The crypto-Jews of Mashhad]. Jerusalem: 1979.

Levy, Azariah. "The British Secret Service Requests Aid from the Jews of Mashhad" (Hebrew). *Etmol*, July 1977, pp. 6-8.

———. "Persian Jews on the Pilgrimage to Mecca" (Hebrew). *Davar*, 1 April 1973.

Moradi, Soliman. "The Disturbances in Meshhed in the Spring of 1946" (Hebrew). *Edoth* 2 (1946-47): 129-31.

Patai, Raphael. "The Hebrew Education in the Marrano Community of Meshhed" (Hebrew, with English summary). *Edoth* 1 (1945-46): 213-26, 262-63.

———. "Marriage Among the Marranos of Meshed" (Hebrew, with English summary). *Edoth* 2 (1946-47): 165-92, 311-14.

Schechtman, Joseph. "The Remarkable Marranos of Meshed." *Jewish Heritage*, Fall 1960, pp. 24-30.

NOTES

1. Joseph Wolff, *Narrative of a Mission to Bokhara, in the Years 1843–1845, to Ascertain the Fate of Colonel Stoddart and Captain Connolly* (London, 1846), p. 395.

2. The most comprehensive collection of these tales is in Kashani, *Anusei Mashhad.*

3. Arminius Vámbéry, *His Life and Adventures, Written by Himself* (London, 1884), p. 279.

4. Qtd. Ben-Zvi, *Exiled and Redeemed*, p. 116.

5. Qtd. Fischel, "Ibrahim Nathan," p. 338.

6. Qtd. Levy, "Secret Service," p. 8. See also *The Voice of Jacob* (London) 4 (25 April 1845): 101.

7. Rabinowitz, *Far East Mission* (Johannesburg: Eagle Press, 1952), pp. 63-64.

8. Qtd. Fischel, "Ibrahim Nathan," p. 336.

9. Qtd. *The Jewish Encyclopedia*, s.v. "Merv."

10. Rabinowitz, pp. 61-62.

11. Qtd. Moradi, p. 131.

12. Recounted by Rabbi Yaakov Goldman, personal interview, 1979.

Chapter Five: Dönmeh

BIBLIOGRAPHY

Benayahu, Meir. *Ha-Tenuah Ha-Shabtayit Be-Yavan* [The Shabbatean movement in Greece]. Jerusalem: Yad Itzhak Ben-Zvi, 1973.

Bent, J. Theodor. "A Peculiar People." *Longman's Magazine* 11 (1888): 24-36.

Danon, Abraham. *"Une secte judéo-musulmane en Turquie."* *Revue des études juives* 35 (1897): 264-81.

Galante, Abraham. *Nouveaux documents sur Sabbetai Sevi; organisation et us et coutumes de ses adeptes.* Istanbul: 1935.

Gordlevsky, Wl. *"Zur Frage Uber die 'Dönme' (Die Rolle der Juden in den Religionssekten Vorderasiens)."* *Islamica* 2 (1926): 200-18.

Molcho, Itzhak R. "Additional Details on the Sabbatians of Salonica" (Hebrew). *Zion* 11 (1946): 150-51.

———. "Material Towards a History of Shabbatai Zevi and of the Dönmeh of Salonica" (Hebrew). *Reshumot* 6 (1930): 537-43.

Nehama, Joseph. *Histoire des Israélites de Salonique*, vols. 6-7. Thessaloniki: Communauté Israélite de Thessalonique, 1978.

Ökte, Faik. *Varlik Vergisi Faciasi* [The tragedy of the capital tax]. Istanbul: 1951.

Rosanes, Solomon A. *Korot Ha-Yehudim Be-Turkiya Ve-Artzot Ha-Kedem* [The history of the Jews of Turkey and the Orient]. Sofia: 1934-35.

Schlousz, Nahum. *"Les Deunmeh: Une secte judéo-musulmane de Salonique."* *Revue du monde musulmane* 6 (1908): 483-95.

Scholem, Gershom. "The Crypto-Jewish Sect of the Dönmeh (Sabbatians) in Turkey." In idem, *The Messianic Idea in Judaism and Other Essays.* New York: Schocken Books, 1971. Bibliography.

————. "Prayerbook of the 'Dönmeh' from the Sect of the Izmirlis" (Hebrew). In idem, *Mehkarim U-Mekorot Le-Toldot Ha-Shabtaut Ve-Gilguleiha* [texts and sources concerning the history of Sabbatianism and its metamorphoses]. Jerusalem: Mahon Bialik, 1975.

————. "Redemption Through Sin." In idem, *Messianic Idea.*

————. *Sabbatai Sevi: The Mystical Messiah, 1626-1676.* Bollingen series, no. 93. Princeton: Princeton University Press, 1973.

Shatz-Uffenheimer, Rivka. "Portrait of a Sabbatian Sect" (Hebrew). In *S.Z. Shazar Jubilee Volume.* Edited by Itzhak Ben-Zvi and Meir Benayahu. Jerusalem: Yad Itzhak Ben-Zvi, 1960.

NOTES

1. See Stephen P. Ladas, *The Exchange of Minorities: Bulgaria, Greece, and Turkey* (New York: Macmillan Co., 1932).

2. Deut. 23:3.

3. Scholem, "Crypto-Jewish Sect," p. 166.

4. In ibid., p. 157.

5. Qtd. Galante, p. 51.

6. Elkan Adler, *Jews in Many Lands* (Philadelphia: Jewish Publication Society, 1905), p. 146.

7. Gershom Scholem, personal communication, 1980.

8. In Gershom Scholem, "The Crisis of Tradition in Jewish Messianism," in idem, *Messianic Idea,* p. 75.

9. Qtd. Galante, p. 50.

10. Schlousz, p. 492.

11. Rosanes, p. 475.

12. Galante, p. 72.

13. Schlousz, p. 495.

14. In Danon, pp. 270, 272.

15. David Farkhi, "Salonica Jews in the Young Turk Revolution" (Hebrew), *Sefunot* 15 (1979).

16. Itzhak Ben-Zvi, *Masa'ot* [Travels] (Jerusalem: Yad Itzhak Ben-Zvi, 1960), pp. 178, 184.

17. See Galante, pp. 77-79.

18. See Benayahu, pp. 105-08; and Nehama, pp. 76-78.

19. Qtd. Gordlevsky, p. 201.

20. Qtd Ben-Zvi, *Exiled and Redeemed*, p. 148.

21. Qtd. Gordlevsky, p. 201.

22. Donald E. Webster, *The Turkey of Ataturk* (Philadelphia: American Academy of Political and Social Science, 1939), p. 282.

23. From the preamble to the law; qtd. Geoffrey L. Lewis, *Modern Turkey*, 4th rev. ed. (London: Ernest Benn, 1974), p. 134.

24. Qtd. C.L. Sulzberger, "Ankara Tax Raises Diplomatic Issues" (last of four articles on the capital tax), *New York Times*, 12 September 1943, p. 46.

25. Ökte, p. 85.

26. Ibid., p. 99.

27. Ibid., p. 195.

28. Ibid., p. 85.

29. Qtd. Ben-Zvi, *Exiled and Redeemed*, p. 149.

30. This paragraph is based on interviews with emigrants from Turkey in Israel, 1979.

31. Scholem, "Crypto-Jewish Sect," p. 166.

Chapter Six: Samaritans

BIBLIOGRAPHY

Ben-Zvi, Itzhak. *Sefer Ha-Shomronim* [The book of Samaritans]. 1934/35. Reprint. Jerusalem: Yad Itzhak Ben-Zvi, 1970.

Bonne, Batsheva. "The Samaritans: A Demographic Study." *Human Biology* 35 (1963): 61-89.

Bowman, John. *The Samaritan Problem: Studies in the Relationships of Samaritanism, Judaism, and Christianity*. Translated by Alfred M. Johnson. Pittsburgh: Pickwick Press, 1975.

Coggins, R.J. *Samaritans and Jews: The Origins of Samaritanism Reconsidered*. Atlanta: John Knox Press, 1975.

Felix, R.; Amit, M.; Bar-Yoseph, H.; and Wintner, I. "A Psychological Comparative Study of the Samaritan Community: Schem (Nablus) and Holon." *The Israel Annals of Psychiatry and Related Disciplines* 8 (1970): 123-35; and 9 (1971): 117-31.

Gaster, Moses. *The Samaritans: Their History, Doctrines, and Literature*. London: Oxford University Press, 1925.

MacDonald, John. "The Discovery of Samaritan Religion." *Religion* 2 (1972): 141-53.

————, and Tsedaka, Binyamim. "Samaritans." In *Encyclopedia Judaica*, vol. 14. New York: Macmillan Co., 1971.

Montgomery, James A. *The Samaritans, the Earliest Jewish Sect: Their History, Theology, and Literature*. 1907. Reprint. New York: Ktav Publishing House, 1968.

Pummer, R. "The Present State of Samaritan Studies." *Journal of Semitic Studies* 21 (1976): 39-61; and 22 (1977): 27-47.

Tsedaqa, Ratson. *Agadot-Am Shomroniyot* [Samaritan legends]. Edited and with an introduction by Dov Noy. Israel Folktale Archives, no. 8. Haifa: Ethnological Museum and Folklore Archives, 1965.

NOTES

1. Qtd. *The Jewish Encyclopedia*, s.v. "Tribes, Lost Ten."
2. *Jerusalem Post*, 8 February 1977.
3. Ibid.
4. Exodus 12:6.
5. In Montgomery, p. 50.
6. II Kings 15:19-20.
7. For population estimates, see Alan D. Crown, "The Samaritan Diaspora to the End of the Byzantine Era," *Australian Journal of Biblical Archeology* 2 (1974-75): 107-23.
8. *The Jewish Encyclopedia*, s.v. "Samaritans."
9. Itzhak Ben-Zvi, *Zikhronot U-Rishumot* [Essays and reminiscences] (Jerusalem: Yad Itzhak Ben-Zvi, 1965), p. 119.

10. Batsheva Bonne, "A Genetic View of the Samaritan Isolate" (Ph.D. diss., Boston University, 1965), p. 185.

11. Montgomery, p. 23.

12. *Masseket Kutim* 28; tr. Montgomery, p. 156.

13. In Gaster, p. 189.

14. Qtd. *Jerusalem Post*, 13 June 1967. See also *Jerusalem Post*, 7 December 1973.

15. Leviticus 12 and 15.

16. See Boruch ben Gamaliel Tsedaka, "The Laws of Ritual Uncleanliness: The Difficulties of Keeping the Law" (Hebrew), *A-B: Samaritan News*, 1 June 1979, p. 6.

17. Felix et al., 1970, p. 133.

18. In *A-B: Samaritan News*, 15 July 1979, p. 10.

19. Qtd. Montgomery, p. 141.

20. Qtd. ibid., p. 156.

21. Qtd. ibid., p. 170.

22. Qtd. ibid., p. 195.

23. Qtd. ibid., p. 192.

24. In Ben-Zvi, *Sefer*, p. 365.

25. In ibid., p. 366.

Chapter Seven: Karaites

BIBLIOGRAPHY

Algamil, Yosef. *Toldot Ha-Yahadut Ha-Kara'it* [The History of Karaite Judaism]. Ramla: 1979.

Ankori, Zvi. *Karaites in Byzantium: The Formative Years, 970-1100.* New York: Columbia University Press, 1959.

Friedman, Philip. "The Karaites Under Nazi Rule." In idem. *On the Track of Tyranny.* London: Valentine Mitchell, 1960.

Green, Warren P. "The Nazi Racial Policy Towards the Karaites." *Soviet Jewish Affairs* 8 (no. 2, 1979): 34-44.

Helman, Boruch K. "The Karaite Jews of Cairo." *Hadassah Magazine*, March 1979, pp. 4-9.

Hirth, Paula. "Maurice Marzouk Makes Trouble." *Israel Magazine*, October 1971, pp. 22-28.

Kohn, Moshe. "Bigamy and the Karaite Schism." *Jerusalem Post*, 13 March 1966.

Loewenthal, Rudolf. "The Extinction of the Krimchaks in World War II." *The American Slavic and East European Review* 10 (1951): 130-36.

Mann, Jacob, ed. *Texts and Studies in Jewish History and Literature*, vol. 2: Karaitica. 1931. Reprint. New York: Ktav Publishing House, 1972.

Nemoy, Leon. "Early Karaism (The Need for a New Approach)." *The Jewish Quarterly Review*, n.s. 40 (1950): 307-15.

————. "Karaites." In *Encyclopedia Judaica*, vol. 10. New York: Macmillan Co., 1971.

————. "A Modern Egyptian Manual of the Karaite Faith." *The Jewish Quarterly Review*, n.s. 62 (1971-72): 1-11.

————, ed. *A Karaite Anthology*. Yale Judaica series, vol. 10. New Haven: Yale University Press, 1952.

Zajaçzkowski, Ananiasz. "The Culture of the Karaims." *East Europe*, August 1971, pp. 23-27.

————. *Karaims in Poland*. The Hague: Mouton and Co., 1961.

NOTES

1. Exod. 3:5.

2. Qtd. Nemoy, "Karaites," col. 765.

3. In Leon Nemoy, "Al-Qirqisani's Account of the Jewish Sects and Christianity," *Hebrew Union College Annual* 7 (1930): 330.

4. Qtd. Nemoy, "Karaites," col. 781.

5. Zajaçzkowski, *Karaims*.

6. Arthur Koestler, *The Thirteenth Tribe: The Khazar Empire and Its Heritage* (New York: Random House, 1976). Cf. Leon Wieseltier, "You Don't Have To Be Khazarian," *New York Review of Books*, 28 October 1976, pp. 33-36; Edward Grossman, "Koestler's Jewish Problem," *Commentary*, December 1976, pp. 59-64; and Bernard D. Weinryb, "Origins of East European Jewry: Myth and Fact," *Commentary* 24 (1957): 509-18.

7. Norman Golb and Omeljan Pritsak, *Khazarian Hebrew Documents of the Tenth Century* (Ithaca: Cornell University Press, forthcoming).

8. Zajaçzkowski, *Karaims*, pp. 20-23.

9. Qtd. Loewenthal, p. 134.

10. Qtd. Friedman, p. 107.

11. Anatoli Kuznetsov, *Babi Yar* (New York: Dial Press, 1967), p. 61.

12. Qtd. Loewenthal, p. 135.

13. Qtd. ibid., p. 136. See also Ben-Zvi, *Exiled and Redeemed*, pp. 101–11.

14. Qtd. Zajączkowski, *Karaims*, p. 52.

15. Qtd. Friedman, p. 99; tr. Green, pp. 37-38.

16. Qtd. Friedman, p. 101.

17. Qtd. ibid., p. 104.

18. Qtd. ibid., p. 103.

19. Ibid., p. 107.

20. Qtd. ibid., p. 113.

21. Kalmanovitch, "Diary," s.v. "15 November 1942" (p. 37).

22. Philip Friedman, "Polish-Jewish Historiography Between the Two Wars (1919–1939)," *Jewish Social Studies* 11 (1949), p. 396.

23. Qtd. Friedman, "Karaites," p. 115; tr. Green, p. 40.

24. *Jerusalem Post*, 1 August 1950.

25. Green, p. 41.

26. Robert A. Lewis, Richard H. Rowland, and Ralph S. Clem, *Nationality and Population Change in Russia and the USSR: An Evaluation of Census Data, 1897–1970* (New York: Praeger, 1976), pp. 170, 175.

27. *Great Soviet Encyclopedia*, 3rd ed., s.v. "Karaites."

28. *Jerusalem Post*, 21 July 1950.

29. *Jerusalem Post*, 19 January 1956.

30. Roshwald, "Marginal Jewish Sects," p. 236.

31. *Jerusalem Post*, 14 September 1967.

32. Qtd. *Jerusalem Post*, 27 September 1976.

Chapter Eight: Falashas

BIBLIOGRAPHY

Aescoly, Aaron Z. *Sefer Ha-Falashim* [The Book of Falashas]. Jerusalem: 1943.

————. *Recueil de textes Falachas: introduction et textes éthiopiens*. Paris: Institut d'ethnologie, 1951.

Halévy, Joseph. "Travels in Abyssinia." In *Miscellany of Hebrew Literature,* vol. 2. 1877. Reprint. Westport, Conn.: Greenwood Press, 1975.

Leslau, Wolf. "The Black Jews of Ethiopia: An Expedition to the Falashas." *Commentary* 7 (1949): 216-24.

———. "A Falasha Book of Jewish Festivals." In *For Max Weinreich on His 70th Birthday: Studies in Jewish Languages, Literature, and Society.* The Hague: Mouton & Co., 1964.

———. "Report on a Second Trip to Ethiopia." *Word,* April 1952, pp. 72-79.

———, ed. *A Falasha Anthology.* Yale Judaica series, vol. 6. New Haven: Yale University Press, 1951.

Messing, Simon D. "Journey to the Falashas." *Commentary* 22 (1956): 28-40.

Quirin, J. "The Beta Israel (Felasha) in Ethiopian History: Caste Formation and Cultural Change, 1270-1868." Ph.D. dissertation, University of Minnesota, 1977.

Rapoport, Louis. *The Lost Jews: Last of the Ethiopian Falashas.* New York: Stein and Day, 1980.

Rodinson, Maxime. "Sur la question des 'influences juives' en Éthiopie." *Journal of Semitic Studies* 9 (1964): 11-19.

Sherman, Arnold. "The Falashas in Israel." *Israel Magazine,* February 1973, pp. 58-62.

Stern, Henry A. *Wanderings Among the Falashas in Abyssinia.* 1862. Reprint, with an introduction by Robert L. Hess. London: Cass, 1968.

Ullendorff, Edward. *Ethiopia and the Bible.* London: Oxford University Press, 1968.

———. "Hebraic-Jewish Elements in Abyssinian (Monophysite) Christianity." *Journal of Semitic Studies* 1 (1956): 216-56.

NOTES

1. *Jerusalem Post,* 3 January 1979.

2. Zimna Berhane, letter to Graenum Berger, 4 March 1979. Mimeographed.

3. Ephraim Isaacs, "The Hebraic Molding of Ethiopian Culture," *Mosaic,* Winter 1965.

4. Jerome Lobo, qtd. Ullendorff, "Hebraic-Jewish Elements," p. 218.

5. Qtd. Ullendorff, *Ethiopia and the Bible,* pp. 73-74, n. 3.

6, Leslau, "Black Jews," p. 216.

7. Graenum Berger, *Black Jews in America* (New York: Federation of

Jewish Philanthropies, 1978), pp. 61-62.

8. Qtd. James Boswell, *Life of Samuel Johnson* (London, 1791), s.v. "April 1, 1775."

9. Edward Ullendorff, "James Bruce of Kinnaird," *Scottish Historical Review*, October 1953, p. 128.

10. James Bruce, *Travels to Discover the Source of the Nile in the Years 1768, 1769, 1770, 1771, 1772, and 1773*, vol. 1 (Edinburgh, 1790), pp. 483-84.

11. Ibid., p. 484.

12. Ibid.

13. Ibid., p. 485.

14. Ibid., p. 489.

15. Qtd. Edward Ullendorff, *The Ethiopians: An Introduction to Country and People* (London: Oxford University Press, 1960), p. 97.

16. Rodinson, p. 19.

17. Job Ludolf, *A New History of Ethiopia, made English by J.P. Gent* (London, 1682), p. 73.

18. Wolf Leslau, "A Falasha Religious Dispute," *Proceedings of the American Academy for Jewish Research* 16 (1946-47): 79-80, n. 16.

19. Azriel Hildesheimer, *Jewish Chronicle*, 4 November 1864, p. 6.

20. Halévy, p. 215.

21. Ibid.

22. *Jewish Chronicle*, 7 August 1908.

23. See David Kessler, "Falashas in a Halutzic Move," *Israel Horizons*, June-July 1971, pp. 26-28.

24. Personal communication, 1980.

25. Rabbi Isaac Herzog, qtd. *Jerusalem Post*, 31 May 1966.

26. *Jerusalem Post*, 23 February 1966.

27. Arnold Sherman, "Today's Falashas and the Dream of Rahamim," *Israel Magazine*, September 1972, pp. 45-53.

28. David Zohar, "Israeli Policy on the Falashas," *Sh'ma* 3 (2 February 1973): 55.

29. Qtd. Howard M. Lenhoff, "Rabbis Embrace Falasha Community," *Israel Today*, 16-29 February 1979, p. 3.

30. In Solomon B. Freehof, *A Treasury of Responsa* (Philadelphia: Jewish Publication Society, 1963), p. 125.

31. *Jewish Chronicle*, 23 March 1973.

32. *Jerusalem Post*, 31 August 1977.

33. *Jerusalem Post*, 11 April 1975.

34. Roshwald, "Marginal Jewish Sects," p. 351.

35. Hannah Malhi, "Problems of a Negro in Israel," *Jewish Digest*, November 1963, pp. 78-80.

36. Qtd. Sherman, "Falashas in Israel," p. 61.
37. Qtd. Lenhoff, p. 3.
38. Qtd. Roshwald, "Marginal Jewish Sects," pp. 350-51.
39. In M.D. Gouldman, "The Falasha Wedding," *Israel Law Review* 3 (1968): 599.

Chapter Nine: Kaifeng

BIBLIOGRAPHY

Dehergne, Joseph, and Leslie, Donald D. *Juifs de Chine: à travers la correspondance inédite des jésuites du dix-huitième siècle.* Rome: Institutum Historicum S.I., 1980.

Finn, James. *The Orphan Colony of the Jews in China: Containing a Letter, with the Latest Information Concerning Them.* London: 1872. (Excerpted at length in White, *Chinese Jews*, vol. 1, pp. 71-94.)

Gallagher, Louis J., trans. *China in the Sixteenth Century: The Journals of Matthew Ricci, 1583-1610.* New York: Random House, 1953.

Kublin, Hyman, ed. *Jews in Old China: Some Western Views.* New York: Paragon Book Reprint, 1971.

————, ed. *Studies of the Chinese Jews: Selections from Journals East and West.* New York: Paragon Book Reprint, 1971.

Leslie, Donald Daniel. "The Chinese-Hebrew Memorial Book of the Dead." *Abr-Nahrain* 4 (1963-64): 19-49; 5 (1964-65): 1-28; and 6 (1965-66): 1-52.

————. "The Judaeo-Persian Colophons to the Pentateuch of the Kaifeng Jews." *Abr-Nahrain* 8 (1968-69): 1-35.

————. "Some Notes on the Jewish Inscriptions of Kaifeng." *Journal of the American Oriental Society* 82 (1962): 346-61.

————. *The Survival of the Chinese Jews: The Jewish Community of Kaifeng.* Leiden: E.J. Brill, 1972. Bibliography.

Pollak, Michael. *Mandarins, Jews, and Missionaries.* Philadelphia: Jewish Publication Society, 1980.

————. *The Torah Scrolls of the Chinese Jews.* Dallas: Bridwell Library, Southern Methodist University, 1975.

Rhee, Song Nai. "Jewish Assimilation: The Case of the Chinese Jews." *Comparative Studies in Society and History* 15 (1973): 115-26.

White, William C. *Chinese Jews.* 3 vols. 1942. Reprint. (3 vols. in 1). New York: Paragon Book Reprint, 1966.

NOTES

1. Qtd. George L. Harris, "The Mission of Matteo Ricci, S.J.," *Monumenta Serica* 25 (1966): 161.

2. Qtd. ibid., p. 18.

3. Qtd. ibid., p. 161.

4. Leslie, *Survival,* p. 31.

5. Ricci told this story twice, in his diary (see Gallagher, pp. 106-12) and in a letter of 26 July 1605. The preferred translation of both versions, by Rudolph Löwenthal, is in Kublin, *Studies,* pp. 209-13. This quotation, from the diary, is on p. 210.

6. Gallagher, p. 107.

7. Kublin, *Studies,* p. 212.

8. From the 1489 inscription in the Kaifeng synagogue; in White, vol. 2, pp. 14-15 (inscriptions hereafter cited by date and by page number in White, vol. 2; e.g., "1489, 14-15").

9. 1489, 11.

10. 1489, 12. Cf. Chao Ying Fang, "Notes on the Chinese Jews of Kaifeng," *Journal of the American Oriental Society* 85 (1965): 127 (repr. Kublin, *Studies,* pp. 85-90).

11. In Fang, "Notes," p. 127.

12. 1489, 13.

13. Qtd. in Leslie, *Survival,* p. 44.

14. Qtd. ibid., p. 45.

15. Kublin, *Studies,* p. 211.

16. White, vol. 2, p. 143.

17. Kublin, *Studies,* pp. 211-12.

18. Jean Domenge, in Dehergne and Leslie, p. 129.

19. Antoine Gaubil, *Correspondance de Pékin, 1722-1759* (Geneva: 1970), p. 94.

20. Jean Domenge, in Dehergne and Leslie, p. 148.

21. Leslie, "Memorial Book" (part I), pp. 29-30.

22. Qtd. Bruno Kroker, "The Chinese Jews of Kaifeng," *China Journal of the Arts and Sciences*, 19 September 1938, pp. 141-46.

23. 1663 (reverse), 89.

24. 1489, 10.

25. 1663 (obverse), 59.

26. Ibid.

27. White, vol. 2, p. 152.

28. 1679, 98.

29. 1512, 46.

30. 1663 (obverse), 61.

31. 1489, 11.

32. 1663 (obverse), 61.

33. Jean Domenge, in Dehergne and Leslie, p. 167.

34. 1489, 8.

35. In White, vol. 2, p. 19, n. 2.

36. 1489, 61. See also *I Ching*, hexagram XXIV.

37. 1663 (obverse), 58.

38. 1512, 43.

39. 1489, 15.

40. Qtd. Robert Bellah, "Civil Religion in America," *Daedalus*, Winter 1967, p. 5.

41. Lin Yutang, *The Wisdom of Confucius* (New York: Modern Library, 1943), pp. 14-15.

42. 1489, 14.

43. Chao Nien-tsu's letter is in Finn, pp. 39-44.

44. Rhee, p. 126.

45. Leslie, "Notes," p. 355.

46. In White, vol. 1, p. 101.

47. In Finn, p. 68.

48. In White, vol. 1, p. 157.

49. Qtd. Pollak, *Mandarins*, pp. 248-49.

50. Qtd. Aline Mosby, "China's Lost Jewish Community," United Press International newsfeature, 18 February 1980.

Chapter Ten: Bene Israel

BIBLIOGRAPHY

Bat-Orin, Josefa. "Report from India: The Jews of Bombay." *Jerusalem Post,* 26 and 31 January and 4 February 1977.

B'*nei Yisrael* Bene Israel: halakhic decisions and sources for the investigation of their laws and the question of their origin]. Jerusalem: 1962.

Ezekiel, Moses. *History and Culture of the Bene Israel in India.* Nadiad: 1948.

Fischel, Walter J. "Bombay in Jewish History in the Light of New Documents from the Indian Archives." *Proceedings of the American Academy of Jewish Research* 38-39 (1970-71): 119-44.

———. "Cochin in Jewish History." *Proceedings of the American Academy of Jewish Research* 30 (1962): 37-59.

———. "Early Zionism in India." *Herzl Year Book* 4 (1961): 309-28.

———. *Ha-Yehudim Be-Hodu* [The Jews in India]. Jerusalem: Yad Itzhak Ben-Zvi, 1960.

———. "Literary Activities of the Bene Israel." *Jewish Book Annual* 29 (1971-72): 5-11.

Gourgey, Percy Sassoon. "India." *American Jewish Year Book* 54 (1953): 416-21.

Gussin, Carl Mark. "The Bene Israel of India: Politics, Religion, and Systemic Change." Ph.D. dissertation, Syracuse University, 1972.

Israel, Benjamin J. *Religious Evolution Among the Bene Israel of India Since 1750.* Bombay: 1963.

Kehimkar, Haeem Samuel. *The History of the Bene Israel of India.* Edited by Immanuel Olsvanger. Tel Aviv: Dayag Press, 1937.

Mahadevan, Meera. *Shulamith.* New Delhi: Arnold-Heinemann, 1975.

Mandelbaum, David. "The Jewish Way of Life in Cochin." *Jewish Social Studies* 1 (1939): 423-60.

Musleah, Ezekiel N. "India." *American Jewish Year Book* 62 (1961): 377-81.

———. *On the Banks of the Ganga: The Sojourn of Jews in Calcutta.* North Quincy, Mass.: Christopher Publishing House, 1975.

Reissner, H.G. "Indian-Jewish Statistics (1837-1941)." *Jewish Social Studies* 12 (1950): 349-66.

Roland, Joan G. "The Jews of India." *Jewish Social Studies* 42 (1980): 75-90.

Strizower, Schifra. *The Bene Israel of Bombay.* New York: Schocken Books, 1971.

————. "The Bene Israel and the Jewish People." In *Salo W. Baron Jubilee Volume.* New York: American Academy for Jewish Research, 1974.

————. "Jews as an Indian Caste." *Jewish Journal of Sociology* 1 (1959): 43-57.

Weil, Shalva. "Bene Israel in Britain." *New Community* 3 (1974): 87-91.

————. "Bene Israel Indian Jews in Lod, Israel: A Study of the Persistence of Ethnicity and Ethnic Identity." Ph.D. dissertation, University of Sussex, 1977.

Wigoder, Geoffrey. "Indian Jewry Seems Reluctant to Leave." *Jerusalem Post,* 23 April 1976.

NOTES

1. *Jerusalem Post,* 6 August 1964.
2. Qtd. Fischel, "Bombay," pp. 138-39.
3. Ezekiel, pp. 26-27.
4. Rabinowitz, *Far East Mission,* p. 78.
5. Kehimkar, p. 166.
6. Qtd. Herbert Lottman, "The Last Indian Jews," *Present Tense,* Spring 1976, pp. 7-9.
7. Israel, p. 6.
8. Hugh Tinker, review of Strizower, *Bene Israel,* in *Race* 14 (1972): 98-100.
9. Qtd. Weil, "Bene Israel in Lod," p. 59.
10. Qtd. Weil, "Britain," p. 90.
11. Rabinowitz, p. 76.
12. Carmel Berkson, personal communication, 1980.
13. Mahadevan, pp. 93-94.
14. Ibid., p. 203.
15. Ibid.
16. Qtd. Weil, "Bene Israel in Lod," p. 70.
17. All quotations in this paragraph are from *New York Times,* 31 March 1952, p. 4.
18. *New York Times,* 1 April 1952, p. 12.
19. *New York Times,* 28 April 1952, p. 5.
20. Qtd. Weil, "Bene Israel in Lod," p. 71.
21. *Jerusalem Post,* 10 May 1961.
22. Qtd. Zucker, *Coming Crisis,* p. 117.

23. *Jerusalem Post*, 18 August 1964.

24. Ibid.

25. *Time*, 28 July 1961, p. 52.

26. Gershom Scholem, *Ha-Kabbalah Be-Geironah* [The kabbala in Gerona] (Jerusalem, 1964), p. 4. This passage tr. in Jochanan H.A. Wijnhoven, *Judaism* 19 (1970): 471.

27. Israel, p. 5. My italics.

Index

BOSTON PUBLIC LIBRARY

3 9999 00315 018 0

WITHDRAWN

No longer the property of the
Boston Public Library.
Sale of this material benefits the Library

6/82 **Boston Public Library**

COPLEY SQUARE
GENERAL LIBRARY

DS143
.R58

9800266532

The Date Due Card in the pocket indi-
cates the date on or before which this
book should be returned to the Library.

Please do not remove cards from this
pocket.